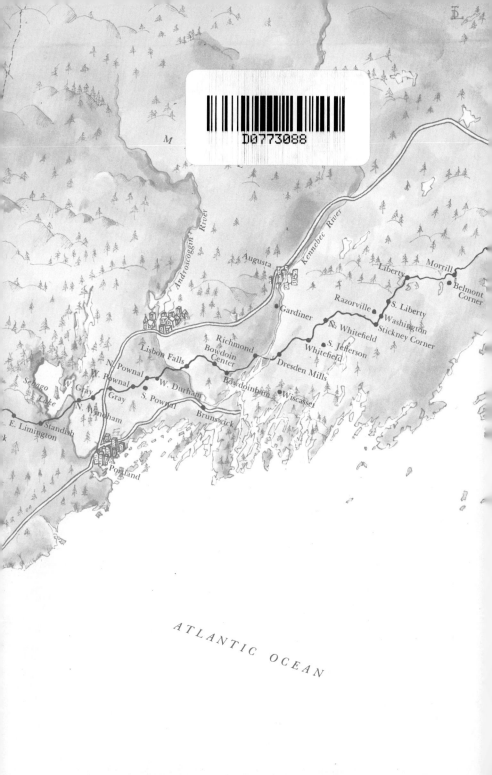

the walk of the conscious ants

THE WALK OF THE

 alfred a. knopf / new york / 1972

CONSCIOUS ANTS

TAYLOR MORRIS

THIS IS A BORZOI BOOK
PUBLISHED BY ALFRED A. KNOPF, INC.

Library of Congress Cataloging in Publication Data

Morris, Taylor, 1923– The walk of the conscious ants.

1. Franklin Pierce College. 2. Outdoor education—
New England. 3. Hiking—New England.

I. Title.   LD1871.F285M6   378.1′7′8   79—171128

ISBN 0—394—47425—2

Manufactured in the United States of America

FIRST EDITION

To the Walkers

There are at least two irreconcilable possibilities:
one, that man should be educated to become what he is;
the other, that he should be educated to become what
he is not.

—Sir Herbert Read
in *Education Through Art*

the walk of the conscious ants

THE IDEA

The idea of a long walk, in place of a semester of courses, came to me as accidentally as most other ideas, great or trivial. My wife had driven me to school, Franklin Pierce College at Rindge, New Hampshire, from Peterborough—a 15-mile stretch—and there was a desultory argument about what time she could get back to pick me up.

"Forget it, I'll walk home."

So I did, carrying a bag of books in one hand, a jacket in the other, on leather soles over a hot highway—a stretch I had driven at least thirty times—and saw more in that walk than in all of the trips by car, saw more, thought about more, realized more. I couldn't help wondering what it would do for a group.

Next day in my classes I put it to them: "Which way do you think you'd learn more, by taking a semester of courses, or by taking a walk for one semester?"

"Taking a walk, of course!"

This answer or some version of it was not only unanimous but given as if no other choice were possible. They sprawled there, answering, "The walk, of course," and yet seemed content, or doomed, to remain sitting through course after course, year after year. Was there even one who disagreed? No. I stood there, feeling like an idiot. What are we doing here, then?

To go into all of my objections to conventional school would take pages. Let it pass. Still, when I broached the idea to my classes that spring I was only wondering out loud; by the fall after the first few faculty meetings and class sessions, I began to make plans for doing it, since my main impulse was to walk straight away from the whole wordy scene.

What the students needed was experience, not words and definitions.

How futile is the definition of "health" if you don't have it!

"I saw that Sufism consists in experiences rather than in definitions," said Ghazzali, the Persian poet and Sufi master, just before leaving the academic world, "and that what I was lacking belonged to the domain, not of instruction, but of ecstasy and initiation." Substitute "truth" for "Sufism" and there was the basis for the walk—whereas "instruction" can only lead to degrees, "initiation" might lead to "ecstasy."

I spoke with the president about the project, and his answer was guarded. "Well, it sounds better than their taking over the administration building and burning records," he said.

I explained that what I had in mind was not to pacify students but to educate them.

"Of course you would take a naturalist along with you."

"Oh no!"

The dean came much closer to understanding it. "For no purpose? Just a walk? . . . It's an interesting idea."

I told a few students about it. They didn't ask why, or even where we'd go; their question was "When do we start?"

By early winter the idea would not let me alone. Those of us in the little conspiracy kept it warm. The plan was to walk, straight out, as far as we could get in thirty to forty days. It didn't matter where—just out of school. I figured we could make about 15 miles a day once we were used to walking. Fifteen times forty is 600 miles. We kept talking. One day I traced a circle with a 600-mile radius from Rindge, New Hampshire, to see how far we could get.

My God! We could get to Canada! We could get to Nova Scotia!

Winter, classes, papers, exams, and suddenly we were out for Christmas. I planned to have the first meeting for our proposed spring walk shortly after we came back.

In school again, I found it more difficult to stick to "the subject." I wanted to talk about the world and *now* . . . our lives. Who does handle that? When is it dealt with? I had no more business dealing with world problems than others had in avoiding them. My only excuse was that I was burning to get out of books and plays and research and into our whole lives: physical, emotional, *and* intellectual.

A colleague in the room next to mine caught me in the hall one day after a class.

"I'm sometimes amused at your political views when you talk to your classes."

"Really? Where do you stand?"

"As a scientist, I can't say one way or another until all the facts are in."

" 'As a scientist'? As a realist you'd better know that all the facts are never in."

One night on the walk we were backed up against the wall. Would we fight? There was no time to study all the angles in a quiet place; we had to act that night, because the facts didn't even start coming in till the next day. People invariably make decisions in their lives—the life decisions—without proper research, for there is not sufficient time. To do proper research before taking a job would be to work there, would be to go to a school before saying yes to it. Not possible. Suddenly Cuba or Cambodia is invaded. Who is right? "Wait till all the facts are in!" Suddenly there is a riot, a plague, or you are in the car with a driver and discover—at 80 miles an hour —that he's drunk and doesn't know what he's doing. A measure of our real education is what we do at these times. And our real education is based on our range of experience, our use of intuition, and imagination. Mark Van Doren once said, "Right use of imagination is to discover the truth." Among other uses, to fore-see and then choose or avoid. And for certain things one has to smell out the truth immediately and without "all the facts"; an ABM-net-around-the-country-for-five-billion-bucks-as-a-starter? One good long sniff. It stinks!

On the walk we would need to awaken intuition. How? Perhaps in trusting the judgment of the students, in not distrusting them, intuition might be born or reborn. In letting the project be about them, in challenging them to prove that they are more than receptacles for pouring ideas into, extracting assignments out of; well ... one has a hunch. Where does the hunch come from? A hunch and a feeling are close together. Let the walkers be free to feel. I had a terribly strong hunch it would work.

January, and the snow came down. Then more on top of that. The walk seemed more remote than ever, but the first meeting was scheduled for the 3rd of February. I wrote a recruiting letter, "Let's Take a Walk," and an invitation to a meeting for those interested. It was geared more to the spirit or emotions than to the intellect, but the idea of its being aimless was there, as well as something about the difference between knowledge and understanding.

I thought back to the time when I had been teaching night and afternoon classes at the same New York school, and about how different the two sets of students were. Afternoon classes brought the usual city college student: grade-conscious, laconic, energetic and burning with issues, or else lethargic, but almost totally lacking in a wide range of experience. To the evening classes—same subject matter—came the adults; often cynical and tired, but when I talked about divorce, love or death, or gaining or losing something long desired, they not only knew, they understood.

At one point during our walk, one of the students was to find himself alone when a thirty-year-old housewife opened her door and let out a big German shepherd: "Bite the shit out of him, Banjo!" she said.

Banjo leaped to the task, snarling and growling all the way. Fortunately Bob, the student, had a knife, pulled it out, and kept facing the dog. When the woman saw that he had a knife and wasn't afraid to use it she called her dog back, for his protection.

Did the student "learn" something? No, that student understood something. Almost everyone knows what "Sic 'em" means, but Bob understands it.

The long walk with its accent on experiences was bound to lessen the gap between knowing and understanding.

Agee, in *Let Us Now Praise Famous Men,* after describing understanding as the key, the all-and-everything for mankind, demolishes education by stating that education "seems indeed the very property of the world's misunderstanding, the sharpest of its spearheads in every brain." He says that *change* is difficult just because education is so linked to the "world's machine" and, since education "could not be otherwise without destroying the world's machine, the world is unlikely to permit it to be otherwise."

But who defends the "world's machine"? Who speaks for this "world"? People who throw stones through strangers' tents? The truck driver who almost wrecked his rig in an effort to make every one of us see that he was giving us his middle finger? State troopers who charged down on us, ready to draw their pistols and start firing? Parents who wanted to couple the idea to something practical ("If you'll lose 20 pounds on that . . . trip . . . we'll let you go")? Townsfolk who phoned people who had agreed to let us put up our tent for the night, telling them that a bunch of hippies or gypsies were using their fields? Owners of fields who backed down after giving us a place for the night and—through sheriffs or constables—told us at the end of a day's walk that we'd have to pack our gear and move on? The locals who cruised by to honk or yell or cut tent ropes, or tell us they'd be back that night to "take care" of us? The people who, just at the sight of a bunch of walkers, shouted names of all kinds? Students who were critical of this idea for no good reason, but who never dreamed of criticizing the soul-killing courses they sat through? People who felt that school-education-learning-becoming were all one big onerous but somehow necessary pill? Fellow faculty members who felt that the whole project was a joke and only part of the "basket-weaving" trend of courses?

Well, better than death courses. Better basket-weaving than casket-weaving.

At the last talk with the president and the dean their objections seemed to be fading away. As long as I set the entire thing up, the school would go along. In all of the talk, however, there seemed to be an element of "humor the madman" and not much understanding of my aimless project, my no-purpose project. As for help, that too was a little vague. When I asked for expenses for a trial trip they scratched their chins and looked at the map. And when I asked for the school VW bus, things became downright uncomfortable.

I put in hours of worry before the first meeting. How many would be there? Would it be a mixed group? Two girls were already involved, but we needed more.

A few minutes before the meeting, a little group of us walked over to the new men's dorm. There were about twenty-five people waiting, five girls among them.

I went over the various points as I had scribbled them down:

1. *Basically, the project involves a walk of about 550 miles —from the school campus to Halifax, Nova Scotia—which will take about forty to forty-five days.*

2. *We will leave on May 2nd, a few days before the beginning of the spring trimester.*

3. *Once under way, we will average about 15 miles a day.*

4. *We will have a truck—to carry our gear, for the "wounded," and for groceries—which we will take turns driving.*

5. *We will have one big tent and will live out the entire time.*

6. *It might be a regular credit course, but that has not been determined yet.*

I mentioned that we *might* get help from the Ford Foundation, so those people who were very interested but broke might still be able to go.

I had a little notation at the bottom of my card: "Drugs, sex, consideration."

Even one person brought to trial for possession would probably kill the trip. So, I told them, drugs were out.

One of the students at the back of the room slowly got to his feet and left. Lloyd of the long red hair. Damn! I wanted him. Didn't he realize that I *had* to say that?

Well, one down. I repeated it. Drugs were out. I told them that sex was sex, that the cardinal rule would be consideration . . . for each other, for the group. There would be no other rules.

In as guarded a way as possible, I did tell them that those who signed up would be taking part in something that might, in some small way, help turn education around. School demanded that they give their minds to books, lectures, assignments, and ignored their bodies. For this they'd give their bodies to the walk for 15 miles a day. Their minds would be free.

While they asked questions, I was able to look them over. They seemed to be a solid, rugged, good-looking bunch; more important, they seemed balanced—neither "brains" nor woodsman types.

After the meeting we collected the 3 x 5 cards with addresses and information and looked them over. Counting two or three who couldn't make the meeting, we had a "definite" group of twelve and about sixteen probables.

The trend in education seems always to go in the direction of more papers, more books, more chores, more hurdles; as if we distrusted free time. I felt that we must give students time to understand—under good conditions. My aim was to create those conditions—conditions which would lead them to their own discoveries.

Although at the time of that first meeting I had not yet written to the Ford Foundation, the hopes for our project were becoming more intelligible. Soon I was able to read to the group: "In addition to walking the back roads, in addition to walking for a part of each day in silence, the trip, for optimum results, must remain aimless. We will not attempt to climb every mountain peak in the such-and-such mountain range; we will not go digging for the remains of some civilizations. This idea is ages old—not a knowledge of chemistry or Appalachian Trail, nor make a study of New England towns. For a project such as this, those aims would only be distractions. This idea is ages old—not a knowledge of chemistry or literature, but a knowledge of oneself."

TRIAL RUN

Early in February it became clear to me that somehow it would be done, but to walk through four- to six-foot drifts of snow while contemplating a 600-mile walk (we thought it was a mere 480 miles), camping out all the way, is a little unreal. Maybe this year the snow won't melt, the leaves won't come back. Maybe it'll never get warm again.

But we did get the VW bus for a scouting trip—the post office workers who objected to our taking their transportation hid the knob that turns on the heater—and two of us actually took off northeastward, as if New Hampshire weren't cold enough.

Three feet of snow on either side of every road we took, no heat in the truck, and Herbie, my copilot and first conspirator to kick education in the ass, confessed to me after 30 miles of erratic driving that he'd never used a stick shift before.

The bus was really beat up and hardly seemed to care any longer, clutch or not. Besides, it wouldn't go any faster than 50 so it was an ideal car for him to learn on.

Gradually we were moving out of familiar territory, looking out on new fields of snow, dead sticks of tree branches. More snow on the way. Would those fields ever have grass again?

For a while we carefully noted the mileage and possible

campsites at each 15-mile "day," then gave it up. How could we say, months ahead, how far we'd get each day? We'd not decide in February how we'd walk in May.

Still, we'd drive on to Halifax, report back: yep, everything's planned, permission for every field granted, every meal, town, mailstop, down to the last penny.

So, what did we accomplish? Nothing concrete, but everything else. We drove through ice, sleet, snow. We froze, until we found the knob to the heater; then we froze with the heater on. We bought peanuts, little cans of fruit juice, cans of Stern-O to heat the truck, and drove east-northeast. We kept all the cans and all the peanut shells in the front of the cab with us, as if they were sacred. I don't think we lost one peanut shell the whole trip. The cans clashing together among two or three inches of peanut shells (drifts of six inches) made a fine sound. If one of us was feeling down, the other had only to thrash his feet around in the mess. It never failed.

And we did find some beautiful walking roads. The first, Pleasant Pond Road, was just out of Francestown, New Hampshire. It was a one-lane winding tree-lined road, barely plowed.

Conception is similar to the birth of an idea, but spirit is life and breath joined to it. At Pleasant Pond Road the spirit joined the idea and the baby began kicking to get out.

That simple tree-lined road is typical of the walk. How did we miss it? . . . The walk just didn't live that way. Perhaps we remember it so well since it was the first real walking road we came across. Because of it we suddenly knew how the walk could be.

Yes, how lovely it would be in the spring, but this was February and we slipped and slid on that skinny road for five miles. Still, it was our real beginning. If we could connect old roads like this, we'd walk to Canada hardly aware that we were walking anywhere.

From some point around Pittsfield the trip became a dazzling collage of country scenes in February; snow-burdened fir trees, quiet white white and quiet fields, smoke from chimneys way off over there, smoke-breathing cows patiently chewing their way through winter, icicled bushes over frozen streams, black branches of trees so cold they're afraid to move. We tool along and I think of Wordsworth and what we should do about him. Should we learn his poetry? Or just read it and then go into streams, glens, on back roads through fields of snow? That's it! Walt Whitman? Yes, and drive on, we'll get there come May.

A dazzling collage and a mood from it: first acceptance, then we're saying yes to all things . . . to the accelerator pedal slipping off its hook wandering over the floor, to no horn, to peanut shells and cans on the floor—scrape them back in— yes to a light snow and hazy sky, to little sweet girls, little boys playing . . . yes to Stern-O cans burning on the floor in front and in back.

The Stern-O raised the inside temperature to about 22 degrees. Herbie would fiddle with the heater knob; "Hey, it's really working now!" Twenty-four degrees. Gloom . . . thrashing cans, and all's well again.

Darkness comes early in February, but there are lights in a store in Limerick, Maine. Ill-fated, violent Limerick, which appeared to us that night as the epitome of quaint New England innocence.

"Do you have any hot soup?"

"Nope . . . and I doubt as you'll find anything open *this* time-a-night!"

It was 6:15.

"Second thought," she actually held up one finger, "Sebago Lake's uh rest'rant stays opin till eight!"

"Sebago Lake?"

"Twenty miles up the road."

By the time we arrived, the snowflakes were as big as leaves. The walk and May seemed more incongruous than ever, but we were inside and warm, our maps were spread out, and we traced the possibilities, happy and lost in Maine and in visions.

From Sebago Lake we eventually picked up Highway 9, which we were not to take again. It is a truck route with hardly a gas station or a store for 90 miles, from Bangor to Calais ("Callous," the natives say) at the Maine-Canada border. It was raining, icing, snowy, and black. The clutch was slipping and the road went over long roller-coaster hills, so we could never tell how much of each we were fighting. But that problem was eliminated when the windshield wipers stopped and we could no longer tell up from down.

Once we stopped, Herb got out and smashed one windshield wiper with his fist. Suddenly it started working again. Great; now do the other one. Okay! It fell off, so we put it in with the peanut shells.

We had already spent one night on the road and were just groggy enough to continue; add one more ingredient or take one away, and we might have stopped.

We drove to the coast and St. John, New Brunswick, discovered that the ferry to Digby wouldn't leave till midmorning, and so went on through the night to Nova Scotia by way of Moncton. The weather was clearing and stars were up there. We could just about make it. Sunrise! Ocean! Halifax at dawn!

Up around Moncton we stopped at an all-night gas station and asked the attendant, "What time is dawn?"

"Ohh, 'bout eight o'clock."

"Eight o'clock?"

"Why, shure! The *sun* don't even come up till 5:30!"

Well, we did make Halifax at dawn of that day, and even saw the sun come up. Here was the planned destination of our walk, and we were grimy, groggy, and disillusioned. As the sun rose, the city came to resemble any city. So much for destinations.

We found a motel, slept three hours, took showers, and stepped outside into a balmy 55-degree day with barely time to appreciate it, since we planned to catch the ferry at 2:30 for St. John. This gave us three hours and twenty minutes to cross Nova Scotia, a drive of 153 miles, in a truck whose top speed was 50 miles per hour.

We caught the ferry with ten minutes to spare, got to St. John late in the afternoon, fueled up, and took off again. By morning we were almost into New Hampshire. At that late date in the exploratory trip, we did begin a concerted search for more dirt roads, trails, forgotten roads.

Just out of Limington, Maine, we drove down a one-tracker, past shacks, huge bare trees, abandoned farms, old cemeteries with only the tallest stones sticking up out of the snow. The road was plowed only up to a lonely little house, maybe the last one on it. The owner told us, "Oh yes, this road goes on into Limerick. This is the old way."

Back around the "new" way and there, just at the outskirts of Limerick, we made the connection. We also came upon a "Directory" tree at a three-way intersection. On the tree were at least twenty-five arrow signs, each with a family name. It is impossible to describe the different lettering styles, colors, sign shapes and sizes, the giant tree itself, and the effect of the homemade announcements, invitations, pleas for those life-changing letters ("You've just won $750,000!" . . . "Mom: I'm coming home!").

"Listen," Herbie said, "we're walking along in silence and we come around that corner and there's the tree. We walk up to it and stand there and *just look*! It'll blow their minds!"

The scouting trip—over 1,600 miles—was not completely satisfying, and yet in a way it was. We had not found enough back roads, but we had something else.

The idea was to sneak up on Canada, to get to Nova Scotia and see *no* cars. The idea was to miss all big towns. The idea was the trip itself, the way there.

We ran the gamut: from the end of the trial run and the recommencement of school till the Ford Foundation came through with a grant that would cover expenses, till the 16-square-foot ex-Army squad tent was bought, till we drank brandy together and toasted the trip two days before leaving, through the last meeting and the weird, building excitement, through exams and last classes and all the interruptions ("L.J. just got some great maps of Maine and New Hampshire!" "Listen! I got the *money*! I can GO!"), till the tent crew had come over and put up the tent three or four times, through the last pledged 7-miles-for-five-days practice walks, till we bought the last sleeping bags, the last ponchos at the Springfield Army-Navy store, had the last hassle with the registrar, who billed the course EN 423, Philosophy of Walking (despite pleas to leave it simply The Walk, under no department), through the last jibes from other faculty members.

I told one that I'd have to be in great shape because the students would be able to bounce back each day. "What?" he said. "They're so soft that they have nothing to bounce back *to!*"

At the very last meeting, held in the new library building—and only at that meeting—was I able to announce that the Ford money had come in. Not only had I previously told the walkers about the application, but I had told them we'd probably get help. A hundred times I could have bitten my tongue off. There were dozens of reasons why Ford might have refused. Well, I *had* felt it in my bones, and this time my bones were right.

As for the group itself, I felt more than lucky. They trusted, they believed, they were smart, quick, they were with it all the way. Not more than a week before we were to start out, a little delegation led by Ann M. came to me. How did I *really* feel about drugs on the trip? I didn't even want to answer. I wanted their freedom . . . I wanted the best for the walk. There was no conflict in my mind; drugs were out. But I wanted them to want that. Their *real* reactions, not theirs through drugs. "We've been feeling," she said, "that between Lloyd, Gordon, and a few of us, we can handle it. On a trip like this, just walking, out in the air, with no one hanging over us, there's no need for it. We'll be high without anything. We'll want *not* to miss anything, to get everything we can!" I wanted to hug her. So I did.

The last days were frantic. At last we found a truck—to haul equipment, to buy food, to scout out roads ahead, and to carry the wounded (I kept thinking of sprained ankles, although we had only one). We bought stoves, Coleman lamps, extra wicks, candle holders, waterproof matchboxes (never used), walking boots (which should have been bought weeks before), pedometers for walking mileage, insect spray (lost until the drive home), and might as well say "and so on" because it didn't matter, it was a buying hysteria, confirmation that we were really going, an attempt to bury two days.

Last day in April. A million things were still undone. Long-distance phone calls had been coming in for days, and now the yard was filling with a weird assortment of cars. The house was full; everybody was off the ground, eyes blazing, not even talking any longer but chattering, laughing, giggling. The balloon was swelling, rising. Our three youngest children were off with their grandparents, our twelve- and thirteen-year-olds were going with us. Seventeen students and the four of us: twenty-one. A good number.

Could we feed them all? Of course. We had air, water, eyes popping, minds blowing, scattering. Even the sanest ones in the group were bowled over and falling away.

"You guys are soft, you'll never make it!"

"WE LEAVE TONIGHT!"

"I'll drink to that!"

We toasted the trip, each other, May, and the mess around us— everything was poleaxed all over the house: duffle bags, ponchos, air mattresses, boots.

"Everybody has to carry his own toilet paper."

"I'll drink to that!"

All of the talk, phone calls, departures for urgent purchases ("Toenail clippers, got to have toenail clippers . . .") was really a very special strange wait-urge for another day and a half to go by.

"What? You haven't seen the truck? Come outside."

The '66 Ford Supervan grinned back at us. Zooommm. Zoooommm. Power!!!

We were already walking . . . floating. To Canada? An incidental, but I must admit it worried me a little.

Next day we sprayed the inside of the truck white, since there were no side windows. Most important was an inspection sticker for it, due May 15th, and the truck would never pass with that crack in the windshield.

May 1st. Suddenly it seemed that nothing was done. We

were scheduled to sleep on the soccer field that night and start walking at 7:00 the next morning. So we sprayed the outside of the truck. In big letters on both sides we sprayed THE WALK.

A. R. Orage once said, "Perhaps man will become more and more like the ants and bees before he becomes extinct."

With something like hope for all of us, I sprayed some additional words underneath, so it was:

THE WALK
of the
conscious ants

The sun kept going down on May 1st, and somehow the mess was being scooped up, folded away, even packed; but if there were to be times of silence, of solitude and tranquil campfires, this day had nothing to do with them. In the final week, two of the most positive students couldn't make the trip, and three additional students *were* going—two of whom I'd never known at all. Well, if the spirit was there, if the feeling for it was in them, the rest could be explained, and all three were championed by students who understood the idea well. Ex–Boy Scouts, campers, hikers were not encouraged. We'd never done this kind of thing before and we didn't want advice.

We had a last meeting that night at one of the off-campus dorms; afterwards Gale (my wife) and I went home and didn't finish there till about 1:30. Then, in the "new" truck, we set out over the same 15-mile stretch which, more than a year before, had begun all this. At the end of this drive was *the* walk.

Jake was in the truck with us, skinny Jake who had hesitated till the last week before deciding to go. He was so excited he was burning himself out, hopping and screaming in the back of the truck.

We turned into the parking lot next to the soccer field. The moon was almost straight up; a campfire had burned down to embers except for an occasional flame. A dozen or more shapes—sleeping bags on ponchos, on space blankets—were scattered to the sides and in front of the tent, which stood like a little brown fortress on a moonlit plain. There was no sound; instead of people it was as if an idea were sleeping. And just that far from being realized.

They had already taken the first step. We were to spend the first night on the soccer field, and there they were. Absolute stillness before motion. The fire was like memories—which are sometimes better than the real. They were one in sleep, and we went down to join them.

THE WALK

May 2nd. At 5:00
a.m., with frost on our space blankets, on our sleeping bags,
on whatever we'd left outside, we woke up. In order to be
warm in a sleeping bag it is best to take off all clothes. I didn't
quite believe this, but I'd taken off enough to feel the zap of
very cold air as I emerged from my cocoon.

We were up on our feet packing, tying, collecting ourselves,
afraid, maybe feeling a little silly now that we were to begin
weaving the first straw in this 600-mile basket. Could we?
Wasn't it a mad scheme—wasn't it high time to admit it?

Several times I thought I noticed students (not yet walkers) looking at me as if they were thinking, "Did he really
mean it? Just walk off?"

Howie hadn't come yet. L.J. (Little John) wasn't there.
Stoney, at the last minute, was out with three abscessed
wisdom teeth.

Howie pulled up in a car driven by a friend and, within
minutes, was doing eggs with the touch of a great short-order
cook. Someone borrowed a car and went off to get L.J., who
can sleep through anything—standing up.

A photographer was there taking pictures, a reporter was
asking questions. Word answers were impossible. We'll see,
we're just taking a walk. *But does it equal a semester?* No,
ten semesters.

At 8:20 we were ready. One hour late. It doesn't seem so

strange now, but it was a little painful at the time. The truck was packed and we'd meet it in Jaffrey, 8 miles away—to cash checks, eat an early lunch, and regroup.

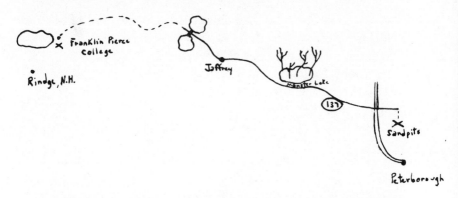

Which was the first step? Off the soccer field? Off school grounds? The back road to Jaffrey is like a green cave, a woodsy dirt road, impassable from late November through early May. Streams were running high and patches of snow were still on the ground. Just before we stepped down that road, the school photographer screamed up. Last pictures, and we traded school for the dark green of the back road to Jaffrey.

President Nixon stated that the moon shot was "The Greatest Adventure Ever Undertaken by Man." But both beauty and adventure are very personal. Whose adventure is the moon shot? Is it Nixon's? Is it MAN's? It is not mine; I didn't do it.

We began on a quiet back road leading, almost meandering, from one unimportant town to another, in a small New England state. Where would we spend the night? How far would we get?

At 9:20 we stopped by a hidden but vigorous stream for one of the only group stops. We were smiling and talking, but the smiles were not so silly. We had done something. According to the pedometer, we had walked about 3½ miles.

Everyone was still full of precautions, warnings, instructions about rubbing alcohol, foot powder, and socks. Almost everyone carried foot powder and rubbing alcohol. Almost everyone carried a knapsack. Almost everyone carried too much.

At 9:30 we began again and, as agreed, walked in silence. What do we know of ourselves? What do we kno of the world? Someone said that "to know ourselves is to ᴋɴow the universe." What does it really mean? Let it go.

To walk together in silence was one of my own aims for the walk. I wondered how Ann M. (There were two Anns— Ann M. and Big Ann) was coming, with her aim not to use her mind for forty days. It is a nice aim. Quite impossible, but okay.

"Osiris is a wish to understand cut into fragments. Our task is to unite the fragments. This is at-one-ment." A. R. Orage said that. Who is he? What does it matter? Put the fragments together . . . the fragments of wishes to understand.

New shoes are beginning to chafe feet. Although everyone had been told to break in new shoes, I am as bad as anyone; mine are only five days old. There are at least six others with brand-new shoes and aching feet.

At 9:30 the first car went by. After it passed, the sounds were even clearer . . . shoes, a canteen clanking, the little click of my pedometer marking time-space in its dumb way (Bill said the noise bothered him). Dan's crazy hat bobs ahead of me. Phil's tired tirelessness. Howie's socked feet. The breeze blows gently past my ears. Birds across the field send their wind song, wind and air song. It erupts from them as naturally as a stream gurgles over rocks. Here we are. Here we are, at a broad field and a gray abandoned house. My son, "the Weasel," just slogs along, loose as goose grease. Lloyd has been barefooted since the first mile. All things register lightly.

Is this school?

We leave the dirt road for asphalt, and it winds down. Two lakes are separated by the road. A rushing stream feeds the two by way of a culvert, over which the road passes. It is a nice open scene with glassy lakes on both sides and, since we are still in silence, no one comments, we simply look, from whatever angle or level we see and appreciate from. No one says it's beautiful. Each of us has it, or doesn't have it.

Once I went to a performance where no one was allowed to applaud. The most beautiful dances were begun and finished and the audience, as instructed, did not make a sound. We were left with our appreciation. It was with such a feeling of thankfulness—well, even happiness—at not having clapped out our enthusiasm that we left the theater . . . that we left two clear lakes separated by a little bridge.

More cars went by as we neared town. The drivers seemed frightened. Of us? Or were these simply their "driving" faces? Tense, anxious, frightened.

Get over! The sound builds up. Is everyone off the road? Zoom! The car's gone, and we're happy and loose again.

More houses and barking dogs. Well, and if we look like beggars, so be it. No one wears his best clothes for a 600-mile stroll.

We entered Jaffrey at 10:25, an average of a little more than 3½ miles an hour—almost 4. Maybe this deluded us as to what sort of pace we could maintain, but there was nothing about our reception which might lead us to think the trip would be easy.

Lloyd, Ann M., and L.J. were standing in front of a general store when a middle-aged man about to pull away from the gas pump screamed, "Oughta hang 'em all!" He drove off quickly, leaving them with his words.

We ate all over Jaffrey while waiting for the truck, which had burst a radiator hose and was being fixed about 10 miles away. We ate, went to the bank, were kicked off the town square, then were kicked off the church lawn (nicely . . . the cop explained he'd had a complaint from two members of the board). I will admit it was a pretty bizarre-looking group. Some were stretched out sleeping, half were doctoring feet, all were wondering (in dreams or out loud) whether we'd really make it.

Finally the truck caught up with us. We took off on 137 out of Jaffrey, due north. Gale was to find a campsite, shop, unload, set up, and come back with directions.

Barking dogs and the outskirts of town go together. Up they come, stiff-legged. Get 'em! They don't drive cars like our masters! Dreamy music leaks out of a house we pass. Music to dream your life away.

The talk is of being pushed around in Jaffrey. " 'Get off the square, we just planted the grass,' he says. 'Go over to the church!' Didn't they just plant *their* grass?"

In the square is a statue of a World War I soldier carrying his wounded buddy, all hewn out of New Hampshire granite: granite heads, granite pants, granite eyes of pride, courage, and coolth.

One day, instead of war heroes and politicians, there might be granite monuments to unsung public servants: John the Newspaper Boy on His Trusty Bike.

" 'Oughta hang 'em all!' " another walker shouted ahead to Lloyd.

The earth to our right rolls down and away in green fields; we're way up striding along on the world. A spring-swollen stream fans out over the road. Country smells. Pines soughing. A dog two miles away. Cow dung on the wind, and sweet clover. We've turned our backs to the south, we're shaking free of the school and its immediate towns, we're alone on the road, only ourselves to contend with. And the little toes on both feet. It's not that they hurt, I just keep thinking about them. Later, I found out that means blisters.

New boots are slung over shoulders and people are into their own slouching, limping survival walks. On we go. Green land sweeps up to a house and we see all the angles.

> BEWARE:
> SMALL DOG

At the next stop, "Monster Lake," an old swamp between Jaffrey and Peterborough with jagged dead trees and a mist hanging over it, we started laughing about our feet, about the whole project. We were sitting, lying around, half on the road and half off, just finding ourselves there. On about five different levels the question came up, "What are we *really* doing?"

The rest of that day is blurred by fatigue. Wooded roads, little traffic, wooden bridges, beautiful country—although I understood as never before that "beautiful" is almost anything seen when you're feeling good. We had walked in a huge semicircle. Our back roads meandered for 16 miles in a jagged curve, while the regular route from the soccer field to the place where we ended the day is no more than 13 at the most. That was okay because it wasn't distance we were interested in; still, I knew many days would pass before we'd begin to get lost along the way.

I remember sitting on a bluff with about five others and feeling the urge, an immediate urge, when the truck pulled up. As nonchalantly as possible I asked the truck for toilet paper. "What?" someone yelled, about five times too loud, "Say you need *toilet paper?*"

I had to own up to that.

We coasted into west Peterborough, which is an area, not a town, and found a breezy hilltop with thick soft grass. Little by little everyone collected there.

"Why not camp here?"

More walkers flopped down, everyone traded sights and pieces of the day: a car that almost hit not one person but four or five at different spots, Howie's fear of dogs and of being chased, who else was lost.

Suddenly Howie was running by, *running* along the road. We called to him and he came up breathless, gave us his story.

Dogs! Wooooahh, he was out of breath.

Don with his Indian hat and Dan came up. Lloyd was on them: "You guys got stuck! You went all the way out to 101 again?"

"Yeah!"

"Well, how did you find this?"

"We figured this was a good place to die."

"I don't know what I'm doing here. I was in the Boy Scouts for two years and I never got past Tenderfoot."

"That's a good sign."

Up came the truck. They'd found a "great" place, the sand-pit near the MacDowell dam, 6 miles away. Everybody groaned. It was finally decided that the truck would take the cooks to help unload and start supper, then would come back for the rest of us, since we'd already walked over 15 miles and the place was "a little" out of the way.

About half decided to walk. We (especially Phil and I) looked on the truck as untouchable. We were *walking* to Canada. I put my boots in the truck and we started off. The 6-mile barefooted trek took us more than three hours, and after getting lost and having darkness drop down on us, we did accept a ride for the last three-quarters of a mile (or was it two?).

Walking barefooted is both a relief and a shock. Suddenly, freed toes stop hurting . . . suddenly the soles of the feet are very tender. I had hold of a great truth: shoes chafe *and* protect.

Almost everyone in camp had foot problems, but it was a good night, a great meal—American chop suey. Chop suey *is* American? Well, this was American chop suey. Don't argue with the cooks. The cooks, Ann M. and Howie, did have one fight but it was a thing of pride, about sauce, I believe. It was also a windy wild night, a wild place; huge banks, hills, and cliffs of sand. The wind was whipping away at our big campfire and our two-burners. We also had a little Optimus backpacker's stove. It was as fierce as a ground rattler and could boil all of the water in the most gigantic pot. It looked and sounded like a little blowtorch, and once it drilled a hole right through a pot. I don't know exactly why, but that made some of us very proud of the Optimus.

Our tent was up but about half the group moved off to sleep under the sky. Someone had very thoughtfully put up the little two-man tent for Gale and me, but it was the first and last night for that oppressive, low-ceilinged tent.

Next morning the dreaded rain greeted us, a steady light rain. I think it dawned on everyone that we'd have to pull off to the side: collect money for food, make a dishwashing list . . . the real specifics. Peterborough was only 4 miles away; we could walk to my house, have coffee and doughnuts and a meeting.

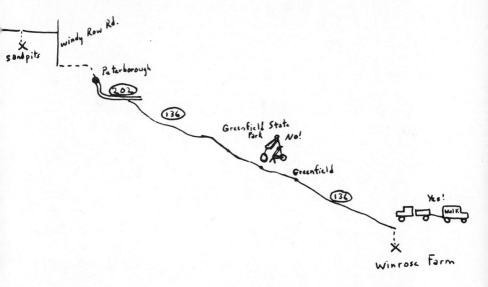

Ponchos were the uniform as we trailed out along the road. One day and a night had gone by, and the question was hanging over us. Could we make it? Would we just split apart *because* of the very lack of structure? Disorganization doesn't bother me—perhaps some would say that it sure as hell doesn't—but even I sensed that it couldn't work like this.

From the sandpit to the house is another nice walk. We saw no more than five cars, passed a tranquil pond, green fields, tar and gravel roads with shade trees on either side which almost touched over our heads. The rain came down steadily, stopped for a short time, came down again. But no matter, for then we were inside a house—with a flushing toilet!

We gathered in the dining room, and it was as if we were breaking a certain kind of silence which had lasted from the minute we stepped off the soccer field till now. Although the words weren't used, we were for the first time admitting out loud: Okay, we've begun. We've really begun.

Lloyd and Ann M. would keep the books. Twenty dollars was collected from each person. Ann M. and Howie would alternate as cooks. The cooks would not wash dishes and would be picked up at 4:30 for shopping and so forth. I made up a list of dishwashers, two for each meal. Lunch would be sandwiches and fruit made by the driver and anyone else on the truck when possible. Bill and Bob D. would load the truck in the mornings. No, they didn't need any help.

All of this was decided unanimously. The idea of unanimity is a Quaker idea. Nothing is done, nothing is decided until there is unanimity. Majority rule is quicker, but usually about 40 percent of a group is dissatisfied with every decision. I was anxious to try it out, even anxious for a time when we would lock horns over something. It would happen soon enough.

The meeting was over. For this beginning, each person had directions for Greenfield State Park, where we planned to stay that night. Walkers left in twos and threes or singly. That pattern was to continue throughout the walk. The sun came out, so we had heavy, cloudy sunshine with a strong southerly breeze.

To walk out of one's house, out of one's neighborhood, on such a project . . . well, it would be good to be long gone.

The houses of Peterborough were stringing out, just as we were. The Contoocook river was on our left, a pine woods on our right, and the wind pushed us along—oranges, peanuts, sunflower seeds, pad, and pen in my knapsack.

A woman is fishing. She casts and . . . she lands a fish!

Here's a nice tree. What kind? One with what we call "branches." I had talked to the walkers for so long about just "seeing" without names and categories that it had become a joke. The game warden at the Audubon sanctuary had told us, in awed tones, that he had spotted a "hooded merganser" out on the lake. Almost any moving object was now a hooded merganser.

Whoooo the wind blows us along. The sun hammers down. We carry our ponchos on arms, over shoulders.

To wish not to change one thing. To will it all.

Come on down, sun! Hurt, feet! Blow, wind!

"Alllllll is p-p-p-*perfect*," the Zen Buddhist said.

We collected at the entrance to the state park and discovered that it didn't open officially until May 9th. Well, how about unofficially? The director sat on his little bike and in perfect composure and with perfect computer logic said, "If-I-open-it-for-you . . . I'll have-to-open-it-for-everyone!" The polished words rolled out and around in our heads.

I must admit he smiled as he said it, but something else escaped in the words, in the tone, from the bicycle seat, and it came out in words soon enough. "Yes, I heard about the trip . . . the police in Jaffrey told me *all* about it."

We pleaded for a spot for the tent, said we'd be gone by morning. Nope, the water wasn't turned on. "We have our own water." But, he said, there'd be no toilets. Could we dig a trench for toilets?

"I told you it's not open. And-if-I-open-for-you-I'll-have to-open-for-everyone."

Perfectly at ease on his bike, he told five of us, "I don't know how you expect to make Canada, anyhow . . . you've only done about six miles a day."

Fiery L.J. leaped over to the bike: "You get off that bike! I'll outwalk you right now and bet any amount on it."

The man smiled coolly. "Oh no!" Why, if he got off his bike for L.J., he'd have to get off his bike for everyone.

We left, straggling away toward Greenfield, or to nowhere, or just on, north. I walked with L.J., who still wanted satisfaction. "Man, I'd have walked till my legs were *bleeding stumps!*" But it was over, he was laughing again, and L.J.'s laughter is a beautiful sound.

Suddenly the truck pulled up. What? We have a place? Just beyond Greenfield?

News like this travels all over the body in instants. Suddenly we could walk ten more miles.

Earlier a friend had stopped her car beside us and stated, "Next time I see you, you'll look like the wrath of God."

Who knows, maybe we'll be angels.

Gentle. Gentle. Walking is a gentle sport.

The site was just off the road out of Greenfield on the way to Francestown. Maybe because I didn't fall in love with our first site (and maybe that was because the sandpit was too close to home), I felt that this was our first real camp. People had said "yes" to us. They hadn't balked at the sight of us. They said yes and then saw us and still said yes. We drove the truck off the road to get the equipment as close to the site as we could, and suddenly we were sinking in a wide bog. With twenty worn-out walkers pushing and one driving, we couldn't budge the truck. I couldn't, or wouldn't, telephone from the owner's house. He had said yes to us, and I wanted no regrets. At a farm a few houses away I asked to use the phone.

"There ain't no wrecker in Greenfield. What's the problem?"

That old farmer just walked out to his truck and dumped a chain in back. "Take the *new* truck," his wife yelled. He just nodded and drove out, in the old one.

It's not so much favors but the way people do them. He did it in style, and almost silently. Our blue van was out. The old man looked at the money as if money and the deed had nothing to do with each other.

While the tent crew put up the tent and the cooks started supper, Bob B. and I went mapping for next day's roads. Bob B. measures about three feet across the chest, is great with maps, and has tiny feet. Already his blisters had blisters, as he put it.

We were out for old roads and, bang, we found them. We passed an old black barn out of Francestown, the biggest barn I've ever seen. It *is* a celebration. Black-ness. Barn-ness. We were goggle-eyed. Just beyond it we turned right, feeling our way down an old gravel road. Darkness was coming on and the trees were hastening it, but before it closed in completely we passed a huge lake. We went over a few bridges and there, almost next to us, was the lake again. We lost it, and there was little light left to the day, but whenever we stopped we could hear streams gurgling, and we could almost feel the presence of the lake. We were giving them a beautiful lake tomorrow and winding, tree-lined gravel roads.

When we had about 13 or 14 miles mapped out, we turned around and raced back. Every house we had been to was empty and unlocked—Saturday night, and they were eating out, going to the movies, or somewhere—we'd get a place tomorrow, around New Boston. Back to camp.

"Great roads!" we told them. "Great roads and a *lake*! Back roads, gravel, trees all over, hooded mergansers!"

It had started raining so we had been invited to eat in the barn. The lamps were hissing, food was hot and good, people chattering and eating. Shiny faces in lamplight, tired, happy, milling around. Stew and half-cooked potatoes. But what a taste! Our cooks, our food, our place for the night, and chocolate pudding for dessert. Some meals are like celebrations. Who knows why?

At the farm was a Canadian musician, a houseguest, who came out to the barn with the owners. A real Canadian! He turned us on. We turned him on. He turned us on. "You're really from Canada?" "You're really walking to Canada?"

"All the way."

"But that's *great!*"

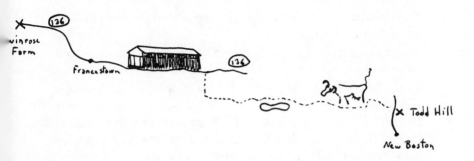

Sunday morning. We were up and off fairly early, but it never seemed early enough. It isn't the same as roll over, get out of bed, look out the window, hmmmm, how's the weather out there?

Diana was our alarm clock. She was to wake me up, I was to wake the cooks and the others, start the stoves, put on water. Some are up quickly and others are slow. Then there is lots to be done, because our home is moving. Besides visits to the woods, and breakfast stuff to be located, there is the tent to be taken down, dishes washed and packed, directions to be given out.

We're off, and that's a relief—even if we feel sore and stiff. Up over that hill, around the bend, who knows what we'll see, or what strange thought will be delivered to us?

We woke up and walked, woke up and walked, woke up and walked. Slowly we were getting into it. Up a hill or two, and something takes over and the mind is free. People drive by in their Sunday best. To worship. Each in his own way. Sunday, Monday, Tuesday, Wednesday.

Within an hour Gale and I were walking alone, close to the end of the haphazard line. Everybody was strung out, two miles or more. But why not? Who really walks at the same pace? They all had directions; let them go. Are there more chances for accidents this way? Probably fewer.

All day people were asking us: What are you doing? Where are you going? What for? You walking for peace? CANADA? Why??

Our answers became simpler. People were out in gardens or driving by, so it was easy for them to look up and ask, or stop and ask. Three or four wanted to join us. One seventy-five-year-old man wanted Gale. "Hey, honey! What are you doin' with that old man?" But he had remarks for everyone. A man in a little VW slowed down and asked the two Bobs and Bill, "What are you doing?" "We're walking to Canada." "Well," he considered that for a moment. "I can't think of a finer thing to do," and he drove off.

In Francestown some of the walkers waited for us. A "cool" couple wanted to see us. They lived in Francestown a few houses off the route. Gale and I walked over and saw John and Kate and had iced tea. "We were talking to some of your students," they told us. "They don't have too good a notion of what this is all about!" He laughed about the different answers they gave him. It didn't matter. Ask us the purpose when we get there.

John, Kate, the baby, and their mindless Afghan joined us for about 5 miles. Out of Francestown we came to the big barn. No sense in drawing or photographing it. It is a wooden wall of China. A little farther on is the gravel road. I put on my shoes and we continue. The commanding colors are yellow, light green, spring red—and they light the air. They dance above and around the unfurling leaves. The earth is cracking open. Bugs are out, the table is being set, the feast is on the way.

Ann M., Don, and Lloyd later told us of an old woman in her little garden, of her sweet smile.

Did she know what she'd done for them? "I can't think of a finer thing to do."

Did he?

They would remember those things; where they happened, with whom they were walking, how they felt.

It's all psychological.

It's all in your head.

If it is, and we could direct it, we could walk off the earth, we could "merge with the miraculous," as Lindbergh said.

Three miles in on that gravel road, we spotted the lake. We were to meet the truck there and have sandwiches and drinks. Another half mile and there they were. There we were. Yes, it's better as we did it; string out, collect at the end or along the way, pass each other or catch up at some country store, and trade back and forth—how delicious the sandwiches were, how freezing cold the water was. Nobody seemed to be very modest, and swimming suits were way down under everything else. The water *burned*: feet, legs, even hair follicles. Once I broke through a layer of ice to go swimming, but that water was no colder than this.

We built a fire and crowded close to it. Everyone was eat-

ing, talking, tending feet. Our blue truck was working fine.
We didn't have a place for the night, but Herbie and the
truck would leave and work on that next. We still had 3 or
4 miles on the single-track hilly, woodsy road, and only a
feeling for the north and east. Only a certainty that we would
miss the big cities. As for the little ones, they were simply
names for us to meet in, get food or white gas for the stoves
from.

To be warm and dry after cold and wet is happiness
enough. To be tying on shoes to walk unknown roads . . .
well, we agreed with that man.

In the afternoon a driver slowed down and asked Bill sus-
piciously, "Is this for peace?" "No," Bill told him. "It's for
nothing!"

We saw a crazy herd of cows that afternoon. They should
have been in a circus. They wheeled, looked, turned their
backs to us, all in unison. It was a great act and the spectators
were only eight or nine walkers on an old road. Our act was
crazy enough to them, I. suppose. We laughed, talked,
clapped for them, turned—almost in unison—and then
walked off, all in the same direction.

By 4 o'clock we had had it. There were some beautiful
fields next to houses which were unused in winter and spring.
There was no one to ask. Who would mind? We flopped in
a field and talked, or giggled. We'd walked only 13 miles as it
turned out, but our feet, legs, and backs told us it was
enough. Even the blackflies were no longer a bother. I remembered earlier seeing Motorhead (he had a head for mo-
tors) doing a dance of frustration, swinging his arms around
his head, jigging up and down, to start life all over again
without blackflies—but that kind of energy had long been
expended.

Across the field a black VW pulled up and stopped. Howie,
L.J., and some local girls came over. Rich and Don and the
two of them had already gotten to New Boston; the girls had
picked Howie and L.J. up, or vice versa, and brought them
over to find us. Rich and Don were still in New Boston. The
truck should be along any minute. We had a place, about 3

miles from where we were. It was in a field, they told us, but
it was "out of the way." L.J. and Howie did not want to go
"backwards" since they'd already made it to New Boston.
Couldn't they sleep just out of New Boston?

I felt downhearted even hearing the question. Instinctively
it was no; we would stick together. I told them that much
then. They went back and talked to the girls, and the rest
of us walked off toward the site. We'd have to have a meeting. The words they had used were disturbing—more than
wanting to sleep apart. Going "backwards"? The campsite
was "out of the way"? We were not trying to *make* it to
Canada. It was exactly what we were *not* trying to do. We'd
do that, but without trying. We had to have a meeting.

We came out of our woodsy road and there, across from a
tar highway on a grass field, was the truck, and a mound of
equipment. We walked across the field and, of course, even
with problems coming up it was good to meet again. All was
familiar except the place. Our tent was going up. But there
was no time to sit around. While people were still tying down
the tent, driving stakes, picking out spots inside, gassing
lamps, blowing up air mattresses (familiar sound: breathing
life into air mattresses in the evening, squeezing it out the
next morning), Ann M., Lloyd, and I took the very detailed
map and set out in the truck for back roads for tomorrow.

Very early it became clear that almost everyone had a
blanket prejudice against students. Not that they knew for
certain, but the chances were that we had just come from
burning all the school records, killing the dean, razing the
administration building, or protesting the war. Ann M. suggested that Gale or I should be the one to ask for a place,
since students were turned away almost automatically. Long
hair or short hair they were turned away, but long hair was
enough to make people bolt the doors, get out guns, and call
the law.

The general plan was to go 15 miles, find a place, then find
the best back roads leading to it; this was not too hard since
we were already off the beaten path. The plan was also to
keep Lloyd out of sight. He has beautiful red hair, very curly,

and it hangs almost to his shoulders. Lloyd is also a great mechanic, great walker, strong, honest, the whole Scout's oath. He is the one who left the meeting when I was talking about drugs ("I had a class," he told me later that day, "I think the idea's great!"). Already he had walked about 30 miles barefoot. But when we were mapping and wanted to get a place for the next night, we kept Lloyd in the truck.

We spotted a great field next to a pond and I went over to ask for the place. They were teachers, and it was a tree farm. Sure, they said; we could even go swimming, "if you're brave enough!" They invited Gale and me for a drink next evening "after the younger generation goes to bed." What? I'd beat them to bed if I possibly could.

"We got it!"

That was always a happy time; with Lloyd's enthusiasm, Ann M.'s smile at Lloyd, we started the drive back.

Keeping track of the mileage while mapping is almost impossible. We leave camp, note the mileage; take off on a side road, note the mileage; turn off again, note mileage to be subtracted; come to a dead end, note mileage, subtract from turnoff mileage; double back another way, begin estimating distance from the original turnoff; then, at another turnoff, just to scout around, junk the whole thing, because it would take a calculus professor to untangle it. Besides, we'll get it "on the way back." Sure, only the way back is also full of experiments, turns, and trial runs.

We had supper and a meeting after it, our first real meeting on the road. I was partly asking for something, partly demanding. Where did my authority lie, especially when I had done everything to convince them that this trip was ours? It was theirs and mine, but there were certain things we had agreed to: that we would go as a group, that we would do things unanimously. If one or two went off for a night, why not twos and threes for two nights? Why not split up and go to Canada in smaller groups, each one picking his way and making it there . . . or not?

During the meeting the girls in their black VW were parked on the edge of the field, waiting—impatiently, it seemed to me. The walk had nothing to do with them. I didn't expect the girls to understand the importance of the meeting, but I did expect all of the walkers to. Everyone was heard. L.J. and Howie agreed: we would stick together. Next came the more important topic of going "backwards," or of being the first to reach camp.

"It's not a race!" They knew it, yet they were caught, or had caught themselves, from time to time, racing. Naturally, I guess, since we all had a lifetime of training in trying to get "there." "We really thought about just striking out," I said. "From school to as far as we could get in forty days— perhaps to western Pennsylvania, or nowhere in particular. I'm not knocking the idea of Canada. It's exciting. But Canada is *wrong* if it hurts the trip. Even to use words like this field is 'out of the way' or you 'made' the town and don't want to go 'backwards' means you're trying to make it to Canada."

Some really didn't understand it, but they were beginning to. It *wasn't* about getting to Canada? They knew but they didn't know. Didn't understand . . . yet. Many of them did, and they tried to explain it to the others. We talked about walking in silence—what it could do, the objections to it. At meetings they could agree to it, but when they were actually out on the road it was more difficult. The meeting ended on a bland note: tomorrow's roads. The way would be marked with toilet paper on tree branches. We doctored our feet and went to sleep. I don't know whether L.J. and Howie kept their dates or slept there part of the night. We had agreed to stick together. On that note I slept well.

It was still too early to think of much besides walking. The part of my brain which registered pain from toes must have been inflamed. My little toes cried to be cut off and left. Phil had the same trouble Someone figured out Bob B.'s problem, and it was as helpful as most word answers: "Bob, your walking area is too small for the bulk it's being asked to carry."

Next day I walked with Bob D. and Bill after they had loaded the truck. They wanted to walk into New Boston. It would add only a mile or two, so we struck out. Various individuals had tried to keep up with Bob B. (or keep down with him). Bob D. had been most successful, because both of them were crippled. They wiggled, hobbled, twisted along the roads. People driving by, and even other walkers, just *knew* it was an act, but no, they were getting along in their own best way. Off we went to town, Bob D. twisting off the miles (it was a football knee from high school he said), me with my tender toes and soles, and Bill, who had little or no trouble with his feet, holding his transistor to his ear.

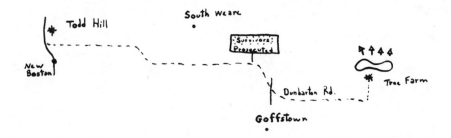

At the meeting the night before, the idea of two hours of silence in the mornings—an idea everyone had agreed to before leaving—had taken a beating. Richie found it very difficult to remain silent for that long. Most wanted it to be an individual thing—the warped American version of external "freedom"—"When you want silence, just drop back or speed up." That would never happen, I argued. Still, everyone agreed to try silence at the same time for four more days and meet again on it. We were due to go into an hour of silence at 9:15.

New Boston was a little farther than we thought, so we didn't get to the outskirts until 9:20 and decided—for the store, or any contacts—that just as good an exercise would be to speak only when we had to, and with as few words as possible.

To walk from country into town is no longer a common experience in the United States; it is a quiet, gradual change:

farmhouse   *field*   *road crossing*
woods   *plowed field*

f a r m h o u s e s
fenced field

intersection—filling station—roads
big-yard houses
road — store — house — shop — houses

streets

blocks

town

Inside the big store next to the post office, the clerk became more and more curious at our short answers.

"You fellers camping?"

"Walking."

"Walkin' eh? Where to?"

"Canada."

"Canada!?°?#!? . . . That's an awful long walk!"

I nod. "Pens?"

"Mean to write with?"

I nod. He walks over, still unsatisfied. "You just walkin' to Canada, eh?" I nod at him. "Any partic'lar purpose behind it? I mean . . . any reason?"

"School."

"Walkin' to Canada to go to school?"

"No."

"Mean it's a school that walks to Canada?"

"Just walks."

We passed the parish house and looked in the windows. On the blackboard was the lesson from Sunday school: "And whatever you do in word or deed do everything in the name of the Lord Jesus."

Well, I was supposed to check in with the school in word and deed "every night." This was the fourth day, so I decided to call. Everything was okay, I told them. We should make our first mail stop—Limerick, Maine—on or about May 9th or 10th.

But why should the freaks report in every night? A phone call is a little thing to someone at home, but on the road it would be an unendurable drag to locate a phone booth every night. I'd call if we needed help. But each day's walk made that less possible. Furthermore, we were trying to escape the usual "conveniences": noisy telephones and mailmen who bring us warnings, reminders, bills, and draft notices.

We set out from New Boston, stopped at an antique place a little way out. The woman was uneasy because we just looked around without a word for about five minutes, then went on with a wave good-bye.

The hour wasn't quite over when a young girl drove up and stopped for us. Suzy Parker, girl reporter from Goffstown, and full of questions. We seemed to turn her down and then off. We posed for a picture, but we weren't a "story." We simply answered questions and let it go. In all, it was the noisiest silent hour we spent.

While the others were walking a car-less gravel road next to little streams and plank bridges, a huge old abandoned chicken "hotel"—gone to seed and almost folded away into the earth—we were on a lined, paved highway with cars zipping by.

We walked until we were giddy, then rested on the side. There was a big stream on our left, and if we hadn't had such a freezing swim the day before we would have gone in. Besides, we'd messed around enough and were certainly behind everyone.

During these early days Bill was still glued to his radio most of his waking hours. He was very touchy about it. He wanted to listen and he'd listen.

A state highway truck passes . . . alert. They sense that we are not the usual campers or walkers.

Gentle contact with a fisherman. His voice seems not to have been used for a few hours. "Straight ahead, about three miles."

"How about the stone bridge?"

"You can go that way."

Three miles? Already we've learned not to trust people who drive cars. If they make a mistake it's no great thing: spin the wheel, press the accelerator, and sit for another two or three minutes.

```
WORMS FOR
   SALE
  1¢ each
```

About fifty yards further on, tacked to another tree, same company:

```
WORMS
50¢ for 50
```

We had missed the truck, and lunch, by going through New Boston, so when we hit the outskirts of Goffstown and our intersection we were ravenous, and not for health foods. Raisins and sunflower seeds are okay, but not for now. We hitched a ride into Goffstown for a hamburger, listened to music, sat in a booth with someone to wait on us. Riding in a car? Sitting in a booth? It seemed dishonest. We walked back to the crossroads and took up our route: 2.4 miles to go.

We were already in what we'd later call the "hate belt"— the *Manchester Union Leader* area—and hostility was on the rise. Although we weren't marching for peace or protesting anything, the school kids in buses would give us the peace sign with no encouragement from us. On the road to the campsite, tacked to a tree, we had our first glimpse of a different attitude:

"I've *got* to have that." So we helped Bob D. pry it loose from the tree.

Up the road we passed some construction workers (they were the most consistently unfriendly, antiwalkers all), but since the three of us are fairly big their remarks were nearly respectable.

We made camp and sure enough, everyone had been there for hours. No, it was not a race but that would have to be said over and over again. Knowledge and understanding: they knew it wasn't a race, but they didn't understand it.

The site was down and away from the road, gear was scattered everywhere, people were sleeping or writing in journals or in groups next to the pond. If it seems dull to just lie in a field and talk, or just lie there, try it after walking 60 miles in three and a half days. We'd done our work for the day, and nothing in the world could be nicer than to lie in a field and talk or sleep and wait for supper.

We studied the map before leaving. The problem was to break through the net of roads leading to either Concord or Manchester. Our great map showed it could be done, but we got no confirmation from the locals, all of whom said we'd have to go to one or the other city first. The filling station maps sided with them and showed no roads running east between the two cities. The wildest-looking walkers came with me: Lloyd, Don (browner and more like an Indian every day, with a squashy green hat and feather), wild-eyed L.J., and Herbie the dancing bear with his black wool ski cap, tremendous sideburns, and Khrushchev overcoat. We had made it from Francestown to our present site without hitting the centers of any towns, large or small. We didn't want to break that record.

Our map led us to Dunbarton, then to a right off the highway just before the town hall, the only other road out of Dunbarton. We took it but found no one to direct us from there to the little junction called Bow Center and on to Hooksett and Suncook. We were like rats trying to get out of a maze. The dead ends were Concord and Manchester.

We pulled up to a house and pored over the map, stared into it. We were not quite on that road, not quite in the map . . . we were literally somewhere between the two.

"I *know* this road will take us there. It's *got* to."

"Go ask that guy."

Don walks over. "Excuse me; do you know if this road goes to Concord?"

"I think so."

"Can you cut off of it and get to Hooksett? Or Suncook?"

"I'm not sure."

"Are you sure it goes to Concord?"

"Well . . . tell you the truth, I've never taken it that way. We always go the other way."

Always? That's what the man said.

Well, It's a great road . . . and it might take us nowhere; then we've wasted the last hour of daylight. We take it for a mile, two miles; no more houses; no more confidence. We roar back the other way, cruising along like tigers behind bars trying to break out, *our* way. We pass a road that seems to be heading due east. Only there's a chain across the entrance. Beyond that chain is, undoubtedly, a great walking road with *no* traffic going all the way to Suncook. Out with the pliers, the hammer, brute strength. Done. We drive the truck through, put the chain back so those evil trespassers won't get in, and drive off into the trees.

My God! There, in a two-acre lot just beyond the trees, were old cars of all makes and models, still as stones, facing in all directions, silent and ghostly as the years gone by; a '37 Packard, a '42 Plymouth, a '46 Ford. Were they stolen? Each of us had his own theory. But we couldn't fantasize about the road; it just stopped. Back to the chain, take it down, drive through, put it back, and off.

Then we found it. An unmarked road to Bow Center; just out of Bow Center, a right on a black-topped two-lane road; across and under the underpass, and into Hooksett. Already we'd gone about 17 miles, but we'd make it tomorrow in style—we'd miss the big cities!

We crossed a river and stopped next to an eight-year-old boy on a bike. We were all feeling a first glow—beer- music-success-glow.

"How do we get to Suncook?"

Lloyd was closest to the window, so the boy explained to Lloyd while the rest of us watched. The boy was off his bike giving us a speech, waving his arms, ". . . and *then* . . . up next to a little, um . . ." We were watching every wave of his arm, ". . . across a big bridge . . . and you go, um, *this* way," every jerk of his head. The sun was on him, the moon was on him. We were nudging each other, waiting.

"Yeahh, okay, thanks a lot!" We raced off.

"Did you get that?"

"Yeahh."

"You know what he was talking about?"

"Of course not."

Two high school girls came out of the town library. "Go ask those girls how we get to Suncook."

"I'm up for that," says Lloyd, and he bounded out of the truck, totally alive, totally wild-looking, and ran toward them.

The two girls screamed. SCREAMED. Clutched each other and fought to get back inside. Lloyd was left standing there, no one to talk to.

Never mind, we'll do it without directions. God will guide us!

Sure enough, not more than two miles later we were confronted by a great brick gothic structure and a tremendous lawn sloping up to it. What is it? That's the place.

Of course there are times when whatever you want will fall into your hands. All that's necessary is the asking—as if the sun really comes out and shines on things for a while.

Up the long driveway. Mount St. Mary's College! "Girls!"

We leaped out, and it's a wonder there weren't more

screams. But no, the girls were older, they had seen more. I talked to the girl at the desk while the others impressed the girls with their exploits. I could hear it all in the background.

"Canada? . . . *Walking?*"

The girl at the desk listened carefully and then called Sister Robert. She gave me the phone and it began all over again. Could we use the field across from the school to pitch our tent? And could she arrange for showers? I mentioned our school, and that the project was for course credit, and that there were girls with us.

It was yes for the field. She *could* arrange showers for the girls. As for the boys . . . well, it might not be possible.

I knew she would work something out. It was there in her voice. It would be her project, and already the project was humming. The girl at the desk was excited, the girls in the lobby were spreading the word. Spring!

"We got it!" ·

Back in the truck and off, another quart or two of beer, music, mapping and getting it just right; under the super-highway, off the main roads, back to our lonely, winding country roads, and 19 miles later we were at camp. It was pitch black and we had to back downhill on the little trail next to the pond. Everyone had eaten but was anxious to hear. What would tomorrow bring?

"Girls!" "Showers!"

"Thousands of girls!!" "And *showers!!*"

"They're waiting for us, already!!!"

Jake was changing his clothes and combing his hair. Down, Jake. And it's a long walk; 19 miles.

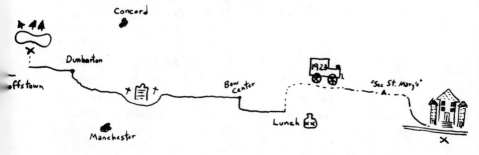

> Left from camp, .5 mile to T intersection.
> Left at T, 1.5 miles to Dunbarton.
> Right, before town hall.
> 5.1 to end of road (bear left, cemetery on left).
> Right on Woodhill Rd.
> 1.4 miles to 2nd left, South Bow Rd.
> 3.9 miles, left at T intersection.
> .4 mile, left at fork (Hackett Hill Rd.).
> Under underpass, take Route 3-A Hooksett.
> At junction take 3-A north (left).
> First right off 3-A.
> Right at RR tracks.
> Straight after bridge.
> Left at first intersection for 1 to 1½ miles to site.

Things were getting a little more organized. Who couldn't walk? Six. That would be quite a load, with all of our junk; but the "truck" would make sandwiches and meet us along the road somewhere. Herbie was driving, let him pick the spot.

One last look at the pond, the fields. Everyone is gone, scattered to the north and east; like a form of wind, we leave no trace of our presence just minutes ago. Already that campsite is only a memory, the "time" of it no longer "really" exists. Or at least, that is what we are taught to believe.

From the camp it was uphill. Down a slope and then up, up, and up. As we suddenly round a bend, still climbing, there is everything. Only the haze stops us from seeing— only the very fallaway of the earth. Many times already we had climbed hills and been rewarded in no way. We would reach the top and just start down again, with trees still on both sides; but here, now, was what we'd been climbing to for miles.

To walk up, still curving, still up, then to catch your breath as you round a bend above it all is to breathe in the whole blue-gray-mountain-town-forest-hill-valley, as far as breath-fed eyes can see. And to stop? To stop walking is nothing. Stop in an instant and have it all, without worries; no parking or waiting for a "scenic site." In an instant, without consult-

ing anyone, stop. It is all yours . . . as spectacular as the
northern lights, and as silent. Breathe it in. Can one realize
it all? Well, in walking there is always that chance. Then
take the names away—bird, flower, cornfield—and just see.

I walked for a time with Gale and Big Ann. We rested.
We were *there*. It was easy, relaxed. Of course, feet ached—
rubbed raw, even powdered and bandaged. If they got too
bad there was always the truck, but that was a last resort, for
you usually had the feeling, while walking along with no aim
other than walking, that in any instant—as close as the air
around your head—you might seize it; you might be there.

And there were showers ahead. Girls and showers at the
end of 19 miles. No one complained. With sore feet, trick
knees, boils, and blisters we scuttled, hobbled, ambled, heel-
and-toe, in bare feet or socks.

What a relief to put school down, just take it down and
walk off . . . not to stand in front wishing it could be different,
but to walk next to them, take the same assignment.

Big Ann and Gale wanted to rest a while, but I had to walk.
I left them and went off. I did about an hour of rhythm walking. What is rhythm walking? It's just rhythm walking. All
by myself I went into a physical-walking-body-cadence, a
walking-body-dance. Suddenly I had the impulse to scream;
it came so suddenly I almost did it without thinking. Next
time I let it happen. The top of my head was open, filled with
sky.

Lunch that day was a balloon going up. Herbie had parked
at an intersection and a whole bunch were sitting, lying,
eating. Each new arrival was cheered. Why? We got up in
the mornings laughing about it. What are we doing? Walking
nowhere? You can't do that!

Herbie had bought a case of beer and a case of soft drinks
for lunch. "Herbie!" He looked a little sheepish. "Give me a
beer."

It was one of the few lunches that almost everyone got
together for. More people came up. Cheers. At one point
fifteen of us were together; then people began taking off.

That afternoon I walked with Phil—steady Phil, who could

walk all day even though every step seemed to be his last. We walked a very old paved road, after a mile or so of dirt roads. In a clearing across from his house an old man was puttering around his truck. A Dodge—1923. It was a well-used, beat-up hunk of rust, but it ran and it worked for him. We stopped and watched him walk over to it in such a way . . . as if he'd begin talking to it, an old trusted friend. He picked up the rusty starter crank; "Where you guys walkin' to?" Inserted the crank and bent to it. Surely it wouldn't start.

"Canada."

He jumped as if someone had goosed him, turned around to us. "What?"

"Canada."

He bent over the truck again and cranked twice. Put the crank down, walked over to a can, poured some gas in the carburetor. "Works better with a little gas," he said. He kicked it over two more times and it started. 1923! We asked him how many miles it had on it, and he turned to us with that chugging background music, put his hands out to the side, smiled in some crazy way: "Who knows? It run through the mileage gauge two er three times . . . Gauge stopped so long ago it could've run around two, three times more."

We were still high but not conscious of it when suddenly the land to our left opened out on miles of hills, fields, towns. At the best spot for viewing it there was a little clump of rocks, a little construction. An arrow, made of rocks! We looked where it pointed. There was St. Mary's! About 8 miles away!

Who had done it? Ann M. and Lloyd? L.J.? Herbie? At the end of the arrow we added SEE ST. MARY'S in stones, and went to hide in the field to watch the reaction of the next walkers. Just as we were about to give up, Jake came ambling along. We ducked and watched. Skinny Jake walked up, saw the rocks, tried to read them upside down, walked back a few paces, stepped across them, read the message, looked, read it again, looked, mumbled to himself, and suddenly, "Yoweeee!!!" he shouted, all by himself. He took off his knapsack, got his camera, snapped a picture, put the camera back, and hiked off.

Bill and Bob D. came next, Bob with his hurt-knee walk and Bill head high and straight on. They were deep in discussion and walked over the stones past the view. They would have gone on unseeing, but we yelled and made them stop.

The four of us made the campsite by cutting across fields, woods, farms and going straight at it. Most of the others were already there. L.J., Don, and Howie had been stopped by the state cops (the stateys) who without any warning had pulled up, blocking them off, and said, "All right, what are you guys up to?" "Walking!" "Walking, eh? Well, you better not cause any trouble cause we're on the lookout for guys like you." "Yeah, we'll be careful," L.J. had told them, "We know we're in the hate belt!" The "stateys" stared at them, then drove away.

A car was racing across the field. It carried Big Ann, Gale, and a reporter from the *Manchester Union Leader*. He was chipper and interested, and he already had his story. To him, our project was an alternative to taking over the Ad. building. Inaccurate, but it was better than I expected from a paper which seemed very ready to hate students, demonstrators or not; a paper whose foreign policy could be summed up in three words: "Bomb the Bastards!" I tried to keep it straight and even asked him to read over his notes before leaving. It didn't sound too bad, but the other walkers had no patience with him. When he asked for their names he got answers like Mike Hunt from Missoula, Montana (in next day's paper it was "Michael"), Dick Hertz from Palo Alto, etc. He took them down, still chipper and interested. He thought it was a swell idea.

While we were talking, our blue supervan came streaking across the field, people hanging from all parts of it. Herbie leaped off, "Fuck the world!" he shouted, and bounded up.

"I'm afraid the world wouldn't stand for it," said the reporter.

"Oh, I'm sorry . . . I didn't know—"

The reporter told him it was okay, he'd heard those words before. He put it down to high spirits and went on with his questions.

Some of the walkers felt I gave too much time to him. But once a reporter had found us, I wanted him to get it straight. Let people like the idea or dislike it on its real merits or demerits.

He left after getting an "intimate" picture of five of us lying in the grass, and another of Bill hanging Christlike up against the truck. We went over to join the others for showers.

It was one thing to see the group in our big tent or in a field, or walking, but twelve of us in a tiled shower room of a girls' dormitory? Too much! The roped-off room was guarded by a beautiful girl—so we wouldn't be molested.

What's that sound? Ohhh yes, a flushing toilet. I remember that sound . . . from my childhood.

After showers the walkers took over the lounge, the halls, the lobby. Don and Dan were screeching at each other from a great distance in some language. Some Slovak language? They cursed, spit, shook their fists at each other.

"Catoo—nawalaiki! Ptui! Kananee TaWanee!"

But the beautiful guard from the shower room understood Dan very well, and they were head-to-head in a long, complicated dialogue. They were to be married that evening in a flower ceremony. Oh, Dan has a way with him. Steel-rimmed granny specs, baggy clothes, and the most shapeless faded brown tramp hat I've ever seen.

While shopping, Herbie had met Sister Robert in the supermarket and she had asked us all to supper, but Herbie, gallant Herbie, refused for all of us. Now she suggested to me that since it was supposed to go down to 20 degrees that night, maybe we could all sleep in the halls of the dorms, outside the rooms. This time I gallantly refused for everyone. Our ideas of what might happen in the halls *had* to be different.

"Well, they could have this room," she said, speaking of the lounge. "We can close it off, and I'm sure it will be fine."

She was really too nice. But okay. Suddenly, there was a stream of ants to and from the tent, lugging space blankets (Norton space blankets, I should add), sleeping bags, and stuff back to the main building. Our girls could be housed in rooms with extra beds.

Gale and I and a few others stayed in the tent; 20 degrees, 10 degrees, what did it matter? Our bags were good—comfortable and warm—even in temperatures down to zero.

That night the locals proved to be more aggressive than the visitors—or this was the report that I got—slipping down to the room for "talks," passing notes ("the girls in 306"), sending poetry, or "poetry," which was, maybe, not typical of that school but seems typical of liberated college first efforts ("Fuck peace. . . . Fuck the Catholic religion," etc.).

Sister Robert had wanted to know when we'd be leaving so she could make plans for the lounge. I told her around 7:00, but since Diana, our alarm clock, was sleeping somewhere in the huge dorm, it was doubtful that we'd make it. We had never made it anyhow—to get off at 7:00 was a recurring dream.

Our destination for the night was "the haunted house," a place we had found in a hysterical search for back roads. The haunted house was on an unused almost impassable road out of Epsom, a very small town, although with a tension behind those calm New England walls which was not apparent to us until the following day. The house wasn't haunted; it had been unused for so long and had such a mundane history that no ghost would have been interested in it, but Diana got a kick out of the idea so we talked it up.

We got stuck, got lost a few times, drove the usual 40 to 60 miles to scout out a distance of 18 or 19 miles from camp to camp, and ran into our first real enemy, unless the Greenfield State Park manager can be counted. She lived on the same road as the haunted house and wouldn't give us her field because they were "scattering"—scattering manure—and we wouldn't be able to stand the smell. She was right, as it turned out.

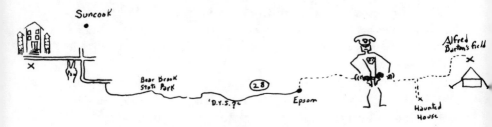

Actually, it was good to leave St. Mary's. They had been very nice to us, but somehow the hospitality split us apart. Our project was to walk and sleep out, together; ours was to walk, so let's walk. We got away about 9:00 on the crowded highway that runs in front of the school. After the first 5 miles, which everyone had been briefed on, we were to follow the white arrows that we had sprayed on the roads the evening before.

Don, Motorhead, Herbie, and I left together, and they told me about their night visitors. "They wouldn't let us alone," said the Motor, in what sounded like a pleased complaint. "They were Catholic jet-setters . . . fashion plates," said Don, fiercely. "They really dug us," Herbie said.

Up the road about a mile from the school we stopped at a gaudy restaurant for coffee. It was a modern truckers' stop; bad food, chrome, glass, and plastic flowers. To have a cup of coffee standing around in a dewy field can be great, but so can sitting down to a cup, with your own spoon. Only there was something else here besides coffee. We were getting some strange looks, stares, snickers, remarks from the truckers and telephone linemen. Was it imaginary? No, it was real. The hate belt. Who started it? Was it the *Manchester Union Leader* with its superpatriotic poison-pen letters and editorials? Or did the people themselves call forth that particular newspaper?

We talked and drank but there was no doubt of it; we were on the other side. We were the unclean, the indecent, the Communists. And they were Americans: hardworking, clean, respectable loyal taxpayers who were, somehow, supporting us. As the signs on many of their cars had it, "Put your heart in America or get your [picture of jackass] out!" They didn't mean America of the '20s or '30s, when—as an old navy chief once told me—if anyone asked you for identification or a "draft card" you told him to "Kiss your ass!" No, they meant a peacetime-draft America, America of Vietnam fame. An America where change has no place—peaceful or otherwise. Yes, we were in the hate belt and would have to pay something to it that very day before we could get our jackasses out. By the time we left the restaurant the looks were threatening, and there were sudden angry glances.

Just as we went out we spotted Dan walking along the road. Dan the lover, at least half an hour behind everyone. Too bad; Sister Robert had kicked him out. "You've overstayed your welcome," she told him. She had seen him kissing his girl in a public place. "No," he told us, "just in the face!" Too bad, because they couldn't have been nicer to us.

Outside we talked more freely of the hostility. It hadn't begun and ended in the cafe: truck drivers were snarling at us, drivers were shouting; the school kids, in strange contrast, screamed and fell out of buses to give us the peace sign.

Since they were impossible to ignore, we worked out a routine for hostile drivers. The one who saw a driver rolling down his window, drawing back his fist, or snarling would count aloud: one-two-three. At three we'd all hit on both feet, knees bent, and present the vehicle with a double peace sign—all five of us. We did it about six times in the next half hour and that was it, but from the reaction and the phone calls, one would think we had terrorized motorists from dawn to dusk.

We split up and talked—Motor and I together—then went into a period of silence which lasted for the rest of the time we were on the main highway.

I dropped behind everyone to tend my feet and to call St. John, New Brunswick, because I wanted to try and set up a party for whenever we'd get there. It was great to be off the big highway and walking through state park grounds, a park full of tremendous trees that didn't have a "park" look but more a look of woods or a forest. Before coming to a phone booth I ran into the park manager. He had talked with a number of the walkers already and he thought the idea was fascinating—a mind-blowing shock to us, after a day of screaming truck drivers and unfriendly cops ("All right, what do you guys think you're doing?" "Walking." "Walking, eh?" etc.). This park maanger was doing cartwheels over the idea. He only wished we could stay overnight at his park so he could talk to us more and get the whole plan.

"I thought the state parks in New Hampshire weren't open till May 9th?"

"Well, technically that's true," he said, "But we can open for special groups, hiking groups, Boy Scouts, and others."

So, the other side of the coin. Human beings make exceptions; to machines it's all the same.

I caught up with Herbie, sitting on a bluff by the side of the road, powdering his feet philosophically. He stopped powdering and leaned over to me carefully and slowly with the can. With his other hand he pointed out the big letters on the side: "IT SOOTHES!" We nodded seriously to each other. He held up the can again, showed it to the TV audience, and *smiled* into their living rooms.

While we were sitting there a man cruised by in his car, went up a ways, turned around and cruised back. He stopped the car just opposite to where we were sitting. The top of the window was just under his nose, just over his mouth.

"Do you screw?"

We looked at each other. What did he say? Sounds like he said "screw."

"What?"

"Do you screw?" The window caught his sallow face just above the mouth. I shook my head and he drove away. He just drooooove away into the night of the day.

We started walking, kept up a good pace, passed Jake sleeping under a tree. We yelled to him in case we were the last walkers, and when his eyes opened we knew he had been in Stage Four. "Hey! Do you screw?" Jake's eyes glazed over.

Not more than a block ahead we passed Gale and Big Ann asleep under some trees. That was sleep corner.

As we walked along past a school yard—the kids yelled "Heyy, hippies!" and "Peace!"—I went over the gamut of reactions so far, or the ones I could remember:

> "*Oughta hang 'em all!*"
> "*I'd love to go with you!*"
> "*Bunch of hippies!*"
> "*I can't think of a finer thing to do!*"
> "*Getta haircut!*"
> "*I think it's fascinating!*"
> "*Do you screw?*"

At a corner antique-junk store Big Ann, Gale, and Jake caught up with us, and we all walked for a while. I had to take off my shoes and go barefooted, and soon everyone was way ahead. I began to walk even slower than I needed to. Up ahead was a bridge; the water of the stream was brown. Nothing's pressing me . . . just sit here till I really see it, really get it. Let the others go. The walk continues but I continue here, looking at the brown, sweeping water. Deeper. I left when I couldn't look any longer.

Blake said: "If the fool would persist in his folly he would become wise."

He also said: "Dip him in the river who loves water."

And "You never know what is enough unless you know what is more than enough."

And he said, "Exuberance is beauty."

And, "The cistern contains; the fountain overflows."

And he said, "Improvement makes strait roads; but the crooked roads without improvement are roads of genius."

We took the roads of genius; we searched out the roads of genius.

Is that what Blake meant? The greatest thing about Blake is that no one can ever be quite sure what he meant. He breaks the machines to decode him. But, I felt, we were coming close.

In half an hour I picked up my pace and caught Herbie again. We walked along for a while, then rested on a high wall, split an orange, an apple, decided to go to the next store and get soup and crackers—it struck us both as the greatest possible dish. We were sitting on the wall thinking about it.

Just then the truck came barreling up "Heyyyy!" Lloyd leaped out. "We got it inspected!" And lunch.

When lunch arrives it is not early or late, it is perfect. P-p-p-p-p-perfect! And the truck is inspected. We're even early!

After lunch Lloyd joined us, we ran into Phil, who joined up, and the four of us headed up a dirt road north out of Epsom, happy to shuck off any attention, looks, threatening gestures, shouts; happy at not even being seen by a lot of traffic—into the shade and peace of a meandering dirt-and-gravel road.

Behind us is the sound of cars coming, fast. Suddenly up roar three state troopers, each in an official state car. They roar up, slam on brakes, skid, and leap out.

We stop and wait as calmly as we can. Three angry-looking stateys jump out, spitting angry. The one in the middle, cherub-faced, with a spit-polish shoeshine, holster-shine, his gabardine uniform crisply pressed, not a crease in it except where a crease belongs, looking waxy and unreal, has his hands at the ready. Let us make one move—false or true— and he will outdraw us. But what would we draw? There isn't a pistol among us. Not one of us has a knife. Even a butter knife. Not even a stick!

"What the hell are you guys up to?"

"Why? We're walking."

"Walking, eh?"

"Yes."

"We've got reports about you guys."

"What kind of reports?"

"All kinds of reports. Let's see some identification!"

Kiss my ass.

They—Herbie, Phil, Lloyd—show their identification.

Mine is in the glove compartment of the truck. I'm guilty. All I can do is remain calm. They are full of questions. All day long they've been getting reports on us. How many of us are there? Where the hell are we going? Are we going to try to take over some town? What's the idea of this walk, anyhow? Where are we from? How do *they* know we're really *from* there?

Some questions are unanswerable.

They roar off, laying rubber, throwing gravel: dissatisfied, angry, insulted, just itching for some action or remark which will allow them to run us all in . . . to . . .

We walked along, goggle-eyed. The one who got us was baby-face, who was ready to draw his guns. And what? Fire? At us? The scene wouldn't leave our minds, that angel-faced statey with his arms bent at the elbow and drawn back, his guns free. Right out of a TV Western—well, here was a real Eastern. We imitated it to each other until we were laughing about it. "Walkin' eh? Pow! Bam!" Marlboro country.

We decided that if, by some chance, they had missed our dirt-lane turnoff we would keep straight, unless we could get up the road without being detected. How innocent we were! We learned later that everyone knew exactly where we were . . . phone calls had informed the best gossips *as* we were passing their houses. Our numbers were tallied and it came to "200 hippies." Maybe the rule of thumb is to divide rumor by 10.

By the time we got to our turnoff, numerous tire tracks convinced us that the stateys had been there, or were there at that moment. Up our little road we trudged. Trouble. How would it work out? What the hell were *they* up to? True, we had not asked permission for the "haunted house," but the place was unbelievably run-down, overgrown, unused. Still, we were trespassing.

Lying on the side of the road in plain sight was Dan's little faded American flag, which he wore in his hat. Had there been a fight? Had it been knocked out? In the same area we found a telephone cable sign, which Bob D. had been carrying. I pocketed the little flag and put the sign under a rock.

At the top of the hill, next to the farm where they were "scattering" manure (take the word of one who likes the smell of manure, it was overwhelming), there were two of the stateys' cars and the truck.

It wasn't really noisy. We had no defense against the charge of "trespassing," just the mitigating circumstances, perhaps, that we had not damaged anything, that we wouldn't have, that we'd have been gone in the morning, and that the house and property, such as they were, would have been intact. But when I told them that we'd pack up and leave, they were not at all satisfied. "We got orders from Concord to get you people out of here." Okay, we'd just get another place.

"I said we're gonna get you people *out* of here."

"What do you mean *out* of here? How far is *out*?"

"Across the state line, or . . ."

"My wife and I are residents of New Hampshire, and these are students in a New Hampshire school! Do you think you can kick us out? For what? What are the charges? Who is making them?"

"Look! We got orders, twenty or fifty phone calls about you people. Disturbing the peace . . . obstructing traffic . . . lascivious and obscene gestures—"

"What? Who signed the charges? Who is making the charges?"

"At least fifty people have called up. We're gettin' you people *outta* here."

Earlier, after Greenfield, I had thought of getting a letter from the Governor, a simple letter saying that he knew of the project and approved of it—which, I believe, he did. I do know him, mainly through our children, and we have been to his house a few times. Now I knew I should have done it.

I told the police I thought they'd gone far enough, that they were harassing us, that they had no right to drive us before them wherever we went without any specific signed charges, that I knew the Governor and I was going to let him know about this.

They were very cool and sure that my threats were empty.

"He says he knows Number One," the state trooper called in to his headquarters, then playfully repeated it: "He says he knows Number One and that we're harassing them." The trooper had a lazy smile on his face. He read off my name from his sheet and waited.

To all staunch defenders of the police and their ways and mannerisms, I suggest that they step off the beaten path just a little, take a walk in old clothes, take a swim in the winter, go against the grain a little, see how the police react to your behavior, and then let's talk. On this particular day, I believe we might have been shot if we had made a sudden move at one point. Of course it would have been for resisting an officer.

"Okay," the trooper turned to me, "the Governor is on the line . . . now are you charging us with harassing you?"

"Yes. You three, at any rate."

"And will you defend your group against the charge of 'lascivious and obscene gestures'?"

"Absolutely!"

We were able to hear only the beginning of the conversation with "Number One" because he rolled up the window.

"Lascivious and obscene gestures?" All day long we had been recipients of obscene gestures and obscene threats from passing car drivers, construction workers, and truck drivers. Fists out of windows, straight arms clutched at the elbows (up yours), the middle finger, and shouts of "Fuck you!"

In a few minutes, the trooper nearest us rolled down his window. His tone was different, guarded, "Our orders from the Governor's office are to protect you within the law. That is all. And you were trespassing, so you have to get out of there." We already knew that.

It had started to rain.

"What other charges do you have?"

"We have no signed charges," he said, almost conversationally.

The trooper in the next car was a little more cautious; he jumped out and walked up close to me. "I hope you don't think we're really harassing you. I mean, we're just doing our job. We've been getting calls all day. Our orders were to get you 'out,' and we were just obeying orders. I hope you understand. We're not after *you* . . ."

Why the change? What *had* the Governor said?

The rain was coming down harder. We gave out ponchos. The stateys were slowly pulling out. It was after 4:00; we had walked 19 or 20 miles and still had no place to stay. I took the truck and went in search of a campsite. Diana told me about the "attack" at the haunted house. This made me more determined to get a letter from the Governor, not to flaunt or even show except as a last resort.

The police had "leaped in through the windows," Diana said, "yelling, kicking us, pulling things around . . ." Yes, the baby-faced neat one had actually leaped through the open window, kicked Diana, yanked her up, yelling all the time. God knows what they expected, but the scene was one of utter tranquillity; tired walkers and people unloading gear, setting up for the night, fixing chicken broth.

"All right, what the hell's going on here? Get up from there!"

Perhaps the police only reacted to the villagers' fear, but where did that come from? For a long time we refused to believe the evidence that the villagers were very frightened. Why? We simply walked along. Everyone who stopped and asked was given a civil answer to any question. But there was the rub. The gossipmongers wouldn't stop and talk. They would peer at us behind curtains and send their fears ahead: "They're coming your way! About two hundred of 'em!"

We sped down the road to get a place as soon as possible. Luckily a woman was just driving into her wide yard only half a mile away from us. She was a teacher coming home from school. She listened patiently. Yes, she told us. In fact, we could stay right across this road; she walked, explaining and pointing. If it rained, we could stay inside their old chicken houses, which they didn't use any more.

"I'll just check with my husband when he comes home, but I'm sure it'll be okay. He's a selectman, you know."

Great! I gave the truck over to Gale and Ann M. after we got back, and the group started walking down the hill. Dan told us he had dropped his flag when the stateys passed by; Bob D. had dropped his sign at the same time. We found the sign, a little tin placard; Dan got his flag, and we continued down to the intersection. When we got to the bridge and the spot where the two gravel roads met, there was the truck and bad news. The woman's husband had come home and refused. Absolutely. First it was one thing, then another. He was afraid of fire, he was afraid of accidents. "You're just afraid of people!" Gale told him finally, and they got in the truck and drove off.

The rain was falling steadily. In another hour and a half it would be dark. All twenty-one of us were together with our truck fully loaded at a bridge and crossroads, and now which way? Together with no direction, 19 or 20 miles under our belts, raining, darkness on the way, and no place to stop. But wasn't this it, too? What happens next?

"I'd just as soon walk all night, find some place tomorrow."

"I'm up for that."

"I'm game."

The rest were silent and waiting. Very brave, but I believe that another two or three hours of walking and people would be falling out. Bill was really down, and he stood off by himself, a little ashamed at all the attention we had called down on ourselves. Somehow it was our fault, he reasoned. We did look pretty strange.

The road going across the bridge was sort of on our route, Ann M. told me. Good, check ahead for a place.

Off they roared.

Off we sauntered after them. Overtime. It was, really, kind of great. What would we do with ourselves?

We didn't have any traffic for another hour, and then suddenly the truck was there—our "eyes," our "ears."

"You wouldn't believe it. We got a place, and then next minute we were out. Refused again! But we have a place. Really, this time. You keep on this road, straight ahead; the field is just off the road. Well, it's really right *on* the road.

The old man is great. 'Sure! I'm up for a good turn,' he says. An *old* man! I could've kissed him. Okay? We'll get the tent up and supper started."

"How far is it?"

"Oh, it's . . ." Ann M. paused; she was split between how it is when one drives and when one walks. "It's nearly four miles," she said, with feeling. As if they'd make an extra good supper because we were walking and they weren't.

We waved them on. About 2 miles later, on a fence post, as if it had sat there for years, was the big pot of half-begun chicken broth. That was a head-opener. What next?

Phil and I carried it for a while, then gave it to two others, and we alternated among our little group of six. Ah, youth! Adventure! Conrad's spirit moved in me—let it be; whatever comes, whatever happens. Rain! Stateys! Watery chicken broth! Come on down!

Still, it was a long 5 miles before we made the field. Through a tumbledown gate and a walk of 20 feet to the tent. A 25-mile day. Regardless of how it had been forced on us, we were all a little proud of ourselves—like any American sports nut, we had a new day's record.

The sun was setting, supper was almost ready. The cooks gave us a makeshift early supper and three of us went mapping; this strange day was far from over.

If cities are oases we were in a desert. There were only gravel roads, farms, and woods. We took off down Tan Road, passed an intersection, asked some people where it led, turned around, and took it. The road was lonely and straight. At another spot we checked at a solitary farmhouse. It was dark now and they turned on the lights to confront us; a gruff old farmer, chuckling, "You ain't hippies are you?" But out of a kind of good simplicity he assumed we weren't, because hadn't we asked and answered him politely? Hadn't we talked, not screamed? Hadn't we walked instead of leaping? Were we carrying placards? It was just his joke. They ain't hippies, they're people, like us. He and his wife even waved good-bye to us, and we felt they were the very salt of the earth. If people would only talk to us, they'd like us.

They'd lend us a piece of their field. We'd give it back the next day with only a patch of bent grass.

It was almost 9:30 by the time we pulled into Pittsfield—with half the mapping done. One place was open: a drug store, grocery, dry goods, cafe, and stationery store—a big, anonymous but still cozy place. I desperately needed some more ballpoint pens (eternal points) and was beginning to feel that anyone could find our path to Canada; just follow the trail of the ballpoint pens.

We had some coffee, and oh boy! Here they came! Two stateys and the local police chief. It was none other than quick-on-the-draw cherub-faced Trooper Harrison himself. Oh, but now they were all smiles. In fact the cherub wanted to pay for our coffee. Too bad, it was already paid for.

Did we feel vindictive? No, embarrassed. They did everything but apologize. For what? Hadn't they been operating within the law? Just "doing a job"? But once out of sight, we chuckled and wondered what "Number One" had said to them behind those rolled-up windows.

As we were walking back to the truck the local police chief, Vaughn Siel, pulled over to us. "Yew lookin' fer back roads? Get in. I know evva road in these parts." What a strange accent for a New Englander. We got in and he listened for a few moments, got our general directions straight, and took off. He used the accelerator as if it were a switch that could only be on or off. He took us to a road that was impassable by car. Then he whipped us over to where it came out. He'd find another where that one left off, take us a quarter mile up the highway, check mileage for us, then scream around to where it came out. We'd note mileage and landmarks, then zoom off to the next road or trail. This transplanted Texan *did* know "evva road in these parts." Twice or more we told him we could work out the rest of it tomorrow. "Oh, that's all right, I've got to be up till two er three ennyways." He'd bomb off again; "Now this road takes ye—" we'd hear his voice in the slipstream, half the words lost to wind and night, long sentences covering 5 or 10 miles punctuated by screeching tires and sudden night stillnesses as we took down directions and mileage. He drove us around for at least an hour and a half before letting us off in Pittsfield again.

How to explain him? That he helped us because he heard about the call to Number One? But he had nothing to fear, nothing to "make up" for. We hadn't seen or heard of him till he stopped us. He's just a good man; let it go.

We were drunk on the whole day. Tired, downed, elated, stomped on, rained on, springing up again like the flowers of the field. We returned to our tent home and told the others. Of course we'd had a few beers, but it was another one of those times: "Gimme a match!" "I'll drink to that!" We had seen the worst and the best of cops—inside of five hours.

Still the reports were coming in. By this time the police were afraid *for* us . . . afraid we'd be attacked. So they kept the watch. Suddenly there was a state trooper in the tent.

"Everything all right in here?"

"Yes."

"I thought you might want to know, we just got a report on the radio that there was a wild orgy goin' on out there in Alfred Barton's field." The police car was getting the report not twenty yards away from the "orgy."

"I told 'em it was a lot of garbage," the statey said.

So ended the long day. Even the most suspicious policemen must realize that there was hysteria in the air.

Next morning, in a wet and chilly field, we gathered ourselves together. The talk was of the day before, of the mechanics of hate, of why and how we could have excited so much attention. "Boy, this country's in trouble!" I forget who said it first, but everyone turned to him with the heartiest agreement.

Even on these first days, which were peculiarly identified with our feet and legs, other problems were being resolved. It was not alone a time of action, sensation, and outward impressions. How does one get along with others? With oneself? There were hours each day with nothing to do but walk and think, and I have copies of walkers' notes in which these problems were turned over, wondered about.

"Today I discovered how much fear is in me . . . am I really like that?" "I noticed the pattern of how I criticize my mother and father . . . It seems so mechanical, and senseless." "In school there *isn't* time to know oneself . . . We are usually tired with those we know best . . . family, roommates; but here I have been exhausted around almost total strangers . . . Wake up the next morning and I feel they are now friends . . ." "The whole group after yesterday—with the stateys—seems to be growing closer and friendlier." "What is a mile? Distance, time. I see someone up ahead. He's right now passing that bush. What will it be like when I pass that same spot?"

Of course these early days' notes were more often about feet; "I still have these strange painful growths on my toes . . . It's very disappointing to have to ride the truck because I'm not a quitter." Or, "I can't wear those shoes. They are completely useless. I can't stand to look at them." And so on.

Too many details? I've left out hundreds. That day—of the stateys and the haunted house—was also the day of the sonic boom, of the Irish setter that followed us, of the lady in the white station wagon (who caused half our trouble), of the English lady who wanted to know what was wrong with Americans, because in England everyone walked; it was the day one man had to almost drag his wife into the tent to show her that we were really normal human beings, and sat her down and made her converse with us. That man, the Englishwoman, old Alfred Barton, and Vaughn Siel were the bright spots in a day of threats and dire predictions.

It was not our project to attempt to allay the fears of the hundreds of people who could be psyched out just by telephone calls and reports about us. We were walking to see, to understand; walking to turn over questions or have them turn over as we walked. Even questions such as: Is there really something to learn? *Or* to teach?

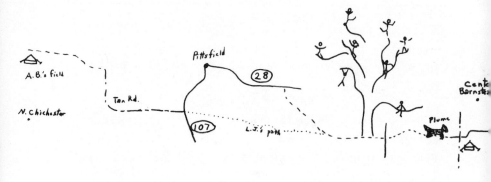

Well, we wanted untraveled roads, impassable roads, and we had them. But this day it was a problem of faith, and most of us were lacking just that.

"It dwindles down to a trail, and then nothing."

But where was L.J.? No one knew at the time, but L.J., on his own, continued over paths that were barely visible, and beat everyone else by hours.

The rest of us fell under the spell of those who had tried to get through and became convinced it was impossible. Were they sure? Had they actually given it a try? Absolutely! It's a dead end! One sight they did report was a house on that old road, house and family, hidden away. Something they would expect to see in the sharecropping South but never in New England. Kids in tattered clothes, poor, fat, ashamed mother. They remembered it vividly three and a half months later.

Was it dew? Fog? Or rain? It was wet, and we stood there on a regular paved highway deciding what to do . . . not a good moment.

Okay, nothing to do but go into Pittsfield and walk it from there. Off we went. Not happily. To put on ponchos meant sweating inside them, to take them off meant a gradual wetting down. By the time we reached Pittsfield, whatever it had been was now a foggy, dewy rain. The big A&P looked good enough to stop all of us; we were like country kids come to town. We cruised the aisle for goodies. Big Ann had a shopping bag full. At first I thought, how generous, she's buying candy and cakes and cookies for the whole group! Guess again, Albert.

Toward the afternoon it cleared a little, and we did find some of the connections between those lonely roads Vaughn Siel had shown us. Gale and I were walking together, a simple time, watching fields come alive, leaves unfold, spring gaining on us. Spring (and so summer) travels north at 13 miles a day, Gale mentioned, and we were heading northeast, diagonally, at 15.

We were completely by ourselves on that old road . . . or were we? It was not exactly a premonition, but something made me look over to my right at a huge and very strange pine tree. A pine tree that grew like an oak. We both looked, open-mouthed.

A human Christmas tree? An egg tree? There in that tremendous pine were at least eight walkers as still as stones; sitting on branches, lying, standing on limbs staring at us: Ann M., Lloyd, Tita, Super-Weasel, Motorhead, Dan, Don, Howie, two or three more.

I took pictures of them but I've never seen the pictures, have no idea whose camera it was or how to get hold of it, although a photograph would be a real treasure. Then again, what does it matter? Heads are better than cameras. The picture hasn't got the day, the mist in our bones, the relief after the day before. The picture doesn't have spring catching up with our northerly walk, doesn't have the absolute silence of those tree statues looking out at us waiting to be noticed; from the picture I couldn't hear the laughter when we turned, stared, pointed unbelievingly at them.

On we walked, in hazy sunshine or in misty rain. This was the first day of relief after days of trouble with either townsfolk or police. Trouble and then relief—of course—but we *felt* it. We knew, too, that we were walking right out of the hate belt, and that was a help. We could also look at the map and astound ourselves. Even ants, if they walk for long periods, cover a great deal of territory.

Again there was no place to stay till three or four that afternoon. The truck found L.J.; he had made it as we'd mapped it the night before, over trails, roads unused for years, straight on course and hours ahead of us. L.J. was the hero of the day. We had gone the long and civilized way. *Back* roads! *Through* the country! All right; it wouldn't happen again.

The truck pulled up. On the right side L.J. had sprayed— memento of the hate belt—(The Walk) *To Look for America*. Well, this wasn't "The walk to look for America," but we were finding it, ready or not.

Another experience in common was the car of four hippie types who kept following us throughout the day, trying to talk, to find out where we'd be staying over. What did it matter if they were hippies and we weren't, or if we were and they weren't? We were walking, they were riding. They were talking about SDS, and we were walking to Canada.

Camp was a small field just off a little-traveled tarred road. We all wanted anonymity by this time, especially at night, but we certainly didn't have it. It was drizzling again. We had two dogs with us now: Plume—for his long plume-like tail—and some other obviously owned dog, which had followed us from Pittsfield. There was only a little traffic on that road, but every car or truck stopped. One of the walkers wanted our truck so he could go into town and call his girl. It was late, because we had started late and because we had walked the roundabout civilized way. I was "down" in general, but suddenly the truck was a clear issue; we had to have a meeting.

All at once the state cops were there, bang! . . . Just friendly, just checking, you know; just in the tent. Well, this time we had something for them. They could take the dog back to Pittsfield. They could hardly get out of that one, so they took him. As for Plume, he had already been with us for two days . . . let him stay.

I was down and going downer. We'd have to get rid of some of the garbage we were carrying—not gear, not food, but mental and emotional excess—family, girl friends, state cops, dogs, rain, the world.

It was an angry meeting, and I began by talking about

our one rule: consideration. Each day there would be an assigned driver for the truck, and he would be responsible for it that whole day. He would have to get the utmost use out of it—mapping, carrying "wounded," fixing lunches, picking up cooks for shopping and gas for lamps—and then, if there was time, fitting in long-distance calls, etc. Barely suppressed was my feeling that we ought to forget the outside world—telephones, families, the college, girl and boy friends. Let's do one thing. Just one thing. Let's do one thing with all our hearts. That was the fury behind what I did say.

On rainy nights, I said, everyone was still spread out. There was not enough room in the tent. This was hardly considerate; everyone would have to sleep closer together and leave nonessentials outside. Even that would have to be in one pile, covered to keep it dry. It was the distressing doom-to-anarchy speech. I knew, also, that I was angry because these things had to be said. Or one fine day the truck, in our loose and carefree fashion, would be smashed, and that would be it.

Then another ugly issue—grades. I had agreed with the school that okay, I would give the walkers some kind of grade. But how could they be graded for something like this? Grades would only cloud the issue. Out the window would go the chance for them to find out how they really were with one another (I included myself and Gale). Grades would take it out of life. If someone *had* to have a grade in order to graduate or to stay in school, then I'd give it to him; otherwise, no grades.

It was late, misty-rainy, no mapping had been done, we still hadn't resolved the walking-in-silence issue, and I had come down on everyone, Ka-rash. Although it had been a mild uneventful day with lonely roads and only one real high, the tree, the atmosphere after the meeting was wild. Not a good wildness but definitely WILD. Tita was crying. I was a bastard for yelling at everyone—although she didn't quite say so—when before that everyone had been so close, had been brothers and sisters. No, it was inexcusable, unforgivable; and I knew she meant it with the pure uncomplicated feeling of a healthy thirteen-year-old. I don't think many others took it so hard. Gordon, Herbie, and Don went outside for a sun dance. With perfect confidence they reported back afterward that for at least two more days there wouldn't be a cloud in the sky. Any listener could be excused for believing Herbie—not because of the crazy dance but because he's enough undiluted insouciant youth for the dance and the pronouncement to pass for prayer, which would be antilife not to grant.

No more than seven slept outside the tent that night. I zipped up the bag—last action of a very different day—with some doubts. How brutal had I been? Maybe I didn't see myself at all as others saw me. Thank God for the sun dance, and the Tree. Still, the keys to the day had been rain, back roads, bare feet, hurt feelings, and missed turns.

It drizzled through the night and soaked the out-of-tent hard-liners: Dan, Don, L.J., Bob B. and Bob D., Lloyd, and Ann M. The drizzle had turned to rain by morning, and we ate breakfast standing around in the tent, wondering. I was driving—the bottoms of my feet were raw. Big Ann couldn't walk, so she would be in the truck too. The tempo of the rain picked up steadily.

"Hey, you know that sun dance?"

"Yes, Herbie."

"Well, I made a mistake. We were going in the wrong direction."

"At least He answered you." •

"Of course! But I'll have to take full responsibility for this weather."

"Can't you dance again? Now?"

"Kimo Sabe no know Indian ways," Don told me. "Never dance before sun makum Tonto's shadow like so."

"Tonto, I think you're full of shit."

"Kimo Sabe!! Tonight, Indians dance *sun* dance! Then see!"

Five sleeping bags were soaked, and all because Gordon, Herbie, and Don had danced in the wrong direction.

Despite all this it was, in a way, a sad beginning. Everyone was aching to go. We decided to just smash everything into the truck, map a partial route, mark it clearly with arrows, and let them get started. I swore it wouldn't happen again; we'd do the mapping the day before if it took us till midnight.

We packed the wet sleeping bags last, so we could get at them as soon as we found a launderette. Then we took off, Big Ann and I.

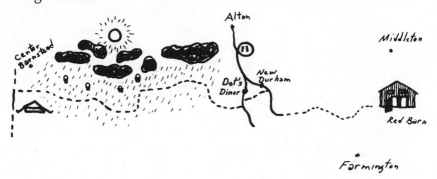

Down came the rain. Dirt roads became mud roads. The shoulders of these roads were treacherous in dry weather, but now they seemed to pull the truck over at every chance. In a lull between rain bursts we passed two state cops in a long car with the big blue dome on top. It was the only traffic I'd seen on this road, and I needed information.

After we drove past, I stopped and got out. They were waiting.

"You're takin' up an awful lot of road! You know that?"

Police never cease to amaze me. It is more than conformity to bow and scrape, to give them free coffee and smokes, to make sure of a hearty good morning—because they don't just stop answering, they start expecting more than half the road. And when they don't get these things after being brought up on them, they think they are being deprived of rights, and the other guy is a dirty Commie.

"Could you tell me if this road goes to New Durham, or close by?"

His eyes glassed over; he mumbled something negative,

asked his partner, "No, I dunno," and looked out at the woods. Then: "How long you guys gonna be in the vicinity?"

"We're not stopping, we're moving through; we just stop overnight."

"Seems like you've been here a long time."

"That's because we're walking," I told him as pleasantly as I could, while kneeling in the mud next to his black racer.

Just get off the earth and let them go back to sleep. Yes, it was natural to connect us with trouble, because there was that connection; but only when looked at drowsily. It was as if everyone was nicely asleep when the mongrels came walking through. A few beagles started barking and woke up the bloodhounds. The bloodhounds woke up the house dogs, and all of them started barking, which woke up the police dogs, who are the keepers of the sleep. They looked out on the scene: there was the quiet band of mongrels and an army of barking locals with papers and credentials and guns. And the key was—and even half-awake, the police dogs could see—that the objects being barked at were just mongrels (which means no-friends-in-high-places and no-money-for-lawyers). Even in their sleep they were smart enough not to tell the barking dogs to shut up; no, they simply told the mongrels to get moving, faster. The mongrels would have to get "out of the vicinity" so the barking would stop and everyone could go back to sleep and watch it on TV.

I went back to the truck and drove off. The stateys took off in the opposite direction. We were into the walk again: our roads, the weather, marking our route in the rain, jumping out of the truck to spray white runny paint on a road, a tree, on a stone.

Maine was not our objective, but in the last day or so we had begun to talk of Maine. It couldn't be helped. If we had walked in a straight line, we would be there by now. We would take Maine (this kind of talk is no more foolish than headlines like THE MOON IS OURS!), but we would not hit the coast so soon. Everyone had the usual exclamations over how far we'd walked, but yesterday and today the rain kept our heads down to the trail and to more basic questions, such as "When will it stop?"

To be driving while a part of your body walks in heavy rain is guilt-producing. We had agreed in meetings that no one should neglect his feet; if they would only get worse by walking, then it was stupid not to ride. Mine were that sore, so were Big Ann's. So were the feet of some others who were still walking, rain or snow. The trouble was that riding was now combined with getting out of the rain, and I was stupid enough to feel guilty.

We found an old general store where, among the shelves of cans and bread, we could almost hear the owner's thoughts. Could they fix us twenty cups of coffee? They could.

The rain was coming down so hard the walkers must be swimming by now. Hot coffee and a candy bar would be good. We got sugar and canned milk on the side. We were ready to go when we saw the newspapers. Two days before, when we could have used some publicity, we got nothing; now that we were out of trouble we had made the front page: N.H. HIKERS GETTING EDUCATION. And two pictures of our relaxed and wild little family. Thirteen-year-old Tita was presented as my wife, there was Mike Hunt and Dick Hertz, some were from Hawaii and some from Alaska. It was billed as a 700-mile trek to Nova Scotia—and although this provided the biggest laugh, it turned out to be very close to what we did walk. The reporter changed things to suit himself, quoted no one and yet quoted someone: "Heck man, what's with burning a building? Sure, it says something, but it's nowhere . . . buddy, when you sit around at night breaking blisters with your friends, you know what it all means . . . you think, 'Why these roads, why these plants, where does it all lead to? Where am I going in the long run?'" No one said those things, but in his mind that's how it came across, and while his quotes were a jumble, somewhere in it, somehow, he had gotten the spirit.

The rain was streaming down when we reached the junction of Highways 11 and 28—and Dot's Diner. Why not have everyone meet there for lunch? At least they could be out of it during the meal.

Making contact was varied and intimate on that day. Only from the truck could we view the whole operation. Ones, twos, and threes were spread out over 3 miles. They were lifted by the coffee, and the candy was a complete surprise. For some the rain was rough, others confided that it was a great day. We'd catch another twosome or trio slogging along in their ponchos, blending with the rain, the road, the trees. Coffee, candy, and a glimpse of the *Union Leader* article. They'd laugh or curse, hang on to the truck for another minute or so.

"How's it going?"

"Great! You know, about the rain . . . somehow it *helps*! I don't know . . . I can't explain it."

We heard those words three or four times. The coffee and candy were great, but they were eager to get back into themselves, the road, the streams on each side, trees, quiet, spring rain, being closed in.

I decided to get a barn for the night. Two solid days of being in the rain, with wet clothes and wet sleeping bags, was enough. I started promising them we'd find a barn. Would we? Yes! We *wanted* one.

We were down to five cups of coffee when we began to hear ominous warnings of a stream which was overflowing the road. Don't take the truck over; you'll never make it. We were hoping to run into everyone before the road turned into a river, but no such luck. There before us was the stream, and sure enough the road had been a low bridge but was now a part of the stream, with huge holes where the little bridge had been carried away. We parked the truck and got out to take a look. A broken axle? Stuck? Turned over!? While waiting for stragglers we began lugging rocks from the sides and building the road up again. We finished it before the last walkers came along, and by now we were anxious to try and ford the stream-road. We eased across. Ha! We still had a truck.

Bob B. was last, a 3-foot-wide poncho-green mountain

cruising along in the rain; no hurry and everything was coming his way.

"I think this is the greatest day yet." The coffee and candy bar were just one more step up.

I was happy but envious. We left him, recrossed our bridge with no mishaps, and headed for Dot's Diner.

At the diner the atmosphere was ours. Dot and her husband were experts on old roads in the area. They had already briefed Gale; we'd have to go to Farmington to dry the sleeping bags first. Big Ann was dropped off for lunch, and Gale and I took sandwiches with us.

Again, we were on roads so out of things that we could only wonder who used them—our feeling was a combination of amazement and thanks. We sprayed arrows on wet rocks and trees and, after 14 miles, began looking for barns. We stopped at a place with a large barn in back. I knocked and a woman answered. After no more than ten words she screamed, without turning her head from me, "MOSES!?!" It almost blew me off the porch. Then she went back and looked for him. We never did see Moses, we only heard him speak. Moses told her we couldn't use the barn because "it's all jammed up."

Off to Farmington to dry the sleeping bags. On the way Gale had a chat with some politico's wife, a Mrs. Tufts. That was just out of Middleton Corners, which should be renamed Tufts Corners, since half the people were Tufts. On coming into the center of this desolate tiny town, we saw a huge sign on the town hall:

WELCOME HOME

Wind, time, years, and faded paint. Not a soul in sight; tree silences; leaves from the fall of '23 undisturbed behind that faded white building, but welcome home.

On the map Farmington looked light-years away, but in the truck it was only twenty minutes—we had made the break, we were more used to walking than riding. I left Gale off with the sleeping bags and drove back for a place to stay. At the house we had kept going back to, they still weren't home. But down the road from it, a little less than 14 miles from last night's camp was a tremendous red barn, well-kept, freshly painted, solid.

I drove in, mustering all the do-it-right forces to succeed. All my ambition was focused on that one thing (not to be President, just to get the barn). The man was home, and he listened. We walked over to the barn; he warned me about fires, told us where we could cook—on the cement ground floor—and said that we could sleep on the hay floor. We went up the ladder to a wide, dry, spacious, sturdy floor with about a foot of hay spread evenly over it. There were small windows, a high roof, barn swallows—a little world, and DRY! In a couple of hundred words he was telling us yes. I said that the group would look a little bedraggled and would begin arriving around 3:00 that afternoon. Fine. Fine.

At the entrance to the house and barn I sprayed the turning-in arrow, the home arrow. Such a simple thing, yet there was nothing more I wanted. Off to Dot's Diner. Can you drive with happiness? Turn with happiness? Shift gears happily?

Just before Dot's I picked up Ann M., who had sprained her ankle. Sure, she would take over and drive; I would pad my feet and walk the 5 miles from Dot's to the barn. I *had* to walk. We met Herbie walking along, and I got out.

"We've got a barn! A beautiful barn for tonight!!"

"Great!" Herbie was looking at me as if a barn was a miracle too remote to be hoped for. All over the world people were happy or sad for all sorts of reasons; we were in ecstasies over a barn for the night. To know we'd wake up dry, that we could move around dry, that whether it was rainy or sunny, we'd be dry.

Ann M. drove off with the noisy truck and its chores. Good-bye!

The bottoms of my feet were almost raw and my toes were sore, so I put moleskin padding next to my feet and walked in socks. What did it matter when we got there? Just savor 5 miles . . . try to walk slowly. Herbie was up for that, so we set off. About a mile along the road, we stopped at The Sportsmen's Grill in New Durham—really just out of New Durham, which is to say almost the same thing. We got a coke but kept eying the fried clams which Ruby, the big cook, was preparing. Oh yes, she'd talked to three or four of the walkers before us, they were all very nice people, she said.

"Ruby, could you fix us two orders of fried clams?" Sure, and she did. She dropped her work for the moment. "I'm secretary to the chief of police here, you know. We've had a dozen calls about you people. Another came through just a few minutes ago, telling me some mysterious looking guys are walking by my place . . . 'mysterious' or 'queer-looking,' and wasn't I scared? I told him, 'Listen, they're perfectly fine. In fact they're *very* intelligent,' I said."

She talked with us about the project and what the others had told her of it. We took her name and address in order to send her a postcard from Nova Scotia.

"Have fun! I wish't I was with you!"

We were down to essentials: old roads, a dry barn, a stranger's welcome—in our world Ruby Shaw was a queen.

The area's capitalist had given us his barn for the night. A sweet old lady had gotten us kicked out of three places, forcing us to walk 10 more miles after a long day. The secretary of the chief of police had silenced the gossipmongers, the bloodhounds. Another chief of police had scouted out back roads with us for two hours. Our faith in people would zoom down out of sight, then without warning, would zoom up just as far.

The weather was drizzly, but it didn't claim any attention.

"Say, what happened to all those great blackfly days?" Dan had asked us earlier, during the heaviest downpour. How we cursed blackflies, and how we'd welcome them back now—with the sun.

A million times we needed to remind ourselves that it wasn't a race, we weren't racing to a place, we were already there. All the time we were there.

Even with the padding, the balls of my feet were so sore I could just barely get along. I told Herbie to go on ahead, and for a time he did. Inside another half hour my feet began to adjust and I was getting along okay. But there was no urgency, that was the saving feature; just move and don't worry . . . be here, now. When that works, your blood turns to spring water and the whole system says yes. Not only the mind, but the palms of the hands, the knees, the top of the head.

Why are these times so rare? Aren't they worth examination? Does education have nothing to do with them? I started to write as I walked along. Why walk out of school?

To find our feet again. To use other parts of our brains beside the memory and low-logic areas.
To preserve our sanity.
Because formal education has outlived its usefulness.
Because the sun is out here.
Because my mind is on the road with me.
Because school is dead and everything that lives is holy.
Because I can't think of a finer thing to do.
Because we are brothers and sisters and rarely act like it.
To find ourselves.
To protest the known fact that education and school have nothing to do with each other.
Because I'm a learner, not a teacher.
Because we're as far away from ourselves as we are from Nova Scotia, and we've gotta get home again.
Because we've lost something precious and there's precious little time to find it.

In the name of science we are taught to forget everything that a child knows, everything that a savage knows. Education makes us more stupid than the brutes. A thousand voices call to us on every hand, but our ears are stopped with wisdom. There are unimaginable wonders everywhere, but we wear blinders of science— Well—I have taken off my blinders. I have unstopped my ears. . . . The darkness that hems us about is only our dullness.

Giraudoux must have locked up all his books, or taken a walk, or both, to have come to that.

I caught up with Herbie and we walked in peace for the

next two hours. When we arrived—great as it was to be there, to see that big red barn, the truck, everyone together —the walk was over and we were sad.

That evening, after mapping the route of our last full day in New Hampshire—with a site ten feet from a lake, a spigot of rushing living water right next to the tent—I realized that my feet were in very bad shape. The moleskin was not just stuck to my raw soles; the moleskin was now *my* skin. Somehow those pads had to come off.

The barn had become transformed. Ann M., Lloyd, and Don were cooking downstairs. Upstairs, that once-empty hay floor was lit with hanging lamps and lined with sleeping bags. Everyone was drying out, singing, talking, writing in journals. The owner had invited the girls to stay in the "playroom"—a two-story house—and to take showers there. Someone had already picked out a room for Gale and me, with a double bed in it, soft, squashy, off the ground, away from the group. I had the same feeling as at St. Mary's— these niceties slowed us down, not to a walking speed but to a different momentum. To split up always seemed to let air out of the balloon. Still, it was a nice favor, a "treat."

Our meal was, as always, prepared with zeal, love, haste, zip, laughs. (Do laughs over stew make it better? Organically better, chemically better, better-balanced? Of course; who needs proof of the obvious?) Don was turning out tremendous salads, Ann M., great dishes; Howie is a born cook.

But those moleskins would have to come off, and I just couldn't do it myself. Ann M. paused in her cooking, grabbed one end, hesitated.

"Just pull!"

She did. And my feet were bloody, bloody, and bloody sore.

"You'll be in the truck for at least two days," someone said.

And miss the walk into Maine? No, I'd soak them in epsom salts, paint them with methiolate, crawl, walk on knees; but I'd had it with the truck. Everyone in the group felt the same way.

That night about ten of us took showers, some watched

television, we sat in real chairs, on sofas. Gale and I showered and fell into our bed. Crisp sheets and all. It was no little thing, but still there was the aura over the group sleeping on hay in the barn. That was where we really were.

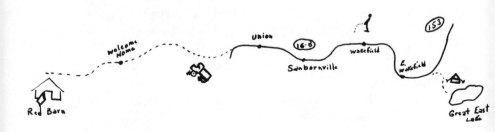

As usual, when we mixed the walk with other people we were slow to round ourselves up next day. The owner was amused because I'd told him we'd be off around 7:30. Those comfortable beds were a drug.

At 10:00 walkers were limping, hobbling, staggering away, leaving the barn. No more than two or three out of the twenty-one looked as if they could walk more than a hundred yards, but part of it was the morning rebellion of feet and legs not willing to give in—yet. If the owner didn't laugh in front of us, he could certainly be excused for laughing till his sides split when we were out of sight. But a few hundred yards later, he might have shaken his head in amazement; everyone began to straighten up and make tracks. I had spent about an hour doctoring my feet, and, by the time we passed through Middleton Corners and *Welcome Home*, even they were not feeling much pain.

It's better not to look back when walking; forget "progress," forget walking, just think and talk. Maybe an hour later, something reminds you: I'm walking, I'm here.

Behind each house there seemed to be an average of ten old cars. My eye fixed on an old International truck on its side in a sea of grass, facing straight ahead on no road. Once it was full of lumber, or kids, or rusty junk from cars ten years *its* senior. Once-mobiles; the once-mobiles of America seem stiller than the trees around them, for the trees are rooted and were never intended to run about.

"I counted twelve cars in back of that house!" someone said.

Bill walked up after a long silence and began speaking to me about the dreamy quality of reality. We even talked about it in our morning sleep. Perhaps it is dreamy and unreal because we have so little time for it.

Our old road from Middleton Corners joined the main highway, and we caught four walkers going the wrong way and turned them around. Up a few miles, a group of walkers was gathered around a police car, which seemed to be parked in a very dangerous place. It was the local police chief. When I was pointed out, he flew up to me. "Can't you keep these people together? They're strung out all over hell!"

"That's the way we walk."

"Well, you'll have to keep 'em together."

"Is there a law that says we have to walk together?"

He didn't answer, he just pulled out his badge. No one had asked if he was chief of police, but he showed us his badge instead of quoting the law. We all looked at his badge, and for some reason he began to calm down. I asked him politely why we should have to walk together, and he told us that we'd have to walk together because, "We *want* you to walk together."

Still, he was much calmer. He was the chief of police and his badge was . . . well, a thing of beauty. The meeting ended, and we were allowed to go our way, but be careful. We would, we told him, as the group began stringing out.

According to the map, Maine seemed to have fewer cities, more blank spaces. Did that mean more fear? Or less?

There was a great old garage by a waterfall where we stopped and had cokes early that afternoon. The truck caught us here and laid sandwiches on us. We ate on a little grassy knoll next to the water under a cloudy blue-white sky. We were inside the whole project, lying in lunchtime clouds and walking free days on all sides of us, up ahead and behind; clouds, sky, roads, and days all balled up and rolling together in our own dance to Canada. And there was something about the old bypassed garage by the waterfall that was unforgettable.

For Bill and me the last part of the walk was uneventful; not so for others. Gale had been hit in the back with a hunk of wood, the cops were looking all over for me, and Motorhead had been arrested. At the campsite Motorhead came up, smiling a pale smile, and confirmed it. The police were coming back to get him.

Suddenly it was innocent early afternoon again, in that big roomy garage with its cement floor darkened by grease, and that dreamy mysterious *there* feeling of doing a simple thing. Walk up to a coke machine when *now*—each instant unlocks its magic—time floats, holds, unfolds, almost stops. The feet walk, fingers hold coins, the mouth wonders, the brain barely ticks over, and hair-by-hair is watching, listening, ready for the next tiny adventure; what next little movement, action, click, will unfold, unfold—the unfolding of a finger, movement of the arm, coin against metal plate adjusting to a slot, release, journey of a coin—while the whole world rolls around.

I've read it, discussed it in school, but here was the experience . . . all the difference in the world: "Whatever is, is right." We sit in class and gobble up mountains, and leave a trail of little goat berries behind us.

But that was early afternoon; total absorption in next-to-nothing, next-to-everything; now came total absorption in a different next-to-nothingness.

What had Motorhead done? They were all stirred up in Sanbornville. And what had the criminal done? Why, he had done nothing less than to walk up to an outhouse, go inside, and urinate. On the walls? No. On the seats? No! Right square in the hole made for the purpose. The crime was that the filling station was closed and had been closed for some months.

We put the tent up, but really we waited for the police to come back. I asked Motorhead again if he was sure that was all. He came over with his wide grin and swore that was it. I began to feel that we were in a foreign country and our real barrier was one of language.

Of all the people they could have chosen, the various flamboyant types, the wild hats and costumes, the free and easy air and the flip walking style of some (although these are not crimes, I'm told), they had picked Motorhead—serious, pleasant, introspective, helpful. I could hardly believe it. "I think," Motor told me, "they're going to try to make some kind of deal, using me as ransom to get us out of the vicinity."

There was the big lake, empty and waiting, but only Richie was up for it. Even Richie, who is built like an oak tree in January, posed on the dock for about ten minutes while the rest stood around and cursed him out, challenged him to go on in. He finally dove, screamed, swam, screamed again and was out huffing and puffing.

I couldn't wait any longer. Jake and Bob B. went with me to check out the roads ahead, to check out Maine. Off we drove, at last heading straight east and across the line. Maine wasn't the object, but it was a little plum along the way. So was the Ox-Head ale.

Maine! It had stores and trees and people, and highways and state cops. Stupendous! What a surprise! At a store we went over and talked to a young state trooper parked out front. We told him about the project, where we were going, how long we'd be, etc. He didn't greet all of this with any relish, but he nodded away and seemed at least neutral. Suddenly my wits came back. Why should people on one side of an arbitrary border be any different from those just the other side?

The post office, a cake for Diana's birthday, mapping. Tomorrow was Sunday, and Mother's Day. Gale was the only mother in the group, but since she is a mother five times, we would go along with the commercial gag and get a cake for her too. We drove into Limerick, bought the cakes, candles, some more Ox-Head ale, drank up, turned the radio on, and went to the post office. Jake was full of giggles: "Say, man, this ale is really Goooooooood!"

Everyone was waiting for money, news, contact. The post office was closed, but I felt the postmaster would open for us if we could only find him. We did and he agreed to. So! We were the mysterious walkers of *The Walk*. Yes, he had quite a bundle of things; packages, telegrams, letters. Across the street we bought a LIMERICK, MAINE sweatshirt and stretched it across the front of the truck.

The postmaster was typical. Small-town postmasters opened up for us after hours, made contacts, wrote to the next postmaster, and helped us cash checks, always in the friendliest manner.

As for roads, there was no problem because there were no choices. It was State Highway 110 into Maine, then 11 into Limerick. We flew back stoned on ale and the idea of Maine —and sea gulls flying over a town dump—hardly noticing the long, straight road we traveled. Maybe it was the first long stretch of straight highway we had come across. We'd find out on the following day what it could do for walkers, or to them.

When we got back, one of those cars with the pretty flashing lights was parked next to our tent. I went over and met my man. He wanted to talk, so I got in; we sat in his car and talked. We talked till it got dark and still sat there. Maybe because I could no longer see his uniform, or maybe because of what we discussed, after half an hour we were simply two men, both parents of thirteen-year-old girls, trading views. He held down two jobs and was exhausted. He worked so many hours that he was completely out of touch with his three kids, the very ones he worked so hard for. And his thirteen-year-old was beginning to pull her own way. He got home for an occasional meal and sleep; after a few words to the children: "Shut the hell up!"

There was no more talk of arresting Motorhead or using him as a hostage, but there was still something on his mind and he finally came out with it.

"Can you tell me why these kids—not just these kids here, 'cause I notice some of these kids *don't* have long hair—but why these kids, a lot of kids, young kids nowadays, want to have long hair?"

Before I could even start to answer he went on, "I don't get it!"

He wasn't with his cronies now and he was really asking—maybe for the first time ever with any hope of an answer—although his tone let me know he'd asked the same question out loud and silently so many times that it had worn tracks in his brain.

"I think you have to turn it around and ask, 'Why not?' Why shouldn't anyone grow hair if he wants to?"

"I just can't see it," he said, still puzzled. Times had changed and he couldn't figure it out; but while he sat there a meal had been served, dishes were being washed, and people were going about selecting where they would sleep —all of it done peacefully and cheerfully by these long-haired kids.

He confessed that he was tired and wished he didn't have to work at two jobs. It was as close as he could come to saying that he'd been rushed into action without much thought. He left on good terms.

The Maine border was about 6 miles away. The night was cloudy and "possible rains" were forecast, although we didn't pay much attention to such reports. The radio was for music; "news and weather" were interests of the unreal world.

Diana, presented with her cake, was overcome. Such a little thing, but the attention of our group was on singing the old song to her and watching her reactions.

We would save Gale's cake for tomorrow, Mom's Day. Later, Mom told me about four of the youths of that good town driving close by Phil, Herb, and her and throwing a block of wood from the car. It hit her in the back, and the three walkers had gone to a house to call the cops. The cops knew from the description of the car who the towneys were —but couldn't do anything because we couldn't furnish the license number.

In the morning it was rain. We quick-breakfasted in order to get out in it—I don't know why, but that was always our feeling. Bob D. and Bill, as usual, stayed behind to load the truck; Jake and I were next to last and hobbled off together with our ponchos over our heads. Maine was 6 miles away, and we'd cross into Maine on our own two feet.

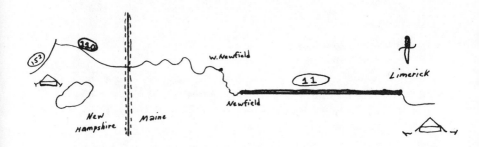

Again the feeling that this hobbling, limping group won't make a mile, let alone the scheduled 16. But we don't consider it walking, this is just what we do, whether it hurts or not. Jake and I are rolling and rocking along, Jake with his bad knee and me with my patch of bare skin which is not healing. As for Bob B. and some of the others, I don't want to *see* their feet—even the bones seem to be bruised from the constant pounding. Gale and Big Ann doctor cuts, bruises, muscles, strains, and sprains every night for an hour and a half or more. It is all very intimate and calm: "How is the heel doing?" But the tone of voice is family on good terms, family or love.

Down comes the rain. The truck passes us, waving, and rocks off toward Maine. We're last, but that can be nice. Down it comes, and we walk. Cold *and* wet. There is always a little world framed by what the eyes see, and now our vision is forced inward even further by the caped ponchos. The changing circle in front is filled with the world of pebbles embedded in tar, not unlike a starry night upside down. Yesterday I had gotten into such a state of peace that when a furious little dog bounded up, I could look on it as that little world of irritation over there, having nothing to do with me.

A wet Sunday and the cars zoom by, but they carry themselves wherever they go, at 40, 80, 150. But 80 is not fast enough, 90 is not fast enough; to go 30 in a car is to die of impatience. With walking, the range of speeds is so slight that impatience runs off and leaves you alone. Walk fast and you'll get there, walk slow and get there a little later; but no truck will hold you up on a winding two-lane highway and no construction gang (unless very hostile) will slow you down.

Jake and I walked and I was thinking, wondering cool about this wall and all the levels of knowing, not even looking up as cars passed. Thinking how you go along and say over and over, Know thyself; hear it, say it—then one day it is on a different plateau and takes on a different sound, when Jake started talking about his knee and how for three days it had not improved. We got on the subject of mind over matter and how, even in our own backward civilization, we had come upon the age-old idea that man can heal himself. That man through his mind and emotions can not only overcome pain but heal himself.

I suggested that Jake try it. Jake can generate tremendous enthusiasm on the instant, and he took it up. "Right now," he said carefully, "I'm sending warm impulses to my knee . . . like warm massaging impulses to my knee . . . *and I can feel it!*"

He kept at it, and inside of ten minutes he was straightening up, his limp was hardly noticeable. Inside of twenty minutes I could hardly keep up with him. Too bad I couldn't put a mental layer of skin over my foot. If I were as innocent and as open as Jake, I probably could.

We got to a store on the New Hampshire side of the border and bought fruit and hats. I found a cheap yachting skipper's hat, Jake got a sand-castle beach hat, and it was off to Maine.

Jake with his mind-over-matter legs was too much for me, so I wished him well and he took off like Big Ann (when she wants to). About a quarter mile ahead, I saw him yipping away and leaping into Maine: Yowee, etc. I found out later that the Super-Weasel had urinated in both states at the same time—pretty good for a twelve-year-old. Into Maine and a gentle elation.

Having absolutely no disturbances, I walked into a state of total concentration, as if all my scattered selves had joined hands. It seemed to me that just from these minutes it was the best day of my life, that I'd walk on forever. Why not? I had the whole walk in my hand, every instant. My whole life was walking with me. I had felt it before—this "walk on forever" sensation—and others had talked about it, but I had never felt it so strongly. At least half of the others had spoken of the moments of clarity, simplicity; discovering that life isn't complicated, *we* complicate it.

I was way behind everyone, but very much with them. At nights we must remind each other to use these hours, that we aren't just walking to Canada . . . what did we bring with us . . . how are we using it now?

I sat on a wet mossy rock, scribbling away inside my poncho. What does it matter where I am? Or when I get there? Sit down! Stick! Grab the moment! The rain had almost stopped. The truck sped by, then pulled over.

"You're way behind everybody. Y'want a ride?"

"No."

"We'll bring sandwiches in about an hour."

"Great."

They were off. Peace.

When the truck was out of sight I started walking again. Over there in that pond is Florida, sticking way out into the Gulf of Mexico. There's New Orleans and here is Texas . . . we're walking down to Mexico.

Walk fast for an hour, slow for an hour, then ask which one did more for you. Come back to each other at the end of the day and report on how these things worked out.

My head was wide open and the winds played through me. Walk to find America? Not good enough. To find ourselves! And some mile along the way, at some bend in the road . . .

Where was I? Out in some field in the southwestern corner

of Maine, debating whether to take a nap and pray for my
sore feet or to keep jotting down things I wanted to tell the
others. The truck whizzed past looking for me, but they were
gone before I could stand up. The sky was lovely blue, soft
clouds white-blue, blue-white. I was in the basin of that long
stretch of clay and tan-brown earth turning green—a 2- or
3-mile straight stretch of road—watching stars, diamonds,
jeweled clouds, all things in sun-eyes.

> *A Phil and a Bill*
> *Two Bobs and a Dan*
> *A Don a Diana*
> *Two Anns and two Taylors*
> *A Herbie a Howie*
> *A Tita a Gale*
> *A Jake a John*
> *A Lloyd a Gordon*
> *An Ed a Richie and*
> *That's the tale.*

Maine is a little wilder, more open; and state cops from
poorer states have shiner, nattier uniforms.

The truck caught me coming back and left a sandwich.
"Boy, you are *way* behind. L.J., Howie, Ann M., and Lloyd
are already in Limerick!"

Good! I hoped they were having as fine a day as I was. The
truck sped off and I started walking. Sunday between small
towns. The day had begun with rain, but now a quiet sunlight
was on everything. And something else . . . more than quiet,
there was almost a vacancy, a forgotten air—a pulse or the
lightest breath of the wreckage of hopes—of too many trees
cut down too early in life because of no money and things to
be paid for. Or the soundless song of wood nymphs still
cruising that hacked-out countryside, lamenting the difference between trees and lumber.

I talked to a young wife, a schoolteacher whose husband
was in "lumber," who had seen the others pass by and wondered about us.

"It's nice behind your house, the trees and the lake over
there."

By her quick and strange agreement I knew she didn't have much talk like this, as if she shared the vacant hunger in the air.

Into West Newfield, Maine; an entire town with that strange vacant bypassed air, a post office–store—at least, the the sign said it was, but not on Sunday afternoon. The people had fled, leaving the flagpole in West Newfield, Maine, of a Sunday flick-rapping in restless wind, that line to the top empty as the graveyard beyond it, empty as the Mason's lodge; just a metal pole and the rope's sound against hollow metal, flick-rap winds knifed by flagless metal pole the ruffled testy flick rap of times-a-changing to leave one empty small-town Sunday still beautiful for spacious skies.

Into this emptiness come the towneys: screech to a stop, motor low and idling, four or five young ginks with so much more energy and time than sense to know even what they *want* to do; idling power they look over at a stranger sketching the Day Spring Lodge of the A.F.-A.M., and suddenly the empty hollow flick-ting rap is a hollow reminder that I'm out of it and way behind the others. Suddenly the car is grinding, screaming; lays out rubber, rocks from side to side and off—with wheeee laughs whistles screams. All for me? There's no one else in West Newfield.

Out of town is a fringe of trees, a lake beyond; trees, cabin, and misty mountain. Sea gulls over the dump at Fisher Downs. We aren't that close to the sea, but there they are.

A car stops and waits for me to walk up. "Hi! What's going on?"

"We're walking to Canada."

"What?" And so on. She has two children with her. She gives me some insect pads—the blackflies are swarming around me—offers me a ride and when I refuse, tells me to stop by for coffee 2 miles up the road on the left. Okay, but my main weakness is directions; sleep automatically closes over my brain when someone says you can't miss it; oh yes I can.

The insect pads don't work, so my little world with thousands of black satellites makes the 2 miles and there's the car!

Found it! Without even trying. The kids take me in, and when she says "coffee" I melt. Even the word sounds sweet. The chair feels great; the table supports my upper body.

She liked our walk very much, and that was a lift; then she told me about the struggles of an art teacher in a small town. Brute courage is my only comment about such people, the brute courage of pioneers. The kids—boys, thirteen and eleven—were funny, alive, literate. They decided they'd walk with me into Limerick, so we set out. Half a mile beyond the house we hit a 2-mile stretch as straight as an arrow. The boys chattered away about their school, teachers, classmates, in the same way my own kids would talk to a stranger who showed tolerance for stories about the school fat kid, strongest kid, strictest teacher ("You know what he did to *one* kid?"), all the time outlining themselves through others. Occasionally I laughed just at the thought of it, the thirteen-year-old, eleven-year-old, exuberance. The walk was nothing to them; they'd climb Mount Everest without asking what they were doing if someone would only walk alongside and listen to the whole tale of their world.

I guess they thought I was the greatest listener of all time. Actually I was too tired to talk. That straight stretch was breaking my back, my arches, and my mind.

Around 4:00 p.m. the truck pulled up and we just piled in. I'd been hobbling all day. The site was a nice field on the edge of town about thirty yards off the road . . . our first campsite whose owner flew an American flag in his front yard.

Mapping was done; the two kids who had walked with me had been picked up by their mother some time after dark; and we were sacked out fairly early. It must have been around 11:15 that Phil and one or two others woke up. Headlights were sweeping the inside of the tent, the car behind the lights was zooming around the field trailed by a sickly "laughing" voice; a humorless scary laugh, an aged childishness. Perhaps we all felt the same way—stay still and it will go away. Well, who doesn't dream at times like that.

After zooming by the tent and just missing it a few times, they pulled over to the side of the tent and got out. There was at least one girl and a few guys. No one has notes of what followed; certainly no one was writing at the time and, maybe out of distaste, no one wrote it up later.

I remember the girl's voice and some of the things she said: they were just trying to be sociable (a Mexican *cantina* sociability which you better, by God, respond to or you'll have a sociable knife between your shoulder blades). I told her we were tired, we'd walked a long way, we wanted to sleep. The guy chimed in: the field belonged to his uncle, did we have permission to stay there? I told him to go ask his uncle. You go ask him, says he. I didn't answer, and the girl came on again. She asked where we were walking to and I told her. She told us, in an eerie coquettish voice, that it was an awful long way. Maybe if we had gone out and talked for a while it could have turned the direction; who knows? Shortly after this, they were leaving. The guy yelled in to us "You long-haired faggots!" And then they left, a little hastily, I now realize. No one, at that point, was really upset. We still wanted sleep more than anything else and were still deep in our sleeping bags—naked for the most part, and that adds a measure of defenselessness, of vulnerability, to being waked up in a strange place with only tent canvas between us and the world.

They seemed to leave, but must have made a big circle and parked in the same spot. The girl came back; by this time Phil, Gordon, Richie, and a few others were awake and getting dressed—crazy, hateful, finding clothes in blackness. "Shall we get 'em?" Phil asked.

"Wait."

Maybe it was this time she was really coming on: how far were we walking, etc.; stupid questions asked without any concern for answers.

Suddenly one of the guys yelled, "Come on, Helen!" He had to yell twice, then just as she started moving away, she tripped—a lovely moment—fell flat over a tent rope, measured her length in inches, and got up cursing. Doors slammed, and they were off. Motorhead was getting up; they'd done something to the tent, he thought. Yes, all of the tent ropes in back were cut. While Helen had been talking to us in front, the others had been cutting the ropes in back.

All the talk had not really bothered us—although the body is shivering in fear and readiness, partly at the unprovoked hatred that this must involve, at the *why* of it,—but in cutting the ropes they had really touched us. And they had gotten away too easily, so they were bound to be back, maybe with a little help.

Yes, they'd probably be back, and the hell of it was that it had little or nothing to do with us—what we had answered or not, done or not—but with their lives: cruelty, neglect, brutality, schools (sacrosanct jails-without-bars), and the lifelong pressure of a competitive society with its unwritten but clear directive to be hard—tricky-hard and armed with dollars, or muscle-hard and armed with hate.

Gordon, Phil, and I decided to make some coffee and stay up and wait. We got out shovels and trench tools, and went around warning all of the groups to come running if we yelled. Even now I shudder at the thought of how easily the car could have run over someone. Ann, Lloyd, and Don were about twenty yards away by a clump of bushes, Dan was in the truck, Bob D. and Bill were on a little hillock farthest away. L.J. and Howie? Someone told me they had dates with two town girls. Too bad, for they were both like fighting cocks.

After an hour of sitting around cursing, we decided to call the cops so we could get some sleep. We trudged across the field to the owner's house and knocked on his door. His wife came down but was afraid to open it. We explained through the closed door ("What? . . . What?"); no, she didn't want to understand. Then he came to the door and finally let us in to call the stateys. I let it ring about fifty times, then hung up. We're on our own.

"They probably won't come back," the man said. Back up to bed for him, in his house behind the locked doors. I gave him a good long look; then we trudged back across the field, just a little desperate. If the cops aren't there when you call them, there *ain't* no cops.

"If I knew how to make a Molotov cocktail . . ."

"I know," Phil said. "Just gas in a beer bottle with a wick. You light the wick and throw it."

I knew Phil had never thrown one or made one. It was, all of it, amusing and at the same time grim. We had talked before about our position and their position—*they* were of the town, we were strangers; there were twenty-one of us (five females) and untold numbers of *them*. Out of any town a group *could* be assembled to overpower us. Not that it would be a likely prospect; but what do we know of Limerick? Pretty Limerick. Or any town we pass through? Who are the people opposing us? Have they gone back for more? What do they feel threatened by?

It was a lonely walk back across the field. How thin and vulnerable our beautiful tent seemed. What did that old man say? "If I'da known it was gonna be such a trouble I'da not let you camp *out* there." Such a trouble. I could still hear the phone ringing emptily of a Sunday night in the state troopers' headquarters or house. Do stateys have houses?

We talked it over. Would they come back? They had pushed and met no resistance—awfully tempting to come back for more. "They probably won't come back," says the owner. I could see him at the inquest—in broad beautiful daylight—"Gee, I didn't think they'd come back!"

We walked across the field wondering what would be best. Would we fight? Somewhere in those hours I realized that at a certain point, I'd fight like ten maniacs. We got out the shovels from the truck—some kind of pacifist, I chided myself—and actually made a Molotov cocktail: white gas in a beer bottle with a paper-napkin wick. I went around once more and warned everybody to come running if I started yelling.

Later we learned that our night visitor had just gotten out of jail for some act of violence.

We waited, feeling foolish and yet ready; wondering whether we'd actually hit anyone with those heavy army shovels, actually throw the Molotov cocktail. Would someone be killed? How long should we stay up? Sleep was out of the question for me; I wasn't being noble, I *couldn't*. I don't know about Gordon and Phil. Of course we were afraid, knowing that if they came back we *would* fight. I also knew I'd hate to come upon such back-to-the-wall desperate rats as we were.

Perhaps it was at the very height of the quiet period, a time of feeling what a waste of sleep those bastards were causing us while they were home in bed, that a car actually swung off the road—at 2:00 a.m.—and onto the field, its headlights lancing out over the tall wet grass and heading straight at us.

No matter how I might want that car to keep going along the nice paved road, here it was bouncing across the field at us. At us? Well, there was nothing beyond us, no towns, houses, roads, just us . . . us chickens. Defenseless (?), harmless, tired, and trapped.

"okay! come on, you guys! here come the bastards; everybody up, let's get 'em! !" I may have cursed a lot more, and evidently I yelled much louder than I thought I did. We were as ready as we'd ever be. I had my shovel and my bottle of gas, and I had just found a cigarette lighter (I realized then I would have heaved it at the car, no doubt about it). Suddenly, from the car we heard frantic shouts of "peace! hey, it's us! stop! peace!"

From fear and wild-eyed hysterical violence the scene changed to amazement, wild relief, and laughter. It was L.J. and Howie, returning with their dates. We told all. The girls offered to take us to the state cop's house. We squeezed into the car and drove off. "It's probably Matthew's gang," they told us on the way to the state cop's house. Helen was Matthew's sister. Being driven to this museum piece, a state cop's house, by other citizens of the town which housed the people who had cut our tent ropes was, all at once, impossible to grasp. We had no name for the laughing, snarling drunk so this is what "Limerick" had done to us. Then, suddenly, "Limerick" is taking us to someone who might be able to help. But not even my talk with the cop of the night before, or the knowledge that he too is the father of a thirteen-year-old daughter, is preparation for walking up on a statey's porch, ringing a state cop's doorbell, watching the light go on in the statey's house, and looking in to see a kid's toys on the floor, a sleepy man in an undershirt, yawning and answering the door—to what? It is now early Monday morning.

We told him our tale and he asked questions. Do we have a license number? No. Description of car? A red Ford, someone said. And the name Helen. Yeah, he knows who it is. But he comes back to what we don't have. No license number, eh?

Gee, we would prosecute those guys but . . . see, we don't have any proof. They *knew*! Everybody *knew*! But they didn't have proof. Was it that, or were they scared of Matthew and his "boys"?

"So call me if they come back," he said, "and I'll get right out there."

I told him that would be too late, there would be no time to "call" anybody. Well, it was the best he could do. Can I blame him? No, it was really all too human. The girls took us back. L.J. and Howie said they'd stay up the rest of the night, so we went to sleep.

Sure, enough, the bad guys never came back.

Next morning, waking up with the same taste of violence done to us, our body, our tent, we were amazed to find that at least half the group had slept through the night impervious to anything . . . except maybe to my screams. "Man, you were really yelling!" I allowed that I was trying to build up my own courage.

The aura in the office of the owner-manager of the general store is the same as years and years ago, old America of rolltop desks and wall hangings, when Limerick was a bustling little town, when tourism was unheard of. The map behind the door showed a fine line between Limerick and Limington; that was our road, a one-laner, snowbound in February, unused for some twenty years. Now we had to check it out. In February, we had gone about halfway, up to some woman's house—it was plowed no farther—this time we roared past her house with a shrug and bounced and charged into the heavy woods that crowded the road.

"Will they make it?" said Don. "Will Harriett ever get back to her mad uncle in Poland Springs?"

"I don't know, man."

The great part of it was that we were all identically concerned—same intensity, same brain, mind, heart; if we could break through to Limerick we'd walk it the other way. The road got narrower, then became a "road" of old autumn leaves twenty layers deep. We followed a winding tree-lined path up and up a turning hill. I shifted down, and since we had been tooling along in second, we would be reduced to backing up if this failed. With a head of steam we made the top and down the other side.

Faith is strange. Months ago, that woman had told us about this road, the old Limerick-Limington road. We had never traveled it before; yet here we were charging through the woods, knowing . . .

"Man, this is *no* road," Don said. But Herb and I knew. That woman had told us once, and our doubts were gone.

Suddenly it began to open up a little. In another few minutes it met a real road. Balboa sights the Pacific!

Instinctively we chose correctly, took a left, drove to an intersection, turned right, and were driving along when suddenly there was the field, the tent, everybody, US, HOME!

Home? That field? To get everything together, all fed, the tent down and out took an agonizingly long time, but it happened. Out, out, away, and good-bye Limerick. Good-bye houses, fewer houses . . . woods . . . gladness, and that woodsy road coming up.

Someone mentioned that a few of the townspeople were on our side against Matthew and his gang, and that we should stay over only a week or so to press charges against them. Just "one more thing" against him, and Matthew would be sent up the river for a good long spell; the eternal gutlessness of a town toward its own problems—let the strangers do it. Later we discovered something more about this lovely-looking little town which made me wonder if the birth of Limerick had not taken place under some violence-producing configuration of the stars: a terrible gun battle, the killing of five or six people a few years before.

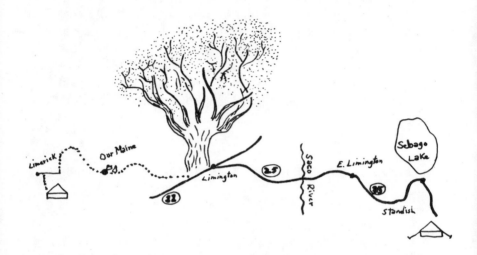

We were leaving, we were happy, happy we were leaving. We were so happy at leaving, at daylight, that we were giddy. The road was ours. We walked past an old cemetery. One of the big stone vaults was ajar. We pushed the door open and went in. Even this was a part of the giddiness, a sort of deliverance from violence, a near-miss of something that could have ruined the trip, which made us turn to anything delivered up to us with a fresh delight—alive and on the move again, although we were physically basted.

I lit a match and held it close to the coffin wondering what we'd find. Three inches from the match was the skull of W. C. Rigby.

At the end of this road we took the woods road and were swallowed up in peace and quiet.

We walked, turning with the trail, each in his own mind, with only the slightest feeler connection between us, a light string from each to each—a period of spontaneous silence.

Apple grove left and below, sloping down to a long meandering lake that went back unendingly, around a bend, back
the other way, with a stand of trees up to the very edge reflected in that calm water, repainted in the lake's eyes. The
first heat was in our bodies, just getting into our day's walk.
I kept wondering and turning to look at the lake through
gnarled apple trees on a hillside, apple grove of young blossoms and tiny leaves unfurling . . . just wondering and then
looking. I hardly knew what I was trying to figure out. Stop
thinking . . . that had something to do with it. Stop thinking
and stop putting into words. For a few moments I was touching bottom, going beyond all of the books I'd ever read—a
stillness I'd never known before.

Not beautiful, not remember, not look. Just there in the
eyes of that lake, and apple grove. Not Limington, not Maine
woods, not apple grove against lake, but ourselves on it, it
in us. To become what is seen without judgment or words, to
accept and thus become those colors, blossoms, water. To be
there in the eyes of tree-edged lake, apple grove on sloping
hill, on leaf-carpeted path through woods in May, to breathe
that apple-blossom air, lake, woods air, to be touched by the
feelers, the noses, fingers, of apple groves, eyes of gentle
lakes. For weren't we in the eyes of the lake, the fingers of
those new blossoms unfurling? Could we emerge without
being part lake? part apple grove? hillside?

Singly or in twos and threes walkers came up that day:
"This walk will never end," "I feel like I've been doing this
all my life;" "I can't imagine what else I did before." There
was also the worry, even this early, that it wouldn't last
forever, that our little world would break up.

Along that impassable trail were old graveyards, former
townsites, old dumps. Ever since Sid (who had stopped
Gale, Gordon, Herbie, had told them stories, sung songs,
drunk beer with them, touched them: "Walkin' to Canada?"
"Nova Scotia!" "Now *that's* what I call *doing* something"),
the walk had taken a slightly new direction. Were we walking to get there? NO! ! ! A thousand times we had an-

swered that question, yet we had to keep turning away from the destination. The most obvious way had been to go inward; but there were other things too, and other ways. Pause along the way; see, feel, experience, talk with each other, but with others too. Our destination *was* the way. That day we indulged it, or overindulged.

We dug through dumps—Phil, Jake, Gordon, Gale, Bob B., and I—and found bottles—oh, maybe fifty years old— dinosaur jawbones, 80,000-year-old-teeth, the cast-iron front to an old wood-burner, OUR MAINE in fancy letters. "Hey, looka this! !" "Wow! "Gee!" "Jesus Christ!" "Hey, whadaya think this is?" "*I don't know!*" "That's a twin-jet carburetor for a 1903 Ferrari!"

The time flew. Great. Who cared? We left our junk on the side of the road for the truck. No one else would have touched it in a hundred years but, as the old joke goes, it was ours and we loved it. We wandered off and stopped at the next graveyard. Ezekiel, Ebenezer, Isaiah, Hepzibah, Jeremiah, Hannah, Patience. Today it is Suzie and Chris. Did our forefathers care what others thought? It was as if they wanted to mark their children—help them be something, someone special.

We made the little town of Limington, but not before an eye feast. As we rounded a bend on entering town, there was an elm tree on the left side of the road, a tree that dwarfed all the others around it. From a huge knot about six feet off the ground, twenty-five main branches flared out in all directions. Each of the branches went up higher than the tops of the highest trees around. The King! In a truly quiet, truly peaceful little hamlet. Limerick and then, the very next town over, Limington. It was as if a range of mountains separated the two.

The stay in Limington was a relief, but I think we realized that the *real* walk was back there . . . stopping, pausing, junking, staring at old gravestones past gray-green fungus: "May 12, 1789, Agatha Clement." Even the ground was rumpled, as if the deaths of these rugged individuals had not set so easy on the earth's stomach.

From the grocery/post office/dry goods store/drugstore we were sending postcards to the south and west. I believe it was a desire to mark the morning, to hold it, although the messages might have contained no clue; it was not something we were unaware of at the time and only remembered later—no, even at the dumps and graveyards we could admit, "*This* is the way it should be."

The old postmaster in the tiny town of Limington blinked at us, humble, vulnerable (although I believe we actually outhumbled everyone that day) as if this little town could muster no gang to beat on us, was a place we actually could have taken over.

We made it to the edge of town before the truck caught us with sandwiches. We flopped and ate by the side of the road, and barely made it to our feet again.

Gordon, Phil, Jake, and I ambled on—Gale went with the truck to find a place. We came to a fair-sized highway and one of those long, straight stretches. No sleep, and digging for junk all morning. We came to a roaring rushing river which at any other time we'd have leaped up and down over. As it was, we laid down to this wildly roaring water music and fell out. I don't know how long we slept, but I'll always remember the feeling, "I'm not really tired but these rocks are so soft." Suddenly I was being waked up. Who? What? I had seen that face in another life, but why are they waking me up? The face didn't go away, and the mouth was making noises at me. I woke up, there was the roaring river . . . had we been there for days? Weeks? Oh, yes, we're walking to Canada. Crazy. Limerick. Limerick was a few lightyears away. Right! This was one of the boys who had walked with me into Limerick; his mother and little brother were parked by the side of the road. Yeah, well, what were we supposed to do? I got up, looked around; Jake, Gordon, Phil were stretched out—dead. If anyone had come upon the scene that would have been his first thought: these guys are dead. I envied them as I hobbled over to the car. I was completely at a disadvantage . . . very tired, walking, just waked up and going over to talk to literate people sitting comfortably in a car—people who were caught up on sleep. I told them what had happened the night before, and they were horrified. So were we, only I guess we didn't quite think of it in that way. She gave me the names of a couple of radio stations and people there, a few reporters for various newspapers who would be interested in the incident, and the walk as well. We exchanged addresses and they left. I woke the others and we slogged off.

The walk was endless. We stopped at an antique store, pushed on, stopped at a grocery store for sweets and ice cream. That was the beginning of a pattern: Tired? Eat junk.

Again the day ended with our being picked up by the truck. The excuse was a good one, though. Our place for the night was 5 miles out of the way—near Sebago Lake, in the side yard of the water commissioner and his wife. Originally he had thought we could stay out by the reservoir, but since it was the local spot for drunks and wild parties he decided that maybe his yard would be better. Much better, we agreed.

Gale and I had another invitation for drinks. The commissioner and his wife were very nice, looked up old maps and roads for us . . . but drinks? I wouldn't have made it past the front door.

Herbie and I mapped and got just about nowhere. We returned with a partial route—we'd camp somewhere outside of Gray, Maine.

It is a big decision to begin sleeping outside the tent but once done, the "decision" becomes silly. It was always as cold inside the tent as out. If a group attacked us, they would surely attack the tent first. Even if it starts raining, there is a good chance that before the first contented smile leaves one's face, a raindrop will land, plick, right on the forehead . . . with the certainty that more will follow.

There is nothing so quietly amazing as to open your eyes in the morning and see as much as you will ever see of the heavens . . . green pine needles and brown branches, early white or light blue sky.

I woke around 7:30, picked up three or four of the others, and we drove into West Gray for gas and ice cream. We cruised into a drugstore tended by a haughty, suspicious manager. Suddenly our eyeballs were falling out. There was an entire large rack of Dr. Scholl's foot powders, corn plasters, bunion rings, shoe cushions, foot pads, cushioned socks, arch supports, bottles of skin toughener, foot medicines, ace bandages, foot creams and deodorants. The man has to be foot crazy. Foot CRAZY! We were looking, poking, smelling, feeling, and the manager was getting furious. So we started talking our language and freaked him out even more. But we did end by buying about ten bucks of stuff. At the grocery store we continued in our language, buying ice cream, chocolate syrup, cherries, crushed nuts, pineapple jam. We got back and woke everybody. "Sundaes for breakfast!"

The day before, the two Anns had gone to a doctor—Big Ann for her swollen and painful feet, Ann M. for poison oak. For Ann's poison oak Gale started using capsules of vitamin E powder, sprinkling it over the redness. "The doctor told me," Big Ann said, "I should stay off my feet for three or four days."

I told her that there probably wasn't one person in the group who wouldn't get the same advice, some for two or three *weeks*. We couldn't do it.

"But the *doctor* . . ."

"I think you should push yourself; walk through it."

"All right, I'll walk." Even as she said this her whole attitude was changing. She even began to straighten up. Suddenly she was out from under the doctor's care, and feeling much better already. For the next six days she rode in the truck less than she ever had, and told everyone that she was feeling great. "I just decided to walk!" And when Big Ann decided to walk she could really cover ground.

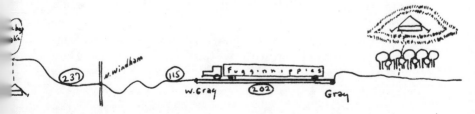

We chose that day to carry out an idea suggested much earlier by Motorhead—to walk in pairs, one leading and one blindfolded. The one walking blind would ask questions and the other would be his "eyes"; then they would switch around.

In more ways than the obvious we are blind—even with eyes and words, touch, taste, smell, and hearing. I walked with Gale and tried to give her the whole picture: sky, earth, walking surface, the changing scene to left and right, curves in the road, houses. When we switched around, it was equally weird; to have to ask for what one needs, a color, a bird call from woods or across a field; to depend on another's words, then to try and pick up through one's pores, through the ears, through the body's radar—clouds, a shade of blue, distances—to grasp things without sight.

We had taken off our blindfolds and were walking along when we passed an old graveyard on our right. There were Phil and Jake, Jake blindfolded and being led slowly through the graves. Phil was talking and Jake's head was cocked attentively as they moved. There was something about the care in Phil's explanation and the intensity Jake was giving it. It wasn't school, we were out of school; this wasn't an assignment, it wasn't homework, they were really doing it. Phil had Jake getting the texture of the stones with his hands, tracing the letters carved in stones. Jake lived through his hands and his ears . . . through his understanding. His eyes were Phil's and he saw only through Phil; for this part of the day they were hooked to each other, responsible for each other.

But it wasn't what we discovered that day—texture of carved stone through the fingers, through having to hear— it was the discovery about what we never discover, not how blind we are for an hour.

We walked into West Gray, a little semitourist town with antique stores, old-bottle stores, and gimmick stores. These places were just dusting themselves off for the summer trade. Ancient buttons and badges were added to costumes. Herbie found a neat little sheriff's badge marked SHERIFF, ELLS-

WORTH, MAINE and put that on his long Khrushchev coat.

In West Gray we saw four or five of the walkers coming toward us on the other side of the street. I must admit we didn't until then realize what we had come to look like. Children of the New Spring: Diana, Dan, Don, Motorhead, Tita.

We joined forces and walked together for the 3- to 5-mile stretch into Gray on a busy highway. Gray is on the Maine Turnpike between Portland and Lewistown, and our course was cutting between the two. Our reception on this fairly well-traveled road was fierce. All the truck drivers would lean out of the windows to show us their fists or their middle fingers. By this time we had stopped waving or looking at cars because it kept us on the surface, neither in a good conversation with each other nor deeper in thought. But these truck drivers were unavoidable; they would come roaring by, sometimes driving onto the shoulder to swing at us, give us the finger, and "Fuck you!" "Faggots!"

Gale left with our truck to find a place for us somewhere out of Gray—let it be way off the road, and hidden.

The hostility in Gray was a tense and quiet thing. They were ready . . . but quiet. No incidents. To get out of town we had to walk through a residential section on sidewalks, no less. While we were walking past a house, a group of townsfolk were getting into a car parked in front. I had said "Good afternoon" to one of them and don't know if it was the same person, but he had mumbled something and then climbed into the back seat. When we were about ten feet from the car, the man in the back seat unrolled his window and with a peculiar pent-up intensity screamed out, "Stick it in your ear!"

The truck caught us just out of town. The campsite was straight ahead, 2 or 3 more miles—for a 17-mile day—and it was well hidden. To face the name-callers in daylight is one thing, but to put up with that crazy friction at night after walking all day is psychically exhausting.

The tent was up and supper was fixing. The field lay a quarter to a half mile from the road, hidden by a bank of trees just off the road and then by another grove which extended into the field, so we were doubly protected. And, it seemed, doubly exhausted.

Maybe it was this field with its peaceful waving grass that made it so natural to think of rest, peace, staying still —but we began to talk seriously about a stopover. I don't remember the meal, but we had such a loyalty for everything prepared by us that our incantations over water would have been food enough. Once Richie made the mistake of criticizing the potatoes in a stew; they were not done, said he. An angry spontaneous murmur arose from four or five people who heard him.

Searching for Bradbury Mountain State Park, we traveled nearly an hour that night in a sort of circle, the park grounds always on our left, but no place to get in. Forget it. Tomorrow we'd walk a short day, and if the park was nice we'd lay over there. We estimated an 8-mile walk.

It drizzled through the night but, as ever, that didn't stop the hard-liners. They'd fix some little house composed of space blanket, poncho, sticks, and leaves, and next morning they'd bring their wet sleeping bags over to be dried at the laundromat.

It was too new for me, and I went inside the tent, talked with Dan, Tita, and Diana for a while, fixed my sleeping bag, lowered the light of the lamp to a glow, and with a great feeling of thankfulness for a safe, dry, quiet place, crawled in.

The tall grass was wet in the morning and looked a ravaged storm-tossed green and silver. Diana waked me early, and we had coffee water going and soon enough, breakfast.

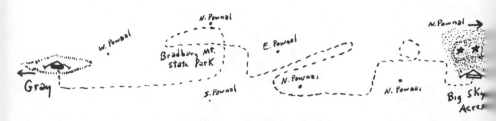

Again Herbie and I tried to find the entrance to that park, which appeared to be as big as a country and as inaccessible as one. When we did discover it, the ranger in charge seemed a little suspicious and sent us on to a private camping area with hot showers. This would add another 2 miles, but it was a good place run by a young couple in their second season. They loved the idea of the walk and pumped us with questions. We sat over coffee and talked. Even at that instant the walk was going on, at that instant they were walking lonely roads, strung out over miles—doing *nothing*. Great! That always split my head open with pleasure. By the end of this semester you will have accomplished essentially nothing. We will know a crooked track across the northeastern part of the United States and a line in Canada up, over, and down to Yarmouth. We will have opened one little crack in the whole world of things to be understood.

But for the truck people, there was a hell of a lot to be done that day. The steering was almost gone. Fully loaded, the truck could not go more than 35 miles an hour without weaving all over the road. So we marked the route to Big Sky Acres, found the others, and went back to Gray. The lamps and stoves had to be cleaned, white gas found, garbage dumped, lunch made, sleeping bags dried, and the truck fixed.

The entire morning was spent trying to track down the mechanic, an old country mechanic . . . very thorough, cranky, always off somewhere, but never failing to leave weird signs on his garage door, completely meaningless to us: "Ch.—at the Hanker C. 12, John's." We finally caught him by calling his number from the parts place in Gray. Yep, he could fix it—tomorrow—but we'd have to get the parts. "Jes' can't do it today. Tomorrow at two, now put Joe on the line." Okay.

While the bags were drying, we wandered around town and heard from school kids that the principal had announced over the school radio that "The Hippies" were invading the town. We heard the story about six times. I went to call the tourist bureau in St. John, New Brunswick, still trying to set up a party for when we'd get there, and came back to find Herbie with an audience of about fifty kids. "And here's our professor!" He told the group.

"He don't look like a professor to me," said one sharp-eyed little kid.

But Herbie was deep into it. "How do you think you'd learn more, in classrooms with books, or taking a walk?"

What's learning got to do with it? You *got* to go to school!

"Tell 'em," Herbie said to me.

"No, you tell 'em."

So Herbie went on. The group dwindled, but of the ones who remained, a core of kids was really interested. It was a good exercise, although most of the students were already brainwashed and looked on us as tall-tale-tellers or just hippies, whatever that meant to them.

Again we got lost going back to the mechanic's, so we stopped at an old farmhouse and asked its aged owner which way to go. That individual picked up a block of wood, reached way inside his old duds, down further, around, stretched, came up with a pencil (all this time we didn't know whether he was going to throw the wood at us or answer the question), then began writing down directions on the block of wood, explaining to us in his very own way: "Take the bend here . . . right up to McKinney . . . double over . . . *past* Chilly Fork . . . Six Rivers" (or "Sick" Rivers), "Not the Gawaggle . . . mile er so more and there is't."

Had we taken this wild walk to get somewhere? No. We watched him making perfect sense on this piece of wood, but his world and ours were just barely tangent, as they used to say in geometry. Was that pencil going like the road went, or was it going with the grain of the wood? It was going perfectly.

When the old farmer finished scratching away with his stub pencil on the block of wood, he turned to us with modesty, largesse, grace, and gave us the wood map. How could we have lost that? After showing it to the others, we put it in the back of the van with boots, jackets, OUR MAINE, candy wrappers, maps of New Hampshire, old bottles, dino-

saur jawbones—a regular witch's cauldron of good magic—
in which it soon enough got lost.

In our travels we heard about a school for retarded children. Herbie's wife, he began to tell everyone, was at the
school in the fourth grade, and we had come to visit her.
Herbie could speak only Spanish, so I was along to help him
translate to the Americanos. I was also to tell the people that
the reason he was very happy was that his wife was on the
honor roll. We stopped at the next house and asked for the
retarded school. The man was explaining while Herbie was
chipping away in Spanish, or mostly Spanish. He insisted
that I explain to the man. I told him why Herbie was so
happy, and the poor man didn't know whether to act sorry
about her being retarded or happy about the honor roll.

We finally got to the mechanic's, and naturally he was out
again: "Back 2:15. Clem at Ch., fix runner & Leg nob."

If it meant he'd be back at 2:15, then he was late by more
than an hour. We locked up the truck, left him a note, and
threw the key under the door. Camp was 6 miles away. It
was as if we had been carrying the truck around on our
backs. Well, now we had put it down.

For a time we went blindfolded. Herb was describing a
man in his side yard washing his little VW. "He's dressed in
bermuda shorts and he has on a little Swiss hat . . . Wait a
second, I think he sees us. He's *running! He's running into
his house!* !" The change in Herbie's voice gave me the scene
as well as my eyes would have.

Later we found out that we'd been reported "on the radio"
and everyone was alerted. All of us now had stories about
people peeking around curtains, ducking back when we
looked at them. Undoubtedly we were "200 hippies" and
were coming "to take over the town." We talked about dropping notes along the road: "It'll be real easy to take over . . .
they think we only have 200!" That's one put-on I'm glad
we never went through with. Cops, lawyers, soldiers, farmers
with pickaxes and shotguns would have killed us in short
order. America is in no mood to laugh at or question the most
preposterous plot.

It had been a strange day full of contrasting scenes: the young mother with staring blue eyes who wanted to study and learn, talking to us about school in front of her house with a big hole in the roof; the search for the retarded school and Herb's wife; the dumb hitchhiker who had quit school (and was congratulated for it, in Spanish); the junky garage and the old mechanic and his notes; the wood map; Herbie's lecture to the school kids.

We walked up around a bend, and everything caught up with us. An abandoned plow on a point of land against the sky, a jointy muscle-bound apple tree, a copse of tall and very slender birches with a growth of new yellow foliage that danced around them, never touching them. The weather-beaten barns, farmhouse, rusty plow on that wind-swept hill, and fields of long, waving, first-crop grass. We stopped, sat on some stumps, and looked—one of those places and times never to be forgotten. Yet in a way, I have forgotten it. Not the feeling, not some of the details, but the exact and entire picture which I swore I'd always remember —only a magic wind and those colors.

It was getting late and a strange sky was shaping up: baby-blue bits through gray through white through pearly pink and white; orange through huge dark clouds with fingers of rain, fingers of sunlight down through heavens to touch us, both sun and rain.

A few miles from us at about this time, Bob B. and Jake were stopped by the sheriff for being "drunk" and "stagger-ing" along the road. Bob had to show the sheriff his blisters before the lawman would believe his story; he was "stagger-ing" because his feet hurt. Jake was limping for the same reason, throw in a bad knee. But the woman who had seen them didn't bother to inquire; she just picked up the tele-phone, that marvelous invention, and called her friend the sheriff. He jumped into his Batmobile and zipped over.

The sheriff let them go . . . with a warning. "Walk straight, and stay out of trouble."

Herb was blindfolded when an old state forest ranger passed by and turned in at his house about a quarter mile

ahead. It was getting pretty late, so I led the victim up to
the ranger's house and asked for a ride. I told him my friend
had rubbed 612 insect lotion in his eyes and that we had
medicine and eyewash back at camp. Okay, he said. I helped
Herb, still blindfolded, into the truck, yanked him around.
Herbie was overdoing it as usual, trying to sit backwards in
the cab. As we rode I explained to the ranger what a fool
Herbie was, how he had yelled and carried on. Later we
found out that the old ranger thought all of us—all us city
folks—were crazy and didn't have enough sense'n to "jimmy
the hawgs," an expression I've never heard before or since.

At camp we were besieged. Television cameramen had
been there, people from radio and newspapers had appeared
off and on all day. Two reporters were still there waiting.
The reaction of the group was mixed; some put up with it,
some were angry.

Two good things came from it, though. We got a beautiful
group picture and a nice interview, and the television footage
was well done. There was a long interview with a reporter
who was so enthusiastic that he even quoted us accurately
(and wanted to drop everything and join us). A quote from
Motorhead is worth repeating.

People can't seem to understand what we are doing. . . . Some
think we are with SDS, others think we are marching for peace.
People seem to think there has to be some reason for our walk to
Nova Scotia. But it is only to look, to think, and to see.

The reporter mentioned the fear and suspiciousness of the
people and the police and concluded, "apparently almost
everyone expects evil of the walkers." The suspiciousness
and fear were no less true of Maine than of New Hampshire, yet we stole nothing, didn't trespass, "took over" no
town.

The TV program, with us on it, would come on at 11:00
that night, and the camp owners had invited us over to see
the show. Again our stopover began to involve other people.
Add another element—an official camping place, a state

park, a school, additional people—and the conveniences they offered were never worth it. But the showers were great; hot water was a joy and a joke.

Gordon, who was very upset about the publicity, showed me his notes on the subject. It was worth a meeting, so I called everyone together before our Coffee Klatch at the Big House and read his notes.

We had agreed earlier that no reporter would accompany us and that no one else would be a part of the group. Up to now there hadn't been many such contacts, but today had been a banner day.

The whole thing should be *our* trip, Gordon noted, and any attempt by people to horn in could only be harmful. We should not get help, either by publicity or in other ways. Even reactions by total strangers should remain reactions by total strangers, untempered by TV or newspapers.

Who could argue with that? I could only thank Gordon for keeping it straight. We agreed unanimously that we would stay over the following day. At 10:15 we broke up for the show.

After coffee and cakes, the lights were turned off and we saw ourselves on TV: a sweep of the whole campsite with everyone lying around, then a shot of Ann M. and Lloyd from the rear, walking into camp, both sort of dragging along. The clothes people wore and their habitual walking ways were so immediately identifiable that everyone in the room started laughing when we saw the rear shot of Lloyd and Ann. But the commentary was misleading; the reporter spoke of the students out on the road gaining knowledge. Knowledge? The world is glutted with it.

It was almost sad that we were not walking the next day. We were derailed. Sleep as late as you want to. That night Ann M. and I wandered back and forth for almost an hour, talking about the school (she had just graduated), her life, difficulties of identifying with the group, how we had to make it vital. She felt that it was her last chance to do something like this. She'd never been forced to live together with people like a traveling family, like gypsies, and so far she hadn't taken advantage of it. She'd really try to from now on.

For some people it is almost impossible not to be part of any group—in one way it is their problem; they *can't* be by themselves. For others it is just as difficult to be a part. Ann M. had come along to help, to give *and* to get something. How different each day was. How different each night was. To be reassured that individual walkers were really trying to pull it all together was, somehow, astounding.

More people slept out that night than ever before. Gale and I were about twenty yards from the tent, just settling into our bags, bodies warm, faces exposed to the frosty night, looking straight up at the sky, when suddenly we became aware of the sky flashing, rippling with lights.

Everything was still, almost everyone was sleep, and this spectacular show played on without a sound. Enormous waves of light rolled across the sky. It was a light symphony, a visual symphony, and my eyes looked so intently that it was as if they were trying to give it sound. Waves and waves of light rippling, rolling on and on.

What is wrong with my mind? I did not and do not care to know "why," what caused it. Just lie there and get it, dig it, roll with it, have it. But what I did want was for everyone else to see it. Should I wake them up? I hesitated, then went to the tent not caring whether they cursed me out, stopping on the way to tell a few others: Get up! Northern lights!

There was an exhausted silence inside the tent, a heavy silence.

"You've got to get up, come see the sky! It's wild! Northern lights! *Northern lights!*" My words met a wall of silence. About half the group finally came out to see; the others claim they never woke up.

Next day the owner let us use his pickup truck—gladly. "You've given me $1,500 worth of free TV advertising." That's all right, keep the change. Lloyd went over to help the mechanic work on the truck; Ann M. and Howie went off with friends from school who lived in Maine; and about fifteen of us took the pickup truck into Brunswick.

People always gaped at one or two of us, but with fifteen together in the back of a pickup truck their eyes fell out of their heads. It was L.J.'s birthday, so we got a cake and some red wine. Diana, Bob B., Tita, and Dan went to a record shop and asked the salesman if he had their latest record album. "Who are you?" he asked. "You don't know? You ever heard of Jim Kweskin's Jug Band? Here we are!" They all bought kazoos and marched out across the street playing the same tune, more or less. Business offices stopped whatever they were doing.

We picked up the truck early that afternoon, and it was working beautifully. The mechanic was impressed with Lloyd. Lloyd could get a job with anyone around there, he said. Things were looking up; Ann M. and Howie were back, so was L.J.; we were getting together. But one of Ann M.'s friends warned us to stay away from Lisbon Falls. "That's a rough town," he told us. In fact he told us in great detail. We were headed right for it.

I had called our school the previous night, and now we needed to have a short meeting. The dean had suggested that some members of the administration get together with us in Yarmouth . . . for "a little celebration." I had told him it was up to the group and I'd let him know.

Meetings always took a while to get going; always one person or another was unreachable. Lamps were brought in, people moved over, there were some quiet jokes, and gradually quiet.

I told them about the dean's proposed "party" and that it was up to them. Around the tent, each person was heard and it was unanimous. This was our project, our accomplishment. If there was to be a celebration it would be *our* celebration. Was it already such an in-group? With such a fierce pride and a fierce privacy? Whatever it was, the answer to the administration was no.

I was glad we were leaving in the morning, that we'd be walking again, not to get "there" but to get with the ever-moving, ever-changing moment. We could be more quiet, more together, more calm than staying here or anywhere. To be under way gave us a great deal. It erased our self-consciousness; our bodies were taken up, which really did allow our minds to be free. But while we were here I felt everything was scattered: friends coming around, walkers off in little groups, reporters. We were trying to realize together, to see together . . . to actually *be* together.

After the meeting we built a big bonfire in the middle of the road, celebrated L.J.'s birthday, and talked. As usual, someone brought up what we were doing. For at least four of the walkers our purpose still seemed vague. I didn't mind. I had suggested in my original letter proposing the walk that we discuss the purpose after we'd done it. The best in-doubt answer came from Charles Fort's *Book of the Damned*: "This whole experiment" (his experiment, but ours too) "might be 'a huge effort, not [so much] . . . to grasp reality in its entirety, as to prevent reality being conceived in a falsely coherent way.'" So stop trying to conclude; just be there for whatever comes our way, even if we are incoherent about it for the moment. As for living together, we must try and accept one another for what we are, without changes. You have a gripe about someone? Your inability to accept it is the first part of the problem. The second part may never even come up.

I liked the fact that Howie was often the one to question what we were doing. He had begun it as a lark, a purpose-less lark, but since no one was questioning how he was taking it, *he* began to question.

Ann M. suggested that each day we choose one thing and contemplate that thing. I had already proposed the difference between knowledge and understanding for tomorrow. She would suggest something for the following day. I didn't even remember that Ann M. was the one who had vowed not to use her brain for forty days.

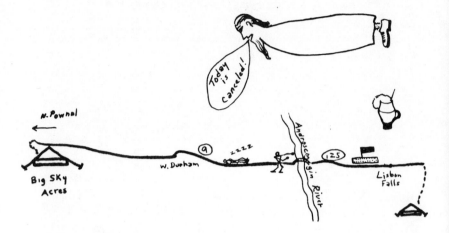

I turn out from the Big Sky sign and know it's right and good to be walking. It's good even though we're headed straight for Lisbon Falls and still have no place for the night.

Herbie, Phil, and L.J. had gone mapping the night before. By 11:00 I was torn between anger and fear. They returned around 11:30 or 12:00 in pretty good condition. They had stopped at a bar in Lisbon Falls, and now they knew "everybody"— the bartender, mill hands, etc. It *was* a tough town, and the mappers hadn't found a place. In fact I don't really know what they did accomplish. Anger or fear? Anger for me. They went to sleep laughing.

I ended up with Phil and Herbie, taking a shortcut which was only about 3 miles out of our way. But why shouldn't I trust them—hadn't they been "mapping" just last night? Never mind, we had good periods of silence and good talks, but by early afternoon we were walked out. We stopped at a spot just off the road and slept for about half an hour on some of the softest rocks in New England.

> *Remember me as you pass by.*
> *So once was I as you are now.*
> *As I am now so you must be,*
> *Prepare for death and follow me.*

So said a tombstone just before Lisbon Falls. Another

caught our eye: "In the midst of life we are in death." All of these little "signs" before Lisbon Falls.

"How are your shoes?" I asked Phil.

"The shoes are fine, but my toes are too big."

"Bye-bye," says a little girl from the door which she had slowly opened and looked out of.

The broad Androscoggin River was before us, and Lisbon Falls just the other side. The river is shallow, with lots of rocks and rapids—a pretty, polluted American river.

Well, there it was: "One of the toughest towns in the state," said Rich, our visitor yesterday. But nervousness was replaced by goofing around. We started yelling across the roaring river (no chance of being heard), "Heyy! We have a guy'll take on any ten of you! Hurricane Herbie!" The threats got louder and wilder. Herbie was dancing around in the road punching the air. "Here he is . . . Hurricane'll beat the shit out of you guys . . . one at a time er all at once!" Herbie was ducking, punching, feinting, ripping the air.

Then we were walking across the bridge, into the dragon's mouth.

As we came off the bridge the first thing we saw, opposite the tremendous mill, was a huge painting: white letters on rock, brown-tan-stained dark rock—

TODAY IS CANCELED!
GOD

It looked like the world's bulletin board. Next to it was a big Nazi swastika. Because of our shortcut we knew the others must already have passed through, or be dead. Guys and women watched us through the mill windows, as though they were waiting for some sign from us. We gave them nothing to work with. Long gone were the times when we would have waved gaily or squatted down one-two-three and a double peace sign. We watched them watching us and kept walking. Apart from some dirty looks and a few curses, which could barely be heard, there was no action; but it was the kind of half-civilized silence which could be broken at any moment.

A little surprised to find ourselves still alive, we stopped at a corner drugstore—as near as anything still left to an old penny candy store with unending bottles, jars, boxes of candies—and sat at the long counter on this clear, hot walking day. Root beer floats! With his first words the owner/manager/worker let us know that practically everyone else had stopped there before us. "Sure they was all in here. They lined up out there with their shoes off. When they left you shoulda heard the comments: 'What was that? Who are they?'"

He described Big Ann and how she was "weaving on the stool . . . weaving all over the stool." Yes, she had a little kitten with her; sat out on the curb feeding the kitten chocolate ice cream. Another girl, he told us, was just a little thing, she didn't belong to the group at all. She'd never be able to make it 'cause she was too young, too little, too fragile. It was either Tita or Diana, "The Waddler," and we told him they were doing fine. Diana was always so afraid she wouldn't make it that she'd take off in the morning with a vengeance and generally wind up first or second in camp. She walked with Dan a lot and he was, despite himself, a very fast walker. "Diana, you're not *waddling* any more!" And Diana would smile from one ear to the other and around the back of her head.

We had another round of root beer floats in his frosted mugs and listened. Above the counter was a little plaque: "If you don't like our town, Ask for a timetable." But he was warming up to us.

"Yep, the people of Lisbon Falls stand together . . . or they used to," he said. If someone from Lisbon Falls was attacked, the others would take care of the attacker. My country, right or wrong; my state, and my town. He was especially proud of the fact that who-started-it didn't even figure. Awful, awe-full, wonderful, and inevitable. Unreasoning and unreasonable; but part of growing up is to understand that it

exists, and to understand that "the law" is at times even
more unreasonable.

In Lisbon Falls they take care of their own. And strangers
better be nice. "If you don't like our town, Ask for a timetable." But the frosted root beer floats were great, and he had
penny candies we hadn't seen for years. He had survived the
onslaught of "hippies" and no one had been condescending.
He showed us his treasures: more rare candies and a coke
bottle collection. He had coke bottles 60 and 80 years old,
some made in South America, some in the Middle and Far
East. And some of his penny candies, he said, were sold in
only three or four places in the whole country. It was as if
he were trying to show us his own goodness, and I think we
all knew it. We parted on good terms and went on up the
street. I had been anxious to put miles between us and this
town. I too had been willing to cancel today and be somewhere else. We still had a few hours before the mill hands
got off, so we stopped again, bought some newspapers, and
saw great pictures of almost the entire group. "On the Road
and Learning by Walking," said the article.

At the edge of town there was a broken windmill with most
of the paddles hanging halfway to the ground. Little stunted
box houses getting farther apart. There was also a fresh
white arrow pointing straight ahead.

"You bad man," said one little boy as we passed by. How
could he tell? I mean, how could he tell so easily?

As we left town, the clouds suddenly cleared away, a
gigantic blue eye opened, and we seemed to be its first object.

We were tired and happy, way out in the open, making
about 3 miles an hour walking the left side of the road, when
a big Cadillac passed us and slowed down. The road was
empty . . . what did they want? They were waving! People
from our past? It was the dean of the college, the head of
sciences, and their wives! How the hell did they find us?

They pulled off the road and we greeted them. They got
out and stood by the car, we flopped in the field. It was
habitual; if we weren't moving, we were off our feet.

They had found us easily, they said, laughing. Everyone

knew exactly where we were, exactly what roads we had taken. In fact there was not one person who *didn't* know, even days later.

"Did you see our arrows?"

"We didn't need arrows."

I felt foolish in my ridiculous skipper's hat. I was one thing at school and another out here—two of my sides had caught up with me.

"Most appropriate," the dean said with a laugh. They commented on how brown we were. Yes, we were brown, and healthier than we had ever been. We had walked through rain, stayed wet all day, had slept in wet sleeping bags—and no one had even had a cold.

"Where are the others?"

"Probably at camp. It should be about two more miles . . . look for the arrow." They were off.

Since we were the first walkers they had come across, we were undoubtedly last in line. We got up groaning. Another mile and a half to the arrow pointing up a dirt road and "⅝ m." We decided to show everyone how "fresh" we were and jogged the last 50 yards, over the bluff onto a beautiful green field and up to the tent.

The scene was a little strange, or strained. The walkers were eating in the tent, the little delegation from school was out of the tent and out of place, just standing around. I got a plate and talked to Howie—had the visitors been offered something to eat? Yes, but they refused. The dean was nice enough to cash a check for me (which subsequently bounced —we were out of Ford money). A few minutes later they said good-bye and left. Almost everyone had felt that we were being checked up on, that it had not been a spontaneous "friendly" visit. I put it down not to the ants' impoliteness but to the fact that we were like a rolling ball, that other people were like pebbles in our way, or gum to impede our smooth rolling. There was also a very private feeling about what we were doing.

"Hey, wasn't that a great road today? That stretch between . . ."

"Yeah, did you pass that old guy hanging out clothes?"

"We *talked* to him!"   And so on.

The night was very bright, filled with stars. The feeling was that we were safe, that we had to deal only with the sky and the earth, the tent and each other. Gale and I slept outside near a little tree. Before they went to sleep, three people came over and asked to be waked up if we saw the northern lights again. Good moments before sleep: a good tiredness, looseness and three stars come over, one by one crouching down next to us under the little tree, saying, "Hey, listen, wake me up if it happens again." Three constellations, then they're gone. No more decisions, no separations. And very clear that sleep is next.

In the morning I learned about the owners of the field. Their barn had burned down recently, their animals had been killed, and they seemed to take it almost as if they were fated to be ruined in just that way. The daughter-in-law offered to patch the tent with an old Singer sewing machine that had once been used to make shoes. There was no talk of money yet, but we agreed to let her do it. It was a good thing, and we'd pay what she asked.

Maybe I should drive, Gale suggested, to see to the tent, mapping, and so on. I was tired enough to agree.

Last look at the field. Incredible that we had lived here and now there wasn't a trace of us. Not a piece of paper, no tent, no people, no sleeping bags, no smoke, no cooking, no sounds, only spots of bent grass. Either we were still there, or we never had been; take your pick.

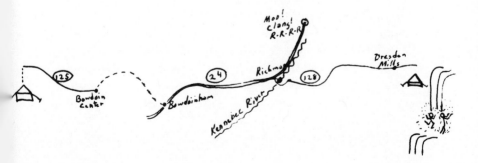

I asked Phil to work with me; Don had to call home for money, so he came along too. We wanted to cross the Kennebec River, which takes a southerly direction from Augusta, but it looked as if we'd have to go north to Gardiner before there was a bridge to cross. On the way to Gardiner, well over our 15-mile day, we saw some nice fields and then some beautiful fields: rolling, unbelievably rich and grassy, they overlooked the Kennebec River. One field knocked us over; we doubled back to find a way to it. An old dirt road led past a dump into some trees, and beyond the trees was the field. The grass was blue-green, a foot and a half high, and the field sloped down, giving us a view of farms, winding river, and sky.

"This is it! We've got to get this. What was the mileage?"

"The hell with the mileage!"

We drove onto the field, up close to the stand of fir trees, then down to a fence. At these times we were always fearful for the truck. The whole walk would come to a screaming halt without it, yet here we were rolling along at a 10- to 15-degree slant through tall grass in an unknown field. On the trip we had already gotten stuck about ten times, the best time still being the first, when not even twenty of us could budge the truck.

We were stopped by a fence. Don was up for dealing with a big herd of frisky cows on the other side, in order to go find the owners and ask for the field. We distracted the cows and he took off, dropping out of sight over the brow of the hill. About five minutes later we heard a call, and the cows, as one, took off toward the voice.

"Good-bye, Don," Phil muttered.

No more voices, no more cows.

In another few minutes we saw Don's wild green Indian hat with red scarf, then his head, Tonto's lean wiry body, flashing brown eyes, brown face. He came up to us exhausted. "I thought I was a *goner*. Those cows are *wild!*"

"Good to have you back, lieutenant."

The owners were across the road at the dairy farm, and

they owned lots of fields in the area. We decided to go into Gardiner and do it on the way back.

Well, the whole thing wasn't mapped and we still had no place, but we had our eye on that field, and when we wanted something it was rare that we didn't get it. And we had a good bridge going across the Kennebec at Gardiner. Bridges are a relief to walk; you can check the river, rocks, trees on the banks, and the water under your feet if it's a see-through metal bridge. Then you're really walking on water . . . right under your boots the water flows by. The view is hardly impaired by the boots at the foreground of the moving picture.

The field was just out of South Gardiner, and the dairy farm was right on the road. It was with the usual semidesperate feelings—the rest are walking now and it's up to us to give them a place to walk to—that we pulled up next to the big barn. Phil wished me well and I hardly had any doubts.

But that barn was chaotic. The farmer-owner directed the manure scrapers, the hungry morning cows were mooing, the man himself talked around a big wad of tobacco. Ptui! Wazzaht? He cups his ear, but it's pretty hopeless. We wanted his field; I guess that got through. Just for the night, I yelled. But I couldn't give him a real pitch; walking to Canada, education, cleaning up afterwards, etc.

"Wal, the one and only rrrrrrrrr I say scrape-clang-Moooooo is becuz Mooooooo that's our Ptui! livin' RRRRRRRRRR them fields scrape-scrape . . . We got to cut hay out them fields RRRRRRrrrMooooommmmOOO. Them kids thow scrape Ptui! Now a tractor c'n crumple a can but them bottles . . . rrrrrrrrr. Cost me $400 to fix a tractor MMMMMooooooRRRRR all 'count of a bottle. But that's the one and only reason rrrrrrrrrrdon't want you to think I'm mean. Ptui! But it's the Mooooooo bottles. That's our livin'." Ptui. MMMMoooo! Rrrrrrrrr. Scraping up cowshit. Awright, let me outta here. No, he loved the yelling scraping scene and wouldn't let me go yet. "Hey, Jake, what about that field a ways up there? Who owns that? Pow! Clang! Rrrrrrr. What? You can?" Ptui! Mooooo.

Back to Richmond. So much of the driving was wrapped up in wrong turns, new searches, alternatives, new connections, dead ends. What now? Gardiner? Someone had heard of a way to cross the river at Richmond. Okay. We scouted around that peaceful little town with wide streets and quiet shops—and came upon a little unobtrusive drawbridge, unmapped, low to the water. We found a bakery for coffee, Danish, and doughnuts. These people were sound asleep in a pleasant dream of running a little bakery in a tiny town somewhere in Maine, making just enough money, serving the same people day after day, watching the outside world on television—growing old so slowly no one kept the score.

What were we like to them? Men from Mars? "Yeah, I seed 'em." Then we were going. On seeing the others later they undoubtedly made the connection but said nothing to us. One part politeness, one part disdain, one part timidity.

At every town we passed through, there seemed to be one store that all the walkers drifted into. At the store in Richmond one of the managers screwed up enough nerve to ask, "What is this? A invasion?" Those were not the ones to fear. The ones to fear hardly looked at us, never questioned, never spoke.

We went across the little bridge and on into Dresden after Dresden Mills—and after getting stuck twice by the river, exploring. Already we'd gone 18 miles from the last site. We had to get a place here. Richmond was about 15 miles from the site, but there seemed to be a smell of trouble about that sleepy little town; besides, it was on the well-traveled road to Gardiner and Augusta. Here in Dresden we were again off the beaten track. We tried a house, and a youngish schoolteacher gave us a hesitant yes but told us to check back when her father would be home.

Just to be safe, I tried one more house. The field overlooked a little muddy river. Everything was still, everything was vibrating. There sat the truck. We were walking to Canada.

It was after ringing the bell and before an answer. I can't resist looking in through the narrow panel window next to the door. An old luminous-eyed bulldog comes into view. The bulldog is cantankerous, old, and uncertain. What should he do? He wanders back and forth looking for someone to come to the door, then forward again, barking. Finally an old woman comes up, and I know the answer is no. The bulldog watches her, then looks at me like an old parasitical lunch lady at a public school in Brooklyn: "Eat, children! Eat!" Sure enough, it is "*no!*" after a good hard look at me, at the truck and the sign on the side (the "Conscious Ants" side).

I gave the truck to Don and Gale and walked with Phil, Gordon, and Motorhead from a point about 5 miles out of Richmond. We began with a great neglected dirt road near Bowdoin Center, which had an unimposing monument "Erected to the Memory of Soldiers of the Civil War, 1861–1865."

> *W. H. H. Small*
> *Joel Small*
> *Joseph Small*
> *Joshua Small*
> *Simeon Small*
> *Zacheus Small*

There were seventeen more Smalls, four Tarrs, two Townsends, three Wilsons, and that was it. Killed in action?

Don and Gale were to pick up the tent, come back to Dresden, and get the place, but walkers and truck met in Dresden, everyone tired, loose, and giddy. Still the father had not come back, so we had no field. For the first time the walkers had made it to the destination before we had a campsite . . . well, first time since Epsom and the haunted house.

When he did get home, he told us we could stay either in their side field or over by a little river which had falls right there. That was the spot. Even the sound was beautiful.

One by one we drifted over to the falls, and one by one

naked bodies were emerging from clothes. The falls were a series of steps with small and large pools between them. The water was rushing through this 40-foot downsloping area, and there was room for ten or twenty in the icy and delicious water. We soaped our dusty, dirty bodies and came out shining. There was one spot where the water cascaded into a 6-foot-long tub. Grab a breath, go under, and be completely covered by pounding icy furious water. It was a gas.

What a feeling to be dry and eating supper after that bath. The others, most of the girls, tried it after supper and came back happy and dripping.

There was every sign that it would rain, so we covered our material and everyone except the hard-liners slept inside the newly patched tent ($8). And the rains came.

Our tent was snug, and except for Jake, who took an early-morning dunking from water trapped in one of the door flaps, everyone inside was dry. For the others it was the same old story: sleepy people dragging wet bags over to the truck—yells and screams as they looked at each other and compared notes.

I took Lloyd and Phil for some early mapping, and about 16 miles away we finally found someone at home. He was a bachelor, something of an alcoholic, who had hardly heard us out before: "Why, shit! You can have *my* goddamned barn! Least I can do for you. Use the bathroom in here. Be fine! Why, hell yes! Come on in! Want a drink?" We went on in. Some people, drunk or sober, just take one look, hear one word, and say yes!

We traced our way back, leaving arrows at every turn, and arrived at camp to pack. Some had already started out, and we stopped to tell them it was marked and to keep moving . . . We've got a barn . . . 16-mile walk.

At a launderette, Open 24 Hours, across from the little diner in Dresden, we dumped nine sleeping bags in the dryer. Herbie, the Weasel, and I shopped for sandwiches and whipped them up in the launderette on the folding tables. The other two left for white gas, and I sat in the diner to "watch" the sleeping bags.

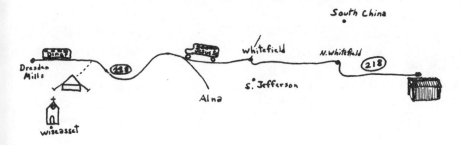

It was always strange to sit somewhere and think of the train of us humping along purposefully without purpose, humping along until Canada would one day be under our feet; but that had its sad side too. Since everyone had finally been convinced that Canada was not the destination but the end of the walk, and since the walk was like a life journey, death was not the destination.

Inside the tiny warm diner in Dresden . . . or was it Dresden Mills? No, Dresden Mills is down the road, but "Makes no difference," says the owner. At the counter they talk about the planet Mars in the breezy way that has become common for Americans, if not all the earthlings, to speak of such things. "Mars is next planet to the sun!" They mull that over, while Mars goes about its business closer to or farther from the sun, unaffected by the talk in the Tip-Top Diner in Dresden, or Dresden Mills, Maine.

They talk way back in their throats about Mars, astronauts, the earth and the sun, rockets and thrust power—scratching an ankle, downing a hot dog, out of a full mouth about planets and the speed of sound, expelling tiny bits of food three feet from the plate, thousands of miles from the launching pad.

Who needs the moon? Here's a celebration. Just sit over coffee and listen, realizing that the line of walkers is even now stringing out toward North Whitefield in a misty rain, and that of twenty-one people involved, I have probably been motionless for longer than anyone.

Herbie and the Weasel returned, the sleeping bags were

dried and in the truck, and I was going to walk. Time: 1:00 p.m.

Within 3 miles my feet had found the road; I was in my own head on this chilly drizzly day, inside of my two sweaters under a poncho. My boots were rounding into shape, but I could feel my right little toe, the ball of my right foot, and the first joint of my left big toe. The big thing, however, is the day: scudding clouds, rainy mist, and a wide-open flat, curving road with no one in sight. The road to Alna, they say; but Alna appears on no map. Maybe it's a state of mind. Such great towns in Maine: China, Mexico, Razorville, Albion, Freedom—all close to our route, but we'd miss them by a little. Instead we'd walk through Stickney Corner, Washington, Liberty, and Swanville.

Suddenly out of nowhere, as if to divert me, my very own guardian angel presents me with a big yellow school bus, empty except for the driver. The drizzle has stopped, the bus slows down and stops opposite me. He leans out this great head toward me—reformed drunk, strong man, with colors flashing all over his face. Gambler? Lunatic? I only know that this face has looked out on some violent scenes and maybe he's up for another one . . . now!

There is an old movie called *The Dead of Night*—the scariest movie ever made—and one scene has a bus driver lean way over to the pedestrian and in a very special voice say, "Room.for.one.more!" The pedestrian—an ex-racing driver fresh out of the hospital, where he has had a dream about death and this face and these words ("Room.for.one. more.")—backs away from the bus. It pulls off, and in no more than half a block plummets through a rail, off the bridge, and kills everyone on it.

Nothing that this driver said, I thought, would have surprised me.

"Are you with the group of students walking to Canada?"

I nodded. Now out comes the machine gun heavy with bullets.

"Well, I'm with the Woolwich-Wiscasset Baptist Church . . . we're having a musical service tonight . . . good music and refreshments . . . and we'd certainly like to have your group come to our service tonight. We'll furnish the transportation, of course."

"I see."

"We'd certainly like to have you come join us . . . there'll be good music, and a good time for all."

"Well, that sounds very nice."

I warned him that we'd be way up in North Whitefield, but that didn't stop him. He copied my little map and arranged to pick everybody up at 7:00. He then told me that "they" had been looking for us for hours. "Sure! We read about your trip in the *Brunswick Times Record*! Sure!" With many waves he wheeled the bus around and took off for Alna . . . or Albion, perhaps.

The sky cleared up and all the problems of the world came down to one. To walk by oneself on an empty road, it is hardly possible not to come upon the idea that what we are taught to believe is only one angle, one body of something *like* knowledge—civilization's prejudices. The feeling washes over one that the body of knowledge stored in books—however little or much one knows of it—is not quite real . . . that it is shot through with the world-exhausts and exhalations of an impure, very human look at the world—as amazing, as wonderful, as touching as that may be. The sciences are not scientific enough, the humanities are not humane enough . . . they miss the mark.

To walk alone with miles and hours ahead, no worries, no aims, something almost touches, hovers overhead; the feeling of "something else" is just behind the ear, just at the back of the neck.

In words, it is like the most serious warning not to take things as they appear to be. That your life is at stake. Look again . . . and look again . . . and look again . . . a look never taken before.

Why is it so beautiful—the brow of a hill, simple view of green trees almost into leaves, a stone wall just at the brow?

I thought of Fort's manifesto, his "furious insistence that there is 'something else,'" that you must "Leave the high road and wander. . . . Even if you have to make wild and clownlike gestures . . . no matter; it's urgent!"

Dance a jig. Laugh at it and start all over.

By the time they found me in the big yellow bus I was rolling along at my own rhythm and at peace with every ant, every toad, even every human in the world. I had been averaging about 3 miles an hour; still, it was a little after 6:00, and there was "Room.for.one.more," leaning over to me, door open. The bus was loaded with walkers, and they were even freshened up for the big event. We roared off to church. How long had this man been driving? Had he been concerned about where we'd have walked to? He'd have driven to hell to pick us up, and driven us back after the service. Sitting up front next to the driver, the woman from the church group gave me a blazing smile and two pamphlets: "The Church that Conquers" and "Let's Go Fishing for Men." I got a glimpse of things to come.

Dan was wild; he was singing nonstop, every rock song he knew, with great imitations of James Brown, the Beatles, Janis Joplin. Bob B., Don, Diana, Tita, and others joined him while we winged it to church. Ann M. and three or four more were in the truck and would meet us there. They had picked up the town hippie, Gale told me. I only hoped they weren't trying to follow the bus, because that mottled-faced reformed gambler-drinker ex-strongman was flying low with his cargo of wild animals, special delivery.

". . . I'll never kiss your lips again, they buried you today!"

The woman up front turned around and beamed her brave blazing smile to us. Tita leaned over, red in the face from laughing, "I'll bet this bus has never heard such songs before."

Into a beautiful Maine seacoast town. Wiscasset.

"Late.at.night.when.you're.sleepin.poison.ivy.comes.a. creepin' . . ."

We pulled up to the big stone church and started piling out.

Smiling, hurt-smiling, girls greet us at the bus: "Glad to have you with us," and they shake, smile, shake-shake-smile.

"Glad . . . Glad . . ." Impossible not to be affected by the sincerity in some, by the greatest imitation of it in others. So consciously doing the Lord's work but (by God) doing it. They smile, almost smile through us. We're not quite human, we're the chance to love, the chance to show tolerance, patience, charity, hospitality too, and they do. Everything was "Sure . . . All right . . . Fine!" The doors swung open for us and we were sucked in. The service was going on; a real jumping bandwagon of a song:

> *Every day I'm camping*
> *In Canaan's happy land!*
> *I'm camping, I'm camping*
> *In Canaan's happy land.*

"Very campy," some walker whispered. But smile! Laugh! Ho! Ho! "Sure! Sure! Welcome! 'Without shoes?' Of course! Why not! That's all right, isn't it, Reverend? Of course . . . why certainly!"

Ann M., Lloyd, Howie, L.J. arrived, caught me at the door talking with the Reverend. I must come out and meet their friend Cliff. Very nice . . . and yes, the hippest kid in Wiscasset.

"What the hell have you got us into? I thought you said music? And food?"

"Well, that's what he told *me*."

Ann M. didn't want to go in, she had no shoes. I told her somebody else had already been welcomed without shoes. They came.

For some reason we were first led downstairs.

"Well, *that* doesn't matter, dear, praise the Lord *anyway!*" a young mother explained to her little boy as we passed them. There was a raging fever in the place.

Downstairs was a question-and-answer session, packed— and very charged up. It was so packed that there were no chairs for Howie, Gale, and me, and since we were very tired (my feet were buzzing) we went back upstairs and sat in the pews. Gale and I sat together, Howie was about five pews ahead of us. The others were scattered perfectly; by design, I found out later.

It was settling-down time after a hymn ("Why Should He Love Me So?"), and after a few more "Amens" and "*Praise a Lords*," an eager voice shouted from the altar, "Now! . . . *Now!* How many are happy in Jesus Christ?!"

Almost everyone raised an arm, "Amen!" and "Praise a Lord!"

"In push-button America . . . in easy-living, easy-going America—"

Nail-a-Commie-for-Christ! said the button on the nicely pressed suit of the man five spaces in from us.

". . . Some have *not* got the spirit of truth, and I speak this to your shame! Then some of you are temperamental! But people who are temperamental are 90 percent temper and 10 percent mental!"

Wild laughter, prolonged. *I'm* not temperamental, not *me*. Ha haaa! Come along, sing!

> *I overlooked an orchid while looking for a rose . . .*
> *It's written in the Bible. It's a message sad but true,*
> *That our blessed savior had to die, to save me and save you.*

"Amen brother and Praise a Lord."

"Amen brother and Praise the Lord!" Howie said in a fairly loud voice, turning around to us with a goony-looking smile, oblivious to the fact that he was in plain view of at least sixty people, including Nail-a-Commie-for-Christ.

Sing!

> *I overtook the savior while wandering the road of sin.*
> *Not thinking of the day I'd have to pay. . . .*
>
> *This world of ours is full of sin*
> *Oh won't you let the savior in.*

"Praise th' Lord . . . Amen! Amen!"

"Amen brother an' praise a Lord!" Howie's goony smile, for all to see.

"We have with us tonight . . ." the voice spoke to the emotional sea, still calming down after the last songburst, "and we're proud to welcome them . . . some visitors from Green-Witch Village! . . . Will you please stand and be welcomed?"

Everybody was turning and craning to see us. We were craning to see the visitors. What? *We* were the visitors from Green-Witch Village.

"Will you please stand up and be welcomed?"

Slowly, with very little faith, we stood.

There was another reason for standing, which we didn't realize at the time. We were being singled out for Christ.

Suddenly a young man popped up on the platform and told an amazing story. He had decided to leave his wife and baby forever, but when he turned the car away from the church, it began sputtering and missing. He fairly yelled: "I'm not lying, I'm not lying, I'm not lying!" He had turned the car around toward the church and it began running perfectly again. Again he turned it toward freedom, and again it started sputtering. "Six times that happened!" So, he returned to church, wife, and baby, and has been there ever since. He was a short, fiery speaker with oiled shiny hair. He stood there exposed, naked really, and spoke again: "*And I love every one of you!*"

"Amen! . . . Amen brother!"

"Amen brother, praise a' Lord." Howie.

Up popped a new speaker; ferocious, square-headed, with big shoulders.

"I used to be a hell-raiser!" Bang, boom! ". . . Through alla these kicks and alla these pills. That's right! And I had a 30-30 and I was firin' at the State Police." Praizalord! "And when I ran out of bullets from my 30-30, I picked up my double-barreled shotgun and kept shootin' and shootin' . . . then I was in Maine State Prison . . . and then the personality of Jesus Christ came into my life. Oh, I used to be a hell-raiser! That's right! I'd put on my stomping boots and go out to stomp in some heads. I loved it! Many's the times we stomped heads, and my stompin' boots would be bloody . . . And then I found Jesus and I don't need to stomp no more . . . no sir, I put my stompin' boots away."

Again Howie with his goony grin, giving a peace sign to

the Stomper. I was praying for Howie to cut it out before
the man put his boots back on again. Nail-a-Commie-for-
Christ was looking over at us with a queer smile. I didn't
know what they would do to someone who made fun of
their religion, but Howie seemed determined to find out.

There was a collection after "He Ransomed Me," then we
sang "The Cleansing Wave," after which everyone was asked
to declare for Christ. To come forward and declare, please
to come forward. A voice at my elbow asked sweetly, "Will
you take Jesus as your personal savior?" I told the young
lady that I wanted to think about it a while longer.

"This may be the time." It was like an ominous invitation
(Room.for.one.more). I can't say exactly what, but something more goes on at these moments. It's very religious and
everything, but . . .

"Please come, won't you?"

I no longer knew what we were talking about, so I just
shook my head. She left.

A husky, busty woman brushed past me and grabbed
Gale, begging her to please come forward for Jesus. Her
right breast was crushing my arm while she was talking to
Gale about salvation and Jesus. I couldn't back up any more.
She was completely unaware of this fact . . . wasn't she?
She talked steadily, and her left hand held Gale's right hand
in hers, and her right breast heaved against my arm like the
ocean against the rocky Maine coast. Jesus . . . personal
savior . . . brotherhood.

Meanwhile Tita, Bill B., Diana, Dan, and Big Ann were
being led forward to declare.

Richie, who was brought up as a semi-Orthodox Jew, was
approached by the most zealous of all, but he wouldn't
budge.

"Look, I'm Jewish!"

"That doesn't matter!"

"It *doesn't?*" Rich has a great "puzzled" look. At any rate,
he won out, or lost out. So did Gale. And Howie, but not
without a fight.

Then it was over, and lost and found sheep were back in

the yellow bus zinging out to refreshments. The house was poor and plain, and the cheese, crackers, jam, tea, and coffee were all part of the sincere offering; good, unadorned, simple, and very much appreciated, since we had left without supper and were starving.

We're walking to Canada. Occasionally the thought crossed our minds, or we caught a glance across the room or a glimpse of a familiar sunburned face in deep conversation with an ardent Baptist, for now it was clear that the strategy was "Divide and conquer."

"You mean *just like that?*" Rich was asking his man. "Just like that, and you're saved? I *can't* believe that!"

"But why not?" the man smiled back at him.

"Jesus . . . I just, Ha, I mean, huh huh, I just *can't.*"

It was 11:00 before we had rounded everyone up and were again in the yellow bus, headed for our barn and sleep. Most of the walkers had never come in contact with this old-time country religion, and they couldn't get over the zeal, the sincerity of the people. For me it was this driver. He was still smiling—glued to wheel and seat—still gracious and hospitable after a twelve- or fourteen-hour day.

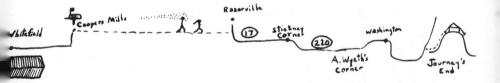

Barns are great to sleep in—despite barn swallows and swallow droppings. Besides, it was raining again. Only people who are outside all day every day realize how much it rains. To others it is a bother, or it is something that changes their plans; to us it meant ponchos, discomfort, and a wet beauty, from which relief was always unbelievably good.

It cleared up early, though, even before I got Lloyd and went mapping. Our first stop was a mail call—Cooper's Mills. The post office was a diminutive house set in a town of dusty roads, old houses, shade trees, a wooden bridge. Not open yet; so we set out for old roads and found a gravel road practically enclosed by trees which went for 7 long miles before it hit a paved road. Beyond Stickney Corner and just out of the tiny town of Washington, almost exactly 15 miles from last night's barn, we found a place—Journey's End. It had a barn, a garage, and a huge field that included the very brow of a hill. The owners were Swedish-American. At one point as I talked, they both started nodding their heads— up and down. We could have the field. We raced back, caught the post office just opening, got the mail, filled out forwarding slips, drove back to our campsite, found a deathly silence. No one was even stirring.

Gale and I were the last to leave. We thanked the owner, who launched into an involved account of his wife, how she had just left him; something he seemed determined not to understand, not even to wish to understand. We were over a mile behind the others when we got away: Thanks again for the barn, we'll write from Nova Scotia.

The day grew hot and sweaty, and the blackflies came down in clouds. That "beautiful" 7-mile stretch turned into a 700-mile death march, without a house or a store or even a hill to distract us. Halfway along it we came upon Ann M. counting out loud. As we passed her she announced, "I've killed 437 blackflies."

Another half mile and we came to a gurgling brook, where Gale took a bath. I watched in amazement as blackflies practically covered her body, but then she was in and bathing. "Delicious!" she said. Okay, baby. But from that point on there wasn't a blackfly around her, while they trailed behind me for half a block. Ann M. passed while I was waiting for Gale to get dressed. "I did 500," Ann said.

Thank God there was an end to it. Our big white arrow pointed to the right and a paved road. Just before it and near some really poor, hopeless houses, two women drove by and stopped for us.

"I'm *curious!*" one said, "I just have to know what all you people are doing."

We were glad to stop and talk.

"Well I declare!" She clucked her tongue, shook her head, and smiled. We waved, they drove off and out of our lives.

In this desolate area we came upon a huge moving van parked just off the road. It had a picture of an elephant with monkeys on his back, and a sign across the top: KING REID SHOWS, "Always a winner!"

We went over and found the King and his wife at home. They were making ready to start on their spring and summer tour of New England. It was a nice life, they claimed, for they earned enough in the spring and summer to pull off the road and just "live" all winter, far from people. "Stay away from Eastport," he told us. "Last year Mrs. Rink's father was shot at in Eastport." We told him of our reception in some towns, and he simply said, "People is going crazy in this country."

We finally came to Andrew Wyeth's Corner in Washington: an open store, cold drinks, and a big barn of a store with a nice combination of junk and antiques. We hiked out of town and up, and came to our destination for the night, Journey's End—1½ miles out of town and ¼ mile up.

I had been planning to sleep outside, but again it looked like rain, so I abandoned my half-built shelter and threw in with the family.

For the next day we had decided to combine a day of walking alone with a day of silence. Everybody was satisfied, although Rich was worried about the silence. Built like an oak tree, Rich is impervious to cold and pain and he slept on the skinniest, flimsiest sleeping "bag" I've ever seen. "Hey, Rich, look what you were sleeping on!" someone would say in the morning. "This big stick!" "Really? I didn't feel a thing." He slept through my screams the night of the Matthew gang raids, and through my efforts to wake everyone for the northern lights. But silence worried him.

That night Tita, Gordon, and the Weasel carried on a three-way conversation in their sleep—not one of them remembered it the next day—and it rained and rained again. At dawn I was awake and so depressed I couldn't get up. If someone had wanted to quit the walk, I would have understood perfectly. What will we do? It was one of those sleepy, silly, direct questions that seemed unanswerable. No one else was awake. Everything was wet. The end. Outside, our cardboard boxes were sagging, clothes dripping.

"Love lifted me . . . Love lifted me . . ." The tune kept going around in my head, one of those rollicking hymns from the Baptist meeting. I had never felt less love in my life.

Maybe if we could have a good breakfast in the garage, it would put things right. I woke Howie up and got L.J. to drive into town for peppers, onions, and eggs. We carried the stoves into the garage, cleared out a space, lit them, put on some coffee water, and things began to lighten somewhat. Back came the truck. Howie was really operating and it was a lift just to watch him. People came straggling down and soon a big hot breakfast was being served. Down came the tent, the truck was loaded (that's the thing . . . move, act, work), and we were ready to go. Everyone in ponchos and no complaints. To me it was a little miracle. Plans, some talk, and we set out individually.

For the first three hours it rained. The whole day was strange, and so vivid that I have only to turn my head one degree and it's there again. Who knows why one day is like that and the next day floats through bone, flesh, and brain without leaving a trace?

I was separated from Jake by about fifty yards and from Tita, behind me, by almost the same distance. My poncho came down a foot and a half from the road. My cotton pants sponged up the moisture, and after a couple of miles both legs were wet above the knees. All three of us stopped at the first store we found, a real old grocery/hardware/dry goods store. Outside is rain. Inside is Lazy-Lizard, with eyes that watch over everything, and three or four strange incestuous products of the back backwoods. I got oranges and apples and stuffed them into my pockets. Because of the looks of these strange people, I let Tita leave first. Down the road we went, still unspeaking.

YOU NEVER OUTGROW YOUR NEED FOR MILK

A truck winged by with a big sign on the back: LIBERTY. Good! Then I realized that we were just out of South Liberty, and to the north of it, Liberty.

SUNSET ACRES   WHISPERING PINES

We were used to cars going by fairly slowly and then, just abreast of us, zooming off, but today every vehicle seemed to be going twice as fast, whether it sprayed us or not. Everyone was hurrying except for us, almost in a line on the left side of the road, living slower . . . walking, thinking, or daydreaming . . . because walking is not a complicated activity, so within ten steps something else takes over.

A telephone truck went by carrying a large roll of insulated wire; the colors were striped white, red, green, black, orange, purple. Maybe it was the wetness, but the colors were burning. Like every detail of the day, these things were going deep. We walk. An apple eaten with all attention on eating an apple: that is a smiling event. Smiling. Eyes plunge into the road. Was it a million times? A billion? One looks up, looks down, wheels the head around, and almost aloud: "Here we are. In our lives." We got no distractions.

Suddenly Jake is sitting down and slowly I come up on him; down, with an out-of-it look on his very young face.

"Did you see those guys in that store?"

"Woooo, did I ever." He's shaking his head, "Some *strange* guys."

We passed a very open-looking house with music coming from it. Across the road was a garage, and next to that a croquet game all set up. How rarely did we pass "music" houses. I was both afraid and desirous of seeing the occupants. I never saw them but . . . they are good people. In my mind they are and they'll stay that way.

Rainy days. Sunny days.

Rainy people. Sunny people.

We went over a low simple bridge and turned into South Liberty—Tita, Jake, and I, still in our separated trio. The man at the store was angry, suspicious; he would barely speak. At first I thought he was just a suspicious Down Easter. Or that it was his bad day. Earlier I had seen a little kid standing by the door of his asbestos, shingled, poor little house, and when I waved at him that ten-year-old only knit his brows and stared. What was he going through? I couldn't know, and I couldn't take on his problems.

But with the old man I did find out something. No, it hadn't been a bad day for him—or not until L.J. and Howie had come by looking for a bathroom. "Over there at the firehouse," the old man had said. Yeah, but it was locked. "Wellllll, but you didn't ast if it was locked, just where it was!" "Well, can you open it?" "Nope, not 'cept in case of fire." "You mean they'll open it up if we start a fire?" Surely a wise answer to go with L.J.'s wild laughter, but under the circumstances . . . Well, Howie could not bring himself to "do a natural," he needed a bathroom. He had not done a natural for the entire trip. In all other ways, though, Howie was undergoing changes. He was one of the late additions, one who had come upon the idea cold, and he didn't really get into the walk until the last week and a half, until the night walk into Canada.

Was the man a little surly toward us? He was. Jake caught Tita and me in the store and got more of the same.

Again we spread out. I was sitting on the steps of the South Liberty Baptist church wondering about the quiet world, this church, religion, the songs, and all the reactions to the Baptists—from Ann M.'s "I've *seen* this kind of thing done

. . . better" to some of the others' amazement at the zealous emotionalism and hospitality. We were at the third intersection, leaving Highway 105 and taking up with 220.

We were heading parallel to the coast, but soon we would turn east and hit the coast around Bucksport. Then we'd have to make a decision: Would we go by the so-called "airline highway" from Bangor to Calais, or continue along the coast as far north as we could? The highway from Bangor to Calais is 90 miles of inland road with eight tiny towns along it. Could we take that? We had just finished 7½ miles of nothing (but blackflies), and it had been hard. Our unanimity would be tested. As the decision came closer, sides were being taken.

It was strange to sit on the steps of this empty church at a three-way road intersection, writing about then and now. Sitting here *and* walking to Canada. I found out later that Phil and Gordon were sitting down at about the same time to a breakfast of pork chops in a stranger's kitchen. He just saw them walking along about a block apart and asked them in for breakfast with him and his wife. They too had had the feeling that they were sitting there and simultaneously walking to Canada.

On how many car trips would we stop and lie down in a field by the side of the road? Or sit in some stranger's kitchen over pork chops at 10:00 a.m., talking about "life"? Walking helps, but a project with no aims assures these things.

Up ahead, we walked into rolling high hills. Tita and Jake were far ahead of me but I could catch glimpses of them across green fields rolling down and away. Swallows dipped in arcs way above the scene of fields, tan roads winding along ten or fifteen miles away. Clouds brush over the entire scene of chittering, playing swallows, fields, and little box houses far away. There is a solemn quiet air which the swallows only accentuate. It was the kind of spot that people would die for. No sooner had the thought entered my head than I saw—as if a smiling (maybe smirking) God had deciphered my wish—a house in a "perfect" spot just up from that view—FOR SALE! I went over and looked in, even took down the telephone number, but the house was miserable.

Bright yellow birds in bunches of eight to ten spring off the ground and fly almost straight up into trees.

Another graveyard; add it to a hundred we've passed. These scenes sit with me. All the poor dear caring departed loved ones, whose remains lie somewhere near these gravestones. All the tears, striving, tension, fears, hopes. And then what? A metal stake with iron words—"Perpetual Care"— already leaning, twisted.

We took the bridge at Richmond because we couldn't get that beautiful field below Gardiner. What had it meant? To turn right there instead of further north? The bath at the falls, and the Baptist church service. But what did we miss?

I caught up with Tita, whose ankles were giving her great pain, so when the truck passed us about 4 miles out of South Liberty, Tita got in and Ann M. got out. Gale was driving and told us we had a giant three-story barn for the night. It was across from a place called The Apple Squeeze on Highway 3 near North Searsmont, another 6 or 7 miles ahead.

I hadn't seen Ann M. for more than a few minutes since Big Sky, so we broke the silence and talked for the rest of the way. By now my pants were wet from top to bottom, but it didn't matter as long as we kept moving, and Ann set a great pace. It was very much like her; she walked herself into the ground, would never quit, but in the process exhausted herself, collapsed, and slept like a log. She had also taken on a great deal of the responsibility of the cooking, washing, shopping. It was her way. It seemed tremendously important for everyone to see his own way of doing things. Ann M. took on so much more than her share, and took it for a long time uncomplainingly. But what everyone had to see was that *he* took on too much, or *he* took on too little and did not realize that someone else was always picking up for him. Ann and I talked about this, the walk itself, and individuals and the group. I had some regrets that she and Lloyd were so often together; in the same way, L.J. and Howie were excluding themselves; so were Bob D. and Bill.

We'd have to change around more, as well as have more time alone.

The last stretch was real highway, a straight road with a constant buzz of cars, then the grand reunion at the Apple Squeeze; sundaes, hot dogs, hamburgers. And then to the barn. An edifice! We were up in the hay on the high second floor. People were milling around looking for places, almost falling through the many holes—no place for sleepwalkers —but we'd have a dry place to cook meals and room left over to move about. Everyone was changing into dry clothes, lying in hay, smiling. There was hardly time to set up a sleeping spot and change pants before we were off for roads for tomorrow. Dry pants were luxury enough . . . and then to trade walking for driving.

At the Apple Squeeze we got directions. We wanted Bucksport by an inland route in order to avoid Belfast. "Well, yes, you can *get* there that way, but the roads are no good." It had that familiar ring. Another mile and we turned off the highway opposite an old Dairy Delight (these little ice cream spots, folded up now with their memories of car hangouts, high school chickies, after-movies' gossip; places which only the wind visits now), and drove toward Morrill. Great untraveled tar roads, but full of turns, crossroads, forks, and branches. At the entrance to Morrill there is a store–filling station, The Blue Seed Store, which separates the roads like a ship parting waves. We took a right on 131 North and ran out of miles. It was probably the most direct job of mapping we did on the entire trip.

We tried a well-kept farmhouse and had the door slammed in our faces, went back about a quarter mile, and found the Freemans. Here was a couple without anything besides their little house and piece of land and apple trees, but their acceptance of us was different. There are such people who almost wait and welcome being asked for things they can give. Who can say "hate belt" or "love belt"? Ups and downs were what we got, and during these days too we were getting our share of abuse. Only two days before, we had asked a man for directions and received for answer a whole load of verbal poison. And here, right across from a woman who slammed and bolted her door in our faces, live old Adam and old Eve in their poor and lovely garden. They had nothing to give, so they could dare to be generous. A glass of water from their well had to be health-giving.

Back with the news, through Morrill, past the Blue Seed Store, and on to our monstrous three-story barn—a walk of almost exactly 15 miles after 18½ in the rain.

Wet clothes hung everywhere, Coleman lamps threw out their green-yellow light, and all the activity seemed gentle. No hissing air mattresses, we'd sleep on hay. Clothes were being sorted, sleeping bags arranged, blisters treated. We four mappers were late for supper, but there was plenty left —barbecued pork chops and a big bowl of salad. For the last time, I decided that when you're tired, hungry, and satisfied with life, it is impossible to tell whether the food is really good or just tastes good.

After supper we had a meeting. We had to make a decision on the route before Bucksport—whether to go by the coast or inland—and I wanted to hear about the day of walking alone. Afterwards Dan, Herbie, Bob B., Diana, and a few others were going to put on a "revival" meeting.

The day had gone well for most, excellently for some. All agreed we needed more time walking alone. Everyone felt that we needed to get around more and walk with different people, so we decided to draw straws for partners. But since some had already made plans for walking tomorrow, we'd do it the day after.

The atmosphere of the meeting was relaxed, slow, lazy. No friction. It made me desperate. Aimless. Okay, but not a forty-day picnic, not a forty-day cookout!

"Perhaps we do our very spirits irreparable harm . . . not our spirits only but our *sight* and our *insight* by not seeing newly. We've got to walk out of our old selves, just walk off brand new.

"Man crawled up out of the slime? From one-celled animals to snakes to toads, to birds, monkeys, apes—and then to MAN?

"Maybe the whole basis is wrong! I'm talking about look-ing—at everything that touches your eyes. Don't look at birds and try to 'see' how they came from snakes! Just *look at birds!* Better yet, just LOOK!

"Suppose in ten years 'they' decide that they made a little mistake, that snakes came from birds. Then all of the *good* kids will suddenly 'see' how snakes 'really' came from birds. *Why do we accept so easily?*

"Right use of the imagination is to help us find the truth.

"Is evolution wild enough? Poetic enough? True enough? The truth for you is *not* through the assumptions of other people, recorded by still others. Swallowed and regurgitated by still others.

"You are free to believe! You are free *not* to believe! You can tell them all to go screw! Are you a fool, then?

"But what do you feel from your stomach? Your guts? That we all came from pine cones? All right!

"That we are really angels? And lack only the belief? Okay!

"And when they tell you you're full of shit, okay, but baby it's your *own* shit, then! And not Darwin's!

"Let's walk out of our old selves. *Leave* yesterday! Let's *do* it tomorrow!"

Was that what I really said? I kept no notes of this kind of thing, and no notes of responses. It's close enough. Our meetings were very much felt. Filled with our own testi-monials. They spoke and I spoke without fear. They knew that they counted. And when they talked over whether or not we'd meet with the president and the dean, they knew they were deciding. And when they decided that it would be inappropriate, it was not a slap at the school or the president or the dean. It had nothing to do with them.

As for taking the inland or the coastal route, certainly I had a stake. So did Herbie, because we'd been over the inland route, and no one else had. Number 9 is a high-speed truckers' road: 90 miles of gentle hills on a big scar of a highway, straight as a ruler, three lanes, with wide shoulders of mud.

Howie argued for the tough 90 miles of Highway 9. "Let's see how it works out. Aren't we trying to challenge ourselves? So what if we run out of supplies and can't find white gas? Even if we have to walk for longer stretches, let's take it." L.J. was with Howie, and he reminded us that we had planned to push ourselves at times "to see our limits."

Ann M. and Lloyd were very much for the coast. So were most of the others.

Deadlocked.

There was a clear majority for the coast, but that didn't matter. Our unanimity would be tested; even one person could hang it up. Some were genuinely shocked and seemed to understand unanimity for the first time.

"What happens if we can't get unanimity?" someone asked.

"Then we stop at Bucksport until we have it." That is unanimity; if we can't go together, we don't go.

Someone muttered, "Well, I'm going by the coast no matter what!"

We went around the group again. No conclusion. The "inland" group had seemed almost ready to go along, but now their pride was involved, since almost everyone had heard the remark.

Again we went round; the coast people wanted "water," "ocean," "beaches," "harbors," "seafood"; the inland people spoke of the "challenge" and pointed out that we'd probably save a day (for what, I don't know) because it was shorter.

I reminded the inland group that we were not trying to beat a deadline, that everyone had been told to count on forty-five days—except for Don, Dan, and L.J., who had spoken to me earlier about jobs. To the coast advocates, as Lloyd said, "The very basis of the whole trip was that we would go to Yarmouth and we'd go together. The purpose was not to get there . . . the purpose was to be *there*, every day and every minute possible. As for water, beach, ocean, seafood, we'll have plenty of coast—from the end of Maine to St. John and then from Digby down to Yarmouth is all coast."

No resolution; now the inland group was piqued that some in the coast group would not compromise. *They* were ready to go along.

Let it hang. We had two more days to decide.

Maybe the revival skit was hurt by the division on how we'd travel. Still, it went well, played to a very appreciative ingroup, with much kneeling and praying, "Amen, Brother!" hoked-up hymns, and screaming testimonies.

I was called on for a "testimony," but the split in the group, and the question whether unanimity would really work, still had my attention. Later I thought about what I could have said for a testimony; there was the "Stomper" and his words: "What a wonderful Savior he is! What a wonderful personality! What a wonderful guy!" He might just as well have added, "What a great Joe! What a terrific son-ofabitch!"

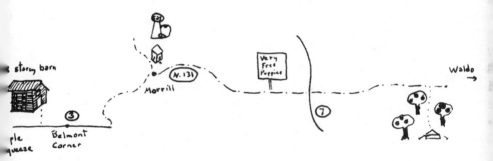

It was a fresh, clear day, wind off the port quarter. We drew straws for partners for the following day. I was scheduled to drive then, so I was out of it. Before leaving we talked to·the barn owners—milk prices, steers and steer-pulling contests, county fairs, and how they might win a free trip to Nova Scotia if their team of steers won.

The truck caught us at the Blue Seed Store at midday with peanut-butter sandwiches. We drank soft drinks, ate ice cream, sat on the steps, and then took off for the last 8 miles.

I was dying, and lay down in a field and went to sleep. Woke up to a fantastic view which I had hardly noticed before: blue-gray clouds low on the horizon, special bronze sunlight on green fields, gray fence posts in a long, crooked enclosure. Got up, went on, caught up with Gale. We walked together, stopped again, lay down.

Each stop seems to make the upcoming miles longer: 6 miles is as far out of reach as 70. We come upon Herbie half asleep by a big tree. We're all dead. Could it be true, the theories about energy in the air? Some days high energy, some days none?

"Some reporter is looking for you. He wants an interview for a radio program. He'll be back in half an hour."

"Okay, we'll wait here."

The man came, and we sat in his car and talked for his tape recorder. He kept calling us "Conscientious Ants." I corrected him three times: "It's 'Conscious!'" Ooookay, he said, laughing; he'd change it. I thought it went poorly, the ideas didn't really come across, but he seemed pleased. It would be on the air (the Maine air) at 4:30 that afternoon on the Belfast station, then broadcast again from Calais on Sunday.

We walked until 4:25 and came to a shaded, rambling, beautiful old house with a sign out front:

FREE PUPPIES !

When we knocked on the door it was opened to eight children, a lamb on the table, kittens, goats, dogs, and FREE PUPPIES! There was no room for worries; just children, just animals. The parents beamed at everything. Her five-year-old, the mother told us, could read "as good as you!" The tiniest girl was tugging at me for attention: "Hey, you know? I can't *read*!" Marvelous!

"She's a mess!" The mother crooned, swept her up, and squeezed and hugged her.

The breezes entered from one side of that house and went clean out the other.

Oh yes, she'd seen the walkers . . . most of 'em had stopped in. The Weasel had come by to see the puppies. "He's a fine boy," she said. She turned on the radio for us, and almost the first words we heard were "the Conscientious Ants."

When the program was over, the old grandmother walked in from the other room and told everybody she'd just heard a news broadcast and an interview with "those walkers" who had been passing all day.

The older children laughed, then the adults, then the littlest children, and finally the grandmother.

We left with their seventeen-year-old boy, who wanted to hear more. We had a good talk for 2 or 3 miles, then parted ways.

At camp Phil, a few others, and I, went mapping. Just 8 miles from camp we found a placid, idyllic (and icy cold) lake near the little town of Searsport. We had walked 18½ miles and then 15; with this 8 miles it would be 41½ miles in three days—only 3½ miles short of three days at 15. A few more "reasons" and we were up for it.

"Let's do it! Tell 'em it's 20 miles away but a great place!"

"No, tell 'em it's 25, but worth it!"

We stopped at a dairy barn and were sent around to the owner, who was milking his cows. The hardy old man stopped, heard us out, nodded, and walked us out to his back field: not in sight of the lake, lots of cow pies, but a nice field. There was something about this old man which touched us. His wife had recently died, and he couldn't keep up with his cows any more and would have to sell them, though they were like pets to him. His fifty-year-old daughter, vague and helpless, had come back to live with him— battered by life, wrecked by the noise and waves out there. He walked to the truck with us, talking. There was no doubt he needed the contact.

"I know you young people are right about a lot of things, but I don't like the violence. The country's goin to *hell*! Still," he paused. "I don't like the violence."

Suddenly there were tears in his eyes. How could it be? Behind his back, between milkings, the country had gone to hell.

Another mile down the road, we saw a wide field with thick grass that went right down to the lake.

"That is *it!*" No need even to say it. We tested the road alongside the field, drove down to the lake. We kept waiting for the balloon to pop. It never did; the man said yes.

We drove back to tell the old dairy farmer, Thayer, that we had found another place; very guiltily, as if we were taking something away from him.

After leaving, we decided to ask him for supper tomorrow night, and we'd buy some of his raw milk tomorrow.

At the field we sprayed the road "SURPRISE" and a big home arrow into the field. A few miles farther back, we sprayed "What's a two?" from Bill Cosby. A mile before that we sprayed "1 and 1 = 2." Let them think it over for a mile.

When we got back we were vague about distances. . . . "It's about 22 or 25 miles." They groaned. "But what a *place!*" They groaned. We'd walk in twos, according to the straws drawn.

After supper that night we played capture-the-flag in the apple grove. Very rough! I could easily picture someone breaking a leg—me. Well, I knew they were much younger, but after 10 minutes I understood it. They could have played all night; we had only walked 15 miles that day.

Evening into night. Peace, calm, smiles, apple trees, soft words, sleep. Did they love Gale and me? Why not, we loved them.

The morning began as peacefully as the evening left off. We had a very pretty young girl come down the road for a visit. Big Ann was giving up Gipsy, her kitten, to the girl—with tears.

I tried to cheer her up, in my way: "Ann, you're just crying because you're losing your footrest."

"No," she said, wiping her tears, "my foot *warmer.*"

For me the day was filled with flying trips: 15 miles to dump garbage (and a talk with the president of the American Mule Drivers' Association), back for water; to the store for groceries; to the dairy for milk; out to the field to unload the truck and lay out sleeping bags, tent, poles, stakes, and set up stoves; back for white gas; light stoves, start bacon, and lay out a board for sandwich making; back later to the store for perishables; still later, out mapping to check the inland highway.

For a week or so I had wanted to fix bacon, lettuce, and tomato sandwiches; well, this was it. But no sooner had I really gotten into them than the first walkers were around the bend and into the field. They couldn't believe the day's walk was over. It shook them up: 8 miles? Only 8 miles? Especially when they had been geared up to do 25.

A bunch of us went swimming in the large unruffled, birch-ringed lake. An automatic frozen scream erupted from each person when he dove in and came up. I've never been in colder water. Tita and Lloyd swam around for five seconds longer than they needed to; the rest of us didn't waste a second getting out; skinny Jake actually ran across the top of the lake to reach shore.

We all agreed to ask Thayer, the dairy farmer, to supper, so a few of us went back to the farm. "I'm very glad to have a chance to talk with you people. I'll gladly come, and I thank you for the invitation; and I have something I want to tell you."

Again, tears came into his eyes. Were we sentimental about him? Yes; he was already a part of the trip. He had something to say; and whether it really affected us or not we needed to be there for him to say it to. "Attention must be paid," goes the line from *Death of a Salesman.*

At times I saw the whole walk very clearly as a huge piece

of sculpture, with sudden unreasonable zigs and zags. Other times it was like a pilgrimage. Was the shrine in Nova Scotia? In bits and pieces along the way. Did I ever say exactly that to the others? They understood. They didn't know it; they understood. Today it was a huge piece of sculpture, a work of art with no practical purpose, and ourselves in the middle of it—working at it, being worked on by it.

Gale and Motorhead came up. Gale reported that Motor had been sick. He was looking very pale. Motor was the lamplighter and stove specialist, and lately he had been out of it. It *had* to be temporary, yet he was quite pale, and his lips were almost colorless.

Split-pea soup was cooking—with garlic, bay leaves, bacon, onions, green pepper, and ham hock. All it needed was time. Off we went for Bucksport to check out the inland "airline highway." In either case, a complicated route for tomorrow: a beautiful bridge, a picturesque fort, into Bucksport, a big town for us, and straight through it to the crossroads. We took 46 out of Bucksport to 9, and even L.J. and Howie had to admit that it was no meandering country road. It was noisy, truck-filled, wide, and ugly.

We still had no place, but we had to get back. I was sick of driving, so Phil took it and I flopped in back. Steady Phil. Herb and Bob B. were up front drumming on the dashboard, ducking, bobbing to the "Pinball Wizard," which came blasting over the radio about three times a day.

Is the shrine in Nova Scotia? Bits and pieces along the way; collect them and put them together. The Walk itself was a song, a long zigzag song, playing all the way to Nova Scotia.

With Lloyd at the spray can, those arrows for turns evolved: flowery arrows became arrowy flowers.

ORANGES!!! Miracle of the ages! We dug about thirty— thirty miracles bouncing bobbing eat-oranges-laughing.

Evening and the old man came and settled into us. The soup was a magic broth; stirred and tasted, stirred and tasted; salt, more garlic, onions. The tent was up. People spread out over the field, but there were twelve or so who would listen. He began talking. For part of the time tears rolled down his face . . . his wife in the hospital, dying, and twice Jesus spoke to him. "There will be no calls tonight," the voice said, while he wondered whether to stay up or not. "There will be no calls tonight." Was it a real voice? Jesus's voice? We listened. The second time Thayer did not tell us the words but conveyed the message; something in him had been touched and he supplied the words: he must make amends, the voice said, and from then on lead the good life. "I'll try," he said, in answer. "I'll try." It was after a long pause. Tears on his face in the yellow glow of lamplight. Not that he would *do* it. "I'll try," his voice said again, to Jesus, to us.

"If I could have known earlier . . . you all here . . . you're *doing* something . . . you've done something for an old man. I don't know if you know it . . . but God is here . . . in this tent, tonight."

We walked him to his car; our grandfather. Bob D. backed the car up for him, set it in the right direction. We shook hands all around. L.J., eyes shining, was one of the first. We waved good-bye unseen, for it was dark; unseen, for he had turned away.

We walked back silently, thought about the old man.

> *Wonderin' if where I been*
> *Is worth the things I've been through.*

Gale and I had a spot below the tent very near the lake. It was a lovely night. I woke up early to a slight fog over the field, absolute quiet. The field was heavy with dew, sleep, peace, wet grass, the spirits of the lake.

I don't know how it happened, but Herbie was up. Did Phil want to go? He was dead. Lloyd was always up for early mapping, but now he was nowhere to be found.

L.J. and Howie had come around. Unanimity: we'd go by the coast. There were *some* reservations, but I didn't find out about them till later.

Herb and I zinged out to Bucksport to look for a place. Through town, out the other end. There was no way out of

Bucksport except by Highway 1—a straight, fast roadway, which can only make walkers feel as if they're crawling . . . add stores, houses, filling stations, and trouble.

Out of Orland, Maine, off the big highway, up a gravel road next to one of the wide reaches of the Penobscot River, and it was a matter of five minutes to get the field. The owners were a little leery, but all day long, unknown to us, they were swinging around toward us.

Back to the campsite, singing "Yes, we have no bananas." We'd open both doors and slam them shut simultaneously.

"Yes, we have no bananas!" BAM.

"We have no bananas today!" BAM.

They laughed at the showoffs, at the bus careening across the field, both doors opening at once, slamming shut perfectly together, all in full flight, with the words of the old song bubbling out ahead of us. Very funny, only the right window dropped down inside the door. We didn't see it again until Canada, where Lloyd fixed it.

We had hot Maypo for breakfast, got things together. Already walkers were streaming across the field to the road. That old man, our grandfather, in just a slightly different context, had said, "Our mortal body is nothing. It is the spirit." Our work for the day was to walk, and we went to work with spirit.

What a relief just to walk. To drive the truck was ten times as hard. To drive the truck was to strike a day out of one's life.

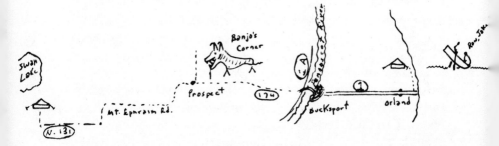

I began the walk alone, thanked the owner for his great field, caught up to Tita, Big Ann, Gale, and Diana, and we walked along together for the first 3 miles or so. The sky was perfectly clear; we were heading due east to the great Atlantic!

The crossroads were so distinct. A hard left onto gravel, a right turn more than 90 degrees, still on gravel. It seemed so peaceful and "country." Well, it was country all right, but at that village-smithy corner Bob B. was almost chewed up. We didn't hear about it till later.

What was Diana doing way back here at the end of the line? She usually charged out at full speed and kept going till she got to camp, flopped, and then was up and around by the time the bulk of the walkers arrived. Maybe it was a sign of confidence—she could make it fast or slow.

"Nice traveling!" some people called to us from their door.

"Yes. It's a beautiful day."

"It sure is."

"The wood smells good!"

"Sure does!"

There was energy in the air.

A simple scene stood before me for half an hour: a big rock on the brow of a hill, down from it a lone but full pine tree secure in the earth. Hill, rock, tree.

I felt too good. I couldn't walk that slowly. Big Ann decided to join me and we took off. In an hour we had clipped off a fraction more than 4½ miles. We rested a minute or so and took off again. We took a chance on a shortcut and it worked out. We had bypassed about eight people, and also bypassed the candy bars and drinks which the truck was dispensing. But we did have some good talk about what we were doing.

We caught up with Dan, Don, and the Weasel. They were amazed! We all stoked up at a corner store, then strung out again. There was a long hill going down, a deep valley, then a long hill to climb. "When you get tired of walking, run!" It was an old joke among us. Dan chose that moment to bring it up, so we started jogging; it didn't last long, but we made it to the top.

Later L.J., Howie, Gordon, and I made miles together and talked about neighborhoods, gangs, changes in attitudes. L.J. and Howie had not known each other, but their backgrounds were amazingly similar. Energetic bantam roosters, witty, sensitive, tough, and competitive, both have known hard neighborhoods.

One of the ideas of the walk was to take students out of the round of pressures—draft, school assignments, home, money, jobs. In L.J.'s case it was only partly successful. Back of every argument over routes was his fear that he couldn't make St. John and still get back to New York in time to find a job before the rush of students. Thus St. John was a goal. He understood it shouldn't be, but it was.

We arrived at the state park, Fort Knox, and explored with flashlights, but it was more of a joke than an "interesting landmark." We sat on the cared-for grounds and watched people drive up, check their maps, and go from point to point reading the metal site markers. Is this history? Culture? Background? Oh yes! Now they knew all about it. When it was built, the purpose, everything. 1765? What the hell is 1765? 1970? What's a two?

"You see, the British came up the river . . . there! The Major . . . let's see, what was his name? Well, he gave the order to fire. One light vessel was sunk, two damaged. Then they headed out to sea."

The area is maintained by the national park commission, directed by the state park commission. And it looks good. Furthermore, the plaques are cast iron. With metal words! It *must* be true.

Up came our beautiful blue truck, with sandwiches! Hard-boiled eggs! Oranges! Watermelon! Walkers were down in the bowels of the fort. Up strode Big Ann. Yes, she admitted, she had caught a "small" ride.

Bob B. arrived and told his story. Just out of Prospect, this big police dog was let loose on him. "That dog meant business! I couldn't find any rocks, so I took out my knife. The dog is circling, and the woman is yelling, 'Bite the shit out of him, Banjo!'"

"What?"

"Then she saw I had my knife out and she starts calling to the dog to come back: 'Come to Mama, Banjo, come to Mama!' "

We walked across the bridge, high and graceful, into Bucksport, all feeling very frisky. Bridges do that to people. Walkers, at any rate. Just off the bridge we stopped at a colonial-house type of restaurant—except for Phil, who was going to lie down in the park and write in his journal. We started talking about how nice it was to be admitted to a strange place and given food, just like that. "Yes, we'll have to thank them for all of this." "Total strangers, too!"

Suddenly the waitress was talking about Vietnam in a loud voice. Lucky we were here and not in Vietnam . . . she had one son over there, and another about to go.

What? We had not mentioned peace, war, or Vietnam.

After crossing the next bridge we saw the truck in the parking lot opposite the big supermarket. Someone had left a note under the windshield wiper, an obvious reference to L.J.'s sign (THE WALK . . . To Look for America). In a neat, careful hand: "If you haven't found it in New Hampshire or Maine, you really *are* lost!"

Oh, we had found it all right, all shades and colors; good, dumb, beautiful, ugly. "Bite the shit out of him, Banjo!" At that very instant Lloyd and Ann M. were having it rough in the supermarket. And the Davises, the owners of the field, passed by, stopped, asked if we wanted a lift, waved, and drove off.

Two more miles and we flopped in their field—and ours, for the night. The Davises had a coffee table set up for us, and their children had moved their hi-fi to the window, beaming music toward the tent.

Everyone had been invited to the high school dance. Don (with his harmonica), Dan, Tita, Bob B., Motorhead (pale as a ghost), Diana, Richie, and Bob D. cleaned up and set off.

While looking for a field for the next night, we picked up a hitchhiker on the road to Surry. He asked where we were going. "Wellll, we have this old map . . . been in the family for over a hundred and fifty years and we're looking . . . welll, for a . . . place."

"Yeah, we ever find that '*place*' . . ."

"Will you guys shut up!"

We took him into Surry, all playing different roles; some cool, some angry that we'd let the "secret" out.

The fields on either side of this neglected road to Surry seemed ownerless. No houses, no people to ask.

Of course it is known that everything, every bit of land, is owned or spoken for, but we came to realize it to another degree—slowly and painfully.

L.J., now officially twenty-one, went into Bucksport with Phil and Herb to buy some beer. When the woman wouldn't sell it to him—L.J. looks about seventeen—he was furious and wanted to wreck the place.

He almost left us that night; the hell with school, credits, the country, and the world. We had a long talk then, and again the next morning, and L.J. agreed to go at least as far as St. John. Still, his tendency was to win, to do it, to *get* there.

That night we paddled canoes and rowed some of the Davises' boats on the quiet calm river. How different from walking, yet very much the same. Effort expended equals distance covered. We got to bed about 11:00; the high school swingers came in much later.

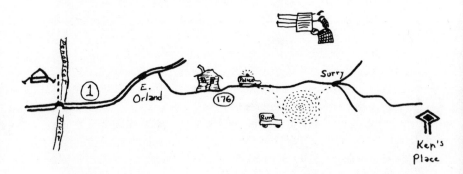

It was a relief next morning to get off the big highway and head for the little town of Surry and the first real glimpse of ocean. About half a mile off the highway we passed an abandoned shack, wide open, full of spider webs. Some of us went in and browsed among old children's books, cheap ornamented candle holders, old yellowed letters, long-overdue bills: "We've given you every opportunity to set your accounts right . . ." If only these smug office authors could have followed the letters out to their RFD destinations; they would never have had the nerve to deliver them.

Half a mile later the police were screaming up to us. When they saw we weren't running they became more polite. They had gotten calls that we were breaking and entering "private houses."

Finally it was straightened out and we were allowed to continue. The truck came by while we were finishing up with the stateys, and I went with them to show them where the field was. We dumped the stuff and were ready to leave when the owner walked up.

" 'At's my field."

"Oh, we didn't know."

"Yep; it's my field!" It was like a game of Territory.

I asked as nicely as I could for permission to use it for the night; we'd keep it clean and leave in the morning. We were on an educational experiment, walking to Canada. His manner changed and he picked out a spot for the tent. At least three times he told us we were welcome, that it was "All right." I said that if it wasn't we'd pack up and leave right away. "Nooo, just when you drive out tomorrow, drive along the edges there, not across the middle."

Okay . . . and thanks very much. We jumped in the truck and went off to Surry for groceries. In the store we found a big barrel full of peanuts and bought about ten pounds. By the time we got back, there were police cars in the field, towneys cruising by honk-honk yelling cars parked, while parking, to see what's stopped more guys dad over getting pull out going let's see why's looking *what's* stopped to *going on over there*!?!

One mountain of equipment; food, boxes, sleeping bags, and tired walkers sprawled in the foothills.

The sheriff greeted us as we drove up. "You got five minutes to get your stuff off this field!" He had a watch, two guns, and a cartridge belt.

"What?"

"You heard me!"

"The owner gave us permission to stay here!"

"Well, he done changed his mind. Says you told him you was a minister . . . an he didn't know what kind of people you was."

" 'Minister?' "

"Minister, preacher! Anyways, you got five minutes to pack your stuff and get off."

"Five minutes?"

To get twenty-one-people and that mountain of supplies packed in even ten minutes would be a feat. But the seconds were ticking away, and his eyes were on the second hand. Would he shoot us at the end of five minutes? He had two guns and a full cartridge belt—that would take care of twelve of us even before he had to reload.

I finally talked him into letting us take the loaded vehicle and three or four people to help unload when we found a place.

The day before, when looking for a barn, I had heard about two "musicians." The man who mentioned them smirked, so I knew they were different. He had flatly refused his barn to us, and it wasn't just his refusal, it was a surliness toward all students and colleges. Maybe I shouldn't have argued with him, but it was rare to come face to face with one of these suspicious recluses. For every accusation he made against us, I asked him where, where, where had he seen it? It was all television. Television had made up his mind! Television with its selected "news." Its "coverage" of the world. No, he said. He had also read the newspapers. He had done everything . . . except go see for himself.

"What are you up to?" he asked me. "Why aren't you in school teaching them? Why aren't they studying? Instead of running around the country causing trouble?"

All this was by way of saying no, he wouldn't give us his

barn because he was afraid of fire. "You're afraid of people," I wanted to tell him, and Gale probably would have.

"I didn't mean to imply that *you're* a Communist . . ."

Toward the end of the argument he had mentioned where the musicians lived. Now I racked my brains to remember.

I told the sheriff about the musicians, and he gave me directions. Go ahead; he'd follow me. Off we went, one loaded truck with five conscious ants looking for America, and one sheriff's car loaded with guns, bullets, and billy clubs right behind.

We found one of the musicians, who seemed hesitant when confronted, in the quietest of Maine towns, by four disheveled and desperate people leaping out of a dirty truck and followed by a gun-bristling sheriff pushing in to hear every word. He started playing coy Zen games with us and wouldn't answer till we'd asked the right question. He sent us to his friend down the road, the other musician. If his friend couldn't put us up somewhere, he said, he knew of a field where we could stay.

Back into the truck for another quarter mile to an entirely different reception. Yes, said the friend, to the sheriff and his guns, they can stay in my side yard. He, Ken, was not awed by badges, guns, or hair. Is it too corny to say *that* is America?

We dumped people and equipment and went back for the others. It was a sorry scene we came upon. The town sharks cruised back and forth, yelling, laying rubber on the road. The group of walkers, very subdued, were just where we had left them.

In another hour we were settled at Ken's. Occasional "cruisers" still came by because it was not very far from the road, but the place was more a garden than a field and, for that reason, private.

Ken's little cabin was crowded with walkers. They were moving in and out of his simple house, his study, peering up at his tiny sleeping quarters. But he could not be interrupted, and he could not be ruffled. Shouldn't they knock before coming in? "Oh no," he said, in the only way he said anything, gently. "I do not have that . . ." he smiled. No, he was not his door, he was not *in* his possessions, he was simply not those things. There was no confusion about possessions. He lived *in* his body, but even that was only a possession. His body was his but not him. He did not tell us that he *believed* in these things, he *was* these things. In his study there were three bookshelves of books on Buddhism. He was working on a book about Japanese farmhouses.

After we had finished supper, he came out with a tremendous kettle of hot water for dishes which had been heated on his stove. It was there and he was gone. He had not done it, it had done itself.

One last person from the town couldn't tear himself away. He was drunk and earlier had asked us to use his field. He hated the man who had kicked us out and told us, about fifty times, "I don't owe that sonofabitch uhh nickel!"

"Well, thanks a lot, anyway."

His generosity was sincere but a little heavy. Finally I told him we were going to have a meeting, thanked him again, and he left.

We talked about the day, about threats and towneys. Herbie had been threatened, Lloyd had been "growled" at. "We were in this store," Lloyd said, "and this guy comes over and asks me why didn't I get a haircut. I told him I didn't want to. He went over and got something at the counter then he turns around and starts growling. He just kept on *growling*! I told him to go to hell . . . his wife was screaming, 'Get in the car . . . Harold! *Get in the car*!'"

The people at the store in Surry: "Sooo, we gonna have visitors tonight, eh?" in oleaginous tones, with many winks and nods, as if they were preparing something for us. As if it would be a stain on the honor of the town if we "got away" scot free.

Of course this worked on us. We didn't know who they were, how much was "humor" and how much was sickness, how far this particular belt extended. Yet in the very eye of the storm, there was Ken. And the night before, that wonderful family in Orland. And right out front was a car with a yellow spotlight that kept cruising slowly by.

We went around the tent: "What shall we do about the towneys?"

We could all agree that whoever was on the truck would have to notify the police in every town we passed through. We *had* to admit that we were causing a great deal of fear. To calm the police first would mean that they could then calm the hundreds (according to them) of phone callers.

L.J. knocked us all over: "I *like* towneys! I really *dig* 'em!"

The Weasel, who is only twelve, reasoned like a man: "Well, I just think that we should answer them in a nice way. I mean, answer their questions and, you know, be nice to them . . . talk to them. Don't give them any wise answers."

Bob D. had had it with the towneys and was ready to throw punches, Diana was very intelligently and specifically vague, Ann M. was a little sad about it, Tita was, as always, more concerned with the twenty-one of us, the family, how we were toward each other. In this context L.J.'s "I really *dig* 'em!" fell like a bomb, a nice unhysterical bomb.

After the meeting, around 9:00 p.m., things settled down. Ken had a great outhouse of two stools about half a block into the woods. People were scattered around, sleeping in the woods, by a little bridge, up under trees, all over the yard. The traffic had slowed out front, and in a lull I parked the truck down a side road, out of sight.

The trouble with classes is that they break up at the appointed hour. If the teacher feels he has started something that should continue, he might not be able to stay, and the students might or might not be able to. Here, though, we were stuck together. We had been through novels, plays and poems in the last twenty-four hours; wonderful hospitality, a high school dance (Don had joined the group with his harmonica—the star of the show), night rowing on the river and tides from the ocean, talks with the Davis family, L.J.'s near-departure, the various hassles with towneys and state cops, the gun-toting sheriff, and now this peaceful (so far) ending, a taste of Zen Buddhism in a Japanese garden in Maine under a clear sky. The little knot of us who were still up (Bill, Gordon, Phil, Herb, Motor, and I) could almost feel the others in their bags turning off, one by one, to sleep.

However we are composed—little worlds within a world, each with stars in his own skies, with an earthly personality turning to different seasons, showing different segments in each season, the different skies of our very selves—however it works, Bill was ready to level, to trust; a certain hesitancy and shyness were gone from his sky, and he told us things that were very close to him. It forced us all to talk with more frankness. We stayed up for so long that I didn't even want to know what time it was.

What did we learn from him, from the day, from Ken, from Surry, Maine? That we must be ready to laugh, and something about *when*: to duck, to smile, to shut up, to venture forth, to hold back, to walk lightly.

"If you see no other part of the Maine coast, you should see Schoodic Point," Ken had said. He hadn't mentioned the naval base.

Gordon knew a man who had a house at Winter Harbor, just a few miles from Schoodic Point. "If he's there, we could have showers and, I think, he would really take care of us."

Of course it was out of the way, but I could feel us leaning, almost veering, toward the Point. I guess it was the mention of showers. Showers were a luxury we had even stopped dreaming of. In fact, once they were mentioned, it was difficult to think of anything else.

So, early the next morning Phil and I took the truck to map a route, but mainly to find showers. Dan was practically begging us to. We had seen signs advertising a place called The Gathering—a trailer camp and picnic spot, with public showers, just out of Surry. "Everyone Is Welcome at The Gathering" said the sign.

Could we make arrangements for everyone to get showers? We'd be in and out within an hour. No, said the manager.

It would cost too much money. The showers were a service to the patrons of the camping area. Well, how much did he charge them? Twenty-five cents. Could we pay him fifty cents for each shower, a quick shower, and agree to be out in one hour?

"I'm sorry, I can't do it. Besides, my regular patrons wouldn't like it."

Trailer people.

"How about seventy-five cents for each shower?" By this time we were putting him on a little. "Nope!" "How about letting us wash our hands for thirty cents apiece?"

"I'm sorry, I just can't do it."

We had to take the big highway again for a stretch to get to Ellsworth, and at a big Texaco sign we saw a notice that advertised showers. Public showers. No camping grounds, no trailers, just showers. Ah!

"No!' said the manager. "No!" That's all. Everyone knows that those longhairs killed Sharon Tate. But I didn't have long hair, and neither did Phil. And Sharon Tate was still alive at the time. Never mind, just look at the truck they came out of.

Suddenly we realized that it was Sunday. Oh, Lord! Sunday traffic and a big highway. Only occasionally did we have any idea what day of the week it was. On Saturdays we walked 15 to 20 miles. On Sundays we walked 15 to 20 miles. On Mondays we walked 15 to 20 miles.

Back to Surry.

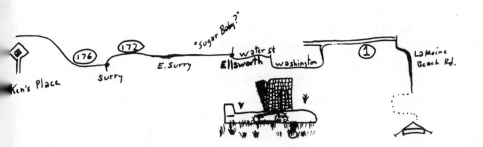

Gale took over the driving. Since we were off the route about 3 miles, we bused everyone—except for Lloyd and Ann M.—into Surry ("Sorry" some called it). We had decided to walk in pairs and to choose someone we had not walked with before. Gordon and I paired off and loped out. Phil and the Weasel were following along.

"Do you like Sugar Babies?" Gordon asked me.

I had never seen or heard of Sugar Babies until he bought some at the store in Surry, but boy, them Sugar Babies were good!

We decided that when we got to Ellsworth we'd ask the chief of police if we could take showers at the jail. Gordon had heard that sometimes it was permitted. Okay, that was set, but we had about 10 miles to go.

We got into such a deep, long conversation that we became totally unaware of the heavy Sunday traffic. We lost our arms, legs, and bodies to the talk. We might as well have been walking in a cave for all we saw. Good? Bad? We talked and walked.

We came out of it a mile or so before Ellsworth and opposite the police chief's car. We went over to his house and rapped on the door. Hi! Hello there! How are you! Good morning! He was a big, serious man. Well, he didn't know about the showers. Had we tried the high school?

Gordon took out his candies: "Would you like a Sugar Baby?"

"No thanks." He scratched his head, tried to come up with some more ideas. Incidentally, he stopped himself, there had been a helluva lot of calls about us. Yessir, a lot of reports.

"Sugar Baby?"

"No thanks." He kept scratching his head. "Showers, eh?"

He told us we could try at the fire station, and we *could* wait over till Monday and ask at the high school. No, we couldn't wait over just for that. "No chance at the jail?"

"I don't b'lieve . . . but you could go over there and ask."

"Sugar Baby?"

"No thanks."

We left. Later we rested with Phil and the Weasel. "Don't forget about Calvin Coolidge's son," Gordon told us as we sat around. "What about him?" "He died of an infected blister."

We went on into Ellsworth. No, they wouldn't let us take showers at the jail. And the fire station was closed.

Later we caught up with Herbie and he told us his story. In addition to his weird-looking cap, his SHERIFF OF ELLSWORTH badge, long sideburns, and Khrushchev overcoat, Herbie had bought himself a long golden sword with a gold scabbard and belt. All for $5.

To go through a minor hate belt dressed as he was, he got off lightly, I think, with only a large vanilla DairyCream cone smashed into his Khrushchev coat. He complained bitterly about the woman ("You sonofabitch hippy! Getta bath you dirty sonofabitch!"). She drove back and forth giving him the finger, telling her children to throw things at him, until finally she pulled up close behind him to give the kids a good shot (they were only youngsters and couldn't throw too well). The big squashy cone hit and stuck.

Just out of Ellsworth we crossed the crowded highway to see a big wooden model of the Titanic in front of a strange little house.

My God!

We walked back past the boat to the . . . contraption/invention. Kind of a wing, wheels, cockpit, flaps. Flaps? The "wings" were about one thousand little flappers. A crank, levers, spools, wire, aluminum of tin-can thickness.

Out of the back of the house, through knee-deep tin cans (real ones) and garbage, a thin seventy-year-old man in a suit was plowing his way toward us. We greeted him and asked him to tell us about it, about . . . them . . . that.

"That's the Silver Wing," he said, as if it was never out of his thoughts, and the only barrier to it was the vocal cords. And now the barrier was out of the way; ". . . no . . . the wing flaps. Principle of bird in flight . . . no propeller . . . plug it up to house battery and she flaps . . ." SHE? ". . . fourteen beats a minute . . . thirty beats and she'll take off

. . . I do it for the benefit of aviation . . . See that one over there? Well, once in a high wind she lifted right up . . . bodily. 'Thout any engine . . . Thought I'd have trouble getting her down but I didn't. I just took hold of the string and down she came . . . gentle as a lamb. Just like that!" He showed us with his gentle old hands, bending almost down to the grass which grew about two feet high all over the yard.

"Has anybody in aviation seen this?"

"Yessir," he said. His eyes alone, just to look into his eyes, could break anyone's heart. "Yessir, some of the smartest men in aviation don't know what to do with this . . . colonels, corporals, doctors, lawyers . . .

"Come over here and see the engine!"

Gordon was already there, looking down into what appeared to be the cockpit. His face was serious enough; he was just gazing away down there at "the engine." I went and looked. It was a big hole with no bottom. The engine was no bigger than my two fists put together, and could hardly be seen through the reeds and tall grass.

I stood there looking and tried to blank my mind. I've never tried harder, and I've never been happier that I succeeded.

We asked about the mysterious seal or sign on the side of the cockpit.

"Don't know what that is, eh?"

No, we didn't.

"That's the key to flight!"

We finally left, after thanking him for showing it. He offered to sell it for $8,000, but neither one of us had enough.

At a DairyCream we got sundaes and met Phil and the Weasel eating banana splits. We told them about the Silver Wing and made the Weasel laugh so hard that some banana went up his nose and he was choking, coughing, spitting, and crying all at once.

We walked in heavy Sunday traffic with no beginning,

no end to it until we came to the Lamoine Beach Road and
left it all. My thoughts were on the inventor of the Silver
Wing and the dreams people have. Garbage and cans spill-
ing out the back of his house, no wife, no children, no one
else in this old house sitting like a rock island between
streams of traffic. And there in that bewildered Silver-
Winged old man's house in late May is a completely dec-
orated Christmas tree with tinsel and colored balls—which
not even the best minds in aviation would know what to do
with.

A thousand cars must have driven by that intersection
while we were there, and not one stopped. *None* out of a
thousand! When we waved good-bye he was reentering his
lonely house between rivers of traffic, inside to his tinseled
Christmas tree. May 25th.

We got to the site; a broad, deep field not far from the
road—a little-used secondary road—to find that Bill was not
there and had not been seen since midday.

The sky was overcast, and we picked out places either
in the tent or somewhere in the field under shelter. There
were pieces of corrugated tin lying around and I decided to
make a little house for Gale and me. It took about an hour
but looked pretty good. L.J. had his spot under a tree. Dan,
Diana, and Motorhead had a spot in the center of the field.
Diana confessed that she and Big Ann had hitched a ride
for a couple of miles. Diana felt bad about it. Big Ann giggled
and wanted to go into town and see *Romeo and Juliet.* It was
a silly little thing to have caught a ride, and yet—we *were*
walking to Canada, weren't we?

Motorhead was very pale, his lips were white, and he was
scheduled to do the dishes with Diana. He almost begged
off, and I told him maybe he should trade with someone for
the night. Later I saw him doing them. He felt "all right."
Very unconvincing.

We had to go out and find Bill. Back to Ellsworth, then
retracing our path beyond Ellsworth and miles to the left
at every possible turnoff. Back to the highway and straight
ahead. We asked at farmhouses, restaurants, everywhere.

Everywhere except the first turnoff out of Ellsworth, because he *couldn't* have gone that way. Perhaps the rule to follow when someone is lost is to immediately go to the most illogical place. I can almost guarantee- 90 percent success. When we got back to camp, Bill was there. Make that 95 percent. He had ended up knocking at doors asking for us. At one place the husband was very friendly but the woman wasn't having any. "You hippy, why aren't you in school? You go to college? Why aren't you studying?" She didn't believe Bill's tall tale about a walk to Canada. No, not for a second. Meanwhile her husband was getting dressed to drive him to the camp. When she discovered *that*, she started screaming and demanding that he come back. "She was yelling at him the whole time we were driving away from the house," Bill said, " 'Come back here this instant! Are you crazy? He'll probably kill you!' "

Bill has a short cap of hair, no beard, no mustache, glasses; wears clean clothes and walking boots.

I was dead and crawled in. Gale, Howie, L.J., and a few others went mapping. They went straight to Franklin, cutting off Schoodic Point. I thought everybody had decided to go and see Schoodic Point. At any rate, this news was our last communication before sleep in our little lean-to hovel: that they'd gone by way of Franklin.

Down came the rain. My nose touched the canvas about 5:00 a.m., and water started dripping through. I scraped an elbow across the canvas and turned on a new leaky faucet. We were drenched by 6:00. Ann M. and Lloyd had been up since 4:00, soaked; L.J. the same. Plume looked as if he'd been dumped in a lake.

Perhaps because of the rain, we were up by 7:30 and ready to decide—again—whether we'd go to Schoodic Point or inland till we got to Cherryfield. It was the original argument all over, with practically the same people on the same sides.

On the one hand: bays, coves, beaches, ocean—and showers, if we could find Gordon's friend. On the other hand: beautiful woods, lonely roads, quiet, shady towns, and a more direct route.

Each point had its counterpoint; every argument met a perfect rebuttal. We went around the room again. Could we split up just for this little section? No unanimity. Could we flip a coin? Three people held out. More arguments were heard. Everyone got sick of the same points rephrased. Some left the tent; they would go either way whenever it was decided, but they'd had it with arguments.

Finally we had unanimity on a flip of the coin. Before the flip I reminded them of what they had agreed to. The coin toss would decide *and* end the dispute. No "feelings," no second-guessing, no more discussions.

Agreed.

Words. I'm sorry now that we didn't take five or ten more minutes to think about it. It was an important time and had a great deal to do with understanding unanimity. To get unanimous agreement to a flip of the coin is an interesting step, and not a small one. Ideally, each side moves somewhat more than halfway. But at the time, their idea of unanimity was more theoretical than real. I didn't want to touch the coin; finally we decided to give it to the Weasel, the youngest walker. As it went up in the air I swore that either way, either way was okay.

Schoodic Point!

The victors were abashed. The losers were silent. We decided (solace to the losers) that after we'd walked to Schoodic Point, we'd bus the group up the eastern side of the peninsula and to the town of Steuben. This was not to recover "lost" time but to give the ones who had to leave early—Don, Dan, and L.J.—the chance to make St. John first.

Down came the tent; we stuffed bags into the truck after lugging them across the wet field, cleaned up, thanked the woman in the snug green and white house—with plastic flag flapping out front—and set off. I could still feel the earth of that field against the right side of my face. Earlier, much earlier, Lloyd and I had gone mapping along the coast and sighted the first real beach, bay, ocean scenes at Frenchman's Bay; now for the same scenes in slow motion.

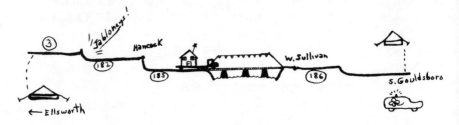

A number of walkers had run across a really great statey just out of Ellsworth. He smiled, stopped and chatted, and, was actually *for* us. He'd wave as he went by, and even volunteered help if we were ever in trouble. Get his name, for God's sake. Ann M., Lloyd, and Don were up for that.

Before walking I had to make a fast mail run into Franklin. It is a beautiful, soft, quiet town. We always had trouble at the coast towns: Belfast, Bucksport, Surry, Schoodic Point, Machias, and so on. The inland towns were greener, softer, quieter, more easygoing. The coast is blue water, picturesque towns, and tough barnacles.

The post office was locked up, but we had the postmaster's name and went to his house, which was wide open and empty. We sat in the truck and I began a note to him. "Dear Mr. Bunker: We tried to—" And just then he drove up, opened the post office specially for us, got our mail, and waved us on. Don't worry, he'd do all the forwarding. Sure! Good luck! Stay loose! Keep the faith! Praise the Lord! We didn't deserve his goodness any more than we deserved the sheriff of Surry.

Howie, L.J., and I left together, hit the main road, and stopped at a little coffee shop, mainly so that Howie wouldn't have to do a "natural." Sure enough, Howie clogged the toilet. L.J. really enjoyed that. Howie had clogged up at least ten toilets since the beginning of the trip. I found a plunger and got the toilet unstopped. However, this wasn't entirely unselfish.

Down the road a couple of miles, some construction workers looked up as we passed by. "Jabloneys!" says one.

"What?"

"You're a bunch of jabloneys."

"You're a jabloney."

The spirit seemed to lighten, though. Along the road we spotted some beautiful strawberries and bought three boxes, eating them as we walked. It was a regular good day of walking in fine weather. Conversation would run for a while, then stop, but it was never uncomfortable. Bill later spoke of this nonverbal communication, a nod at something or just letting it register, silences that just happened and lasted for an hour or more, then fierce conversations that went on and on.

Perhaps we had broken the hump of the project, the physical "hump," the night we played capture-the-flag, proving that we had something left after the day, that a little game wouldn't stop us tomorrow. But there were other humps we had hardly started on.

Maybe bridges should always be walked, especially spidery bridges like the one connecting Hancock and West Sullivan. But there was a distraction for us; a big trailer truck was taking a house across the bridge at the same time. Naturally, Howie had to start directing things: whistling, signaling, pointing. He's like one of the Marx brothers, except that people are actually taken in. He stares with impenetrable brown eyes, blank face, points, directs, shrugs, gives up, turns away, comes back to try again . . . gives it up, walks off.

The house was too high for the bridge, and there was a loud crunch as each successive girder hit the top of the house. The girders didn't give an inch. Howie told them about it. Sure, they could hear it; but what should they do, raise the bridge?

No, let some air out of your tires.

The truck driver shrugs. Howie shrugs. Casts him off with

his hand, walks away. Crunch. Crunch. Crunch. A blind man a block away could tell how many girders the bridge had. If the house wrecked the bridge, or the bridge wrecked the house, it didn't concern the truckers. Their job was move the house—or the nails, lumber, paint, and glass that had once been a house.

We missed the baby seal and the monkey and the clam diggers—maybe because of the house. It was at this spot that Herb (the sword was now in the truck), Phil, and Motorhead sighted the clam diggers, joined them, and dug up about 25 pounds of clams.

Along the way were antique shops, junk shops, and a pottery barn.

We came to a little bay of green grasses, brown sand. It was low tide and the tide was still going out: that pull and sucking out which can be felt, followed by the glorious rush back in till the water of the ocean fills every nook and cranny and packs in even more; then again the period of doubt, of indecision, before the grand exhalation begins, slowly at first then more rapidly, until the waters are whistling out to sea again. Before us were bay, islets, lighthouses, promontories, lobster boats.

"This is like a postcard!"

"Yeah, but they don't put blackflies in the postcard," some cynic answered.

Be
ye

man   woman
early or late
goin   comin

Shut this gate!

Just out of West Sullivan some little kid on a bike began tagging along. ". . . Jeff came back, finally. He went out into the woods to get his head straightened out." Everybody laughed. He asked if we were hippies, and, "Do you know what grass is?" Much laughter. He was no more than nine years old.

"My father smokes grass!"

Howie gave the boy directions to our field for the night.

The walk that day was 20½ miles; the day before, we had walked 17½. But the 17½-mile day was a Sunday with lots of traffic, on straight roads, and we were exhausted. The next day, over untraveled roads, with views of bays, beaches, sand, and water, we walked 3 miles farther and finished fresh. Energy is not expended like gas or money. A different kind of mathematics is involved: mathematics plus emotions, which makes it as tricky as calculus.

We're in a thick grassy green field between Ashville and West Gouldsboro on the Schoodic peninsula. Supper is cooking—a stew of beef and vegetables, along with the 25 pounds of clams dug up near the bridge. Same bridge, different time: for them it was the clam diggers and their baskets, for us it was that house and crunch! crunch! For others it was the tide rushing in or out. For others lobster boats. For others, sky, ocean, and the baby seal. For still others, a train of thought. All over the same bridge.

The tent is going up now. It is going up slowly, but if they had to they could put it up in five minutes: Phil, Dan, Rich, Jake, Don, Gordon, Motorhead. All work leisurely, joking and talking. Rich, the oak tree, holds the center pole. One night the pole fell on Rich's head. Thirty pounds of wood. Ow! says he. It hurt the ones who saw it more than it hurt Rich.

Earlier there had been trouble getting a site because people who had offered their fields were intimidated by phone calls from "friends" and neighbors. This man too was getting his share of phone calls, but he was rugged: Go to hell! Yes, they're using my field and "they" are okay.

We were going to try and locate Gordon's friend that night and make it to his place for the next day. First we ate supper.

"I hope he remembers me," Gordon said. "I guess he will

. . . One time we were out sailing and I ran his yacht into the dock."

"Good God," I said, "Is that his only memory of you?"

"No. I think I dropped the anchor on his foot, the same day."

Lots of cars were driving by and, just as in Limerick, there were sick laughs and sickly screams coming from them. The darker it got, the more concentrated the traffic became. Base workers and sailors from the naval base at Winter Harbor were cruising by and cursing at us. I decided we'd call the cops first. If the cops decided to look the other way, it would undoubtedly be a rough, sleepless night.

We had the name of the friendly state trooper, Libby, and I called and asked that he be advised, that it looked like trouble. As for Scotty, Gordon's friend, we found only his huge and empty house.

By the time we returned, the traffic along the road was crazy. We could hardly get back onto the field, and even then we couldn't drive too far because the ground was mushy. We'd already been stuck once. The local hippies were there, the owner of the field, State Trooper Libby, the banker, one of the selectmen, and of course, the cruisers driving by.

They thought I was Scotty's friend and were very impressed. Scotty had gone to England to pick up his new yacht, they told us, and wouldn't be back till late spring or early summer. The banker was offering to cash any and all checks, the owner was ready to do battle for us (both he and Libby had shown their colors before Scotty), and Libby would stick around all night if necessary.

We had mixed feelings about the sudden attention, but mainly it was a welcome relief. As for the walkers, I always knew they would come through in any emergency, because it was a great group. If people would talk with them for a while, they would know this . . . but what chance did we have with those cruising sharks, who hated us at long range?

Libby left the coffee circle and went back to the road to direct traffic, to warn a few to move on. The banker and the owner of the field left, then the hippies—after asking me, with all sorts of undertones, if we *needed* anything . . . I told them no thanks, just sleep, and we settled down for the night.

It was a night of taunts, threats, screams from the road, and frequent sallies by our knight of the flashing blue shield, whose car would come charging out of its hiding place to stop the screamers and give-em-a-ticket if they came back. That made us chuckle.

It was also an absolutely clear and star-filled night. Everything was quiet by one or two in the morning, and by sunrise there was nothing to mar the peace.

After loading up I went to the owner's house, rang the bell, and spoke to a young girl. "Thanks for the field . . . I hope it wasn't too much trouble."

"Well . . ." she said. And who can blame her? Phone calls and threats are no fun.

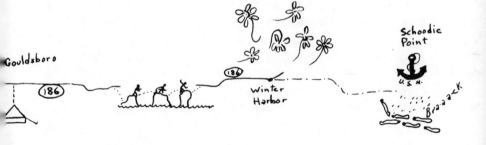

For a long time we walked the beach, zigging and zagging for miles and miles, making almost no forward progress. There would be a spot of beach, then huge rocks. We maneuvered the rocks until it got too close to 11:00, at which time I had to attend the check-cashing ceremonies at the bank.

The rocks, Jake said, exhausted him. Might as well say he lost a day's energy in an hour of rock climbing. There were spots we could jump to only after a wave receded, and we had to go on to the next rock before another wave came in. Some laughed, others froze up. What would it mean if we didn't jump in time? Just a soaking, at worst. Jake *knew* it, and faced it, but the fear was still there—unresolved, irrational. But maybe we cracked it a little because we were working on it—putting his fear next to what he knew were the real risks involved. He would consider, then jump again, scramble up, think about it, jump again. Finally he turned to us. "I'm exhausted!" At 10:30 a.m. He was, too. On to the bank.

No sooner had we reached the road than two cars pulled up to us: the banker, a captain in the Navy, and a few others. The captain introduced himself—he was the commander of the naval station at Winter Harbor—and invited us to use the base camping grounds, as well as their hot showers. We accept!

We gave out directions to the base, then took off looking for a place and roads for the next day. We went through Steuben, Milbridge, and almost to Cherryfield before we got a down-rolling hayfield at the edge of Pleasant Bay. To drive across the field was like taking a boat through long rolling waves. It resembled the location at Limerick, but here the road was behind the brow of a gentle hill. The field rose very slightly and then went down to the water in a graceful bend. The dairy farmer had been saving this lush field, and it was almost ready for his cows to graze on. Before lending it to us he warned us about his wife's conservative ways, her fear of long hair, hippies, and students. I was determined we'd give him nothing to be sorry for. "Well, I'm sure you'll do right . . . but we're lookin' fer no trouble." I'll drink to that.

Back to the Navy base, a delicious supper of spicy meat sauce and spaghetti, visitors with beer, and about five walkers. And a pile of dirty dishes and pans. The list of dishwashers was posted in the truck, and no one was quite sure who was supposed to do them. Ann M., cook for the night, had blown up. The hell with the list! Why doesn't somebody just take over? She and Lloyd were gone, others were on the base watching television, others were playing basketball, some were taking hot showers, and some had left to avoid our three visitors and their case of beer to "share"— in return for atmosphere, "freedom," and a love-in (we furnish the girls, of course). These three seamen were convinced that the most far-out thing anyone could do was belch. And there was one who could, I'll admit, belch louder and longer than anyone I've ever heard. Jake and Rich laughed on cue. It was an impossible situation: it was "their" (the Navy's) camping grounds, and they had brought a gift, the beer. Okay, never look a gift horse in the mouth; but at least count his legs, because some gifts come very high.

I finally told them that no matter how loose the setup appeared, it was a course, that we had another 15 miles to do tomorrow. They got the idea and after fighting down the first urge to react with anger or sarcasm, since they knew the commander had welcomed us—and after trying to find out where we'd be the following night (lotsa-beer-big-party) —they left, belching. Later, according to Herbie, they were calling me the Führer and were still trying to find out where we'd camp the next night.

We slept in a grove of trees. Since we had left the tent in the truck it started sprinkling. Let it fall. The day had been a good one. We had cashed checks in Winter Harbor around noon, just as the grammar school kids were getting out for lunch. One or two started it; without a word to us they ran off and came back with some flowers. Others ran off and did the same; then all these little kids were coming up with armloads of yellow field flowers. Some were so shy they wouldn't come closer than five feet but threw the flowers. They must have brought a million flowers. Blushing, smiling little flowers dropped flowers at our feet and ran! More! More!

Why? From somewhere, from TV or somewhere, children have made the connection between decorative clothes, long hair, flowers, and the words "peace" and "love." We must have gotten five thousand peace signs from the kids on school buses, even through the hate belts. But that was the funny part about it. While many of their Navy parents cursed us out, their children brought armloads of flowers to us. A little rebellion? A child's innate good sense and desire for the things they thought we represented—however well we really did? The first revolutionary, the one they didn't stop quickly enough, was the one who said, "Love one another."

These children loved us with flowers, and hardly a word—as though we didn't speak English—and by the time we walked on, the little yellow field flowers were all over the streets and sidewalks.

It was a night of short naps but of waking up each time contented. The rain was gentle, the tiny drops floated down almost like snow. And I had floated through the night. At the crack of dawn I was watching some animal in a tree. Bear? Panther? Whatever it was, Plume had the thing treed. I'd doze again, then look over. Was it a bear far away or a cat close by? Another nap, then I was awake and watching the thing come down the tree—with such grace, such absolute control, and straight down; if Plume fought with it he'd be hamburger meat in a second. Sure enough, crazy Plume woke up again and barked it back up the tree. About six naps later I could see that it was a giant raccoon, about twice Plume's size. Once again I dropped off, and next time I woke up it was gone.

The commander had invited us to eat breakfast at the Navy mess. Should we do it? We were almost the first in line. We had eggs any style, steak, milk, toast, ice cream, doughnuts, toast, and coffee. At breakfast Gale and the commander discovered they'd gone to college together, along with his wife. After packing up, we went over and had coffee with them.

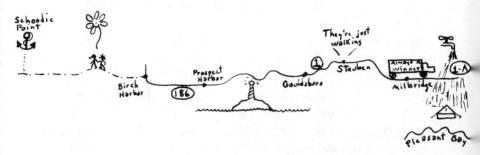

Everybody had been bused out, we thought, but while we drove to Steuben away from Winter Harbor we saw Ann M. and Lloyd walking blissfully down the highway, garlands of flowers in their hair. They piled in laughing. More than that, they were glowing. They were so blissful, bliss-full, so gentled, so beautiful, that they were like people from a better planet. No, they said, laughing, they were not "high" on anything. They had walked up to the top of the point, looked at everything, then were just walking along feeling good. I believe we saw the best Lloyd, the very best Ann—of all the thousands of Lloyds, the thousands of Anns. There was a glow coming from them that could be felt at least five feet away.

Before Steuben, Gale and I gave over the truck and walked with Gordon.

Tunk Lake, off to my right, was named by an Indian chief who stood on the highest surrounding ground and threw a rock in the middle of the lake. Tunk!

Why not? It makes as much sense as most of the history we are taught in school . . . and it might even be true.

Fishing boats, quaint villages, lobster traps, houses out on spits of land, waves crashing on rock, salt spray, lighthouses, the moody power of the sea, the same wind which sweeps over any level unbroken surface of the earth. There it is, and all of it has been painted so often that it makes one tired; yet who can blame the painters?

From Steuben, Maine:

SHERIFF'S REPORT

A group of walkers from Boston has raised alarums from the day they entered the county on their way to Canada. The twenty walkers, whose ages range from 14 to 40, have covered about nine miles per day and calls began coming into the Sheriff's Office from the minute they crossed the Waldo County bridge on Sunday. "Hippies!" say the complainants. A Volkswagen bus that accompanies the walkers carries their tents and luggage. The group has camped in Surrey, Lamoine, and Gouldsboro. They were expected to reach Steuben last night.

"They aren't bothering anybody," says Sheriff Fitch. "They're just walking."

Good for Sheriff Fitch. As for the reporter, there were nine inaccuracies, possibly ten, depending upon whether to have "raised alarums" is looked on as active or passive.

Conversation with a stranger: "Well, I've walked quite a bit, too. I've walked from New Jersey to Maine!"

"Really? How long did it take you?"

"Three or four days . . . but I accepted a few rides."

Gordon, Gale, and I were resting in a field near Steuben when a man in an old station wagon came by slowly, looking at us. His voice couldn't have said it any better than his face: I want to get out and sit down and join you, but how? He finally just turned off his engine and walked over. It's no fun, he said, drinking beer by yourself. So we shared crackers and two quarts of beer. He told us that if we could only stay over till Sunday, he could get his brother's lobster boat and we'd go out to sea, since all the lobster fishermen had agreed not to fish on Sundays. We kept passing the quarts around and around, and he kept talking it up. Impossible, but we really did want to go. "Why . . . we could go out there . . ." he said, "We could go . . . all over the ocean . . . drink . . . halfadozenbeers . . . and have a *helluva* time!"

In the afternoon we talked about seeing without categorizing and tried it.

Blake said: "How do you know but ev'ry Bird that cuts the airy way, Is an immense world of delight, clos'd by your senses five?"

What do we stop in ourselves when we say "red-winged blackbird"? Or to scenery, "It's lovely!"? Language is a conspiracy, says Fort. If it's lovely, let it *be* lovely.

Funny, tragic, lovely, sad . . . and 9 miles to walk before nightfall.

At Milbridge we caught up with Ann M., Lloyd, and Big Ann. Milbridge seemed to be a medium-rough town, but a bunch of high school football players came along, crossed the street, and went past us, without a word.

In the middle of town we ran into none other than KING REID SHOWS, "Always a Winner!" They gave us an old friends' hello, and we had a cup of tea with them. We also met "Jingles" and "Heavy," who ran the girlie show. Jingles invited our girls to see his wardrobe. First Big Ann accepted, then Gale, and then, with a sudden apologetic smile, Ann M., the cool intellectual. Everybody laughed at the way she did it, but after ten minutes we were all there, looking at Jingles' wild collection of shirts.

No, I told Big Ann, we were not encouraging visitors to the campsite, so Jingles was not welcome. But when we left, there were Jingles and Big Ann leading the way. Quite a picture: Big Ann with her mincing steps towering over little Jingles in modern dude cowboy black; Ann M. and Lloyd both barefooted—Ann with her loose long blond hair waving, Lloyd of the long curly red hair—Gale and I next, Gale in her stomper boots, marching along, me in my super boots scuffing along.

At camp everything was so peaceful—only green fields, the bay, and the tent—that I almost hated to go mapping. It was such a great site and I knew that by the time we got back it would be dark, so dark the tent might as well be in a parking lot. Ann M., Howie, Lloyd, and I cast it out ahead, found a good back road (and a fine little bridge) from Cherryfield to Harrington. At the junction of the back road and the main highway was a big sign: WE LOVE OUR CHILDREN!

At Columbia Falls, next to a graveyard, we settled on just about the most depressing, tiny, bug-infested site of the entire walk. That night it didn't seem so bad, though, and we had done it—roads, mileage, and a place—get back! On the way home, just as it got dark, the skies opened wide and we were hit with the heaviest downpour of the trip. Blinding rain. Off the side of the road we saw lights: BEER, EATS, CLAMS! We gave up and stopped. Ann M. was convinced that this was what mapping had come to while she waited at camp to feed us. Swearing wouldn't convince her. I think it was the only time we ate while mapping, but we made up for all the other times that night.

Why ever go back? The rain had driven a wall, not a wedge, between us and the tent. We had beer, fried clams, onion rings, french fries; and everything but the beer was soaked in tomato ketchup. We sat in the back of the truck, lights on, heater going, and had a long talk about the "break-down" at Schoodic Point, the night no one knew who was to wash the dishes and no one would take over. Ann M. and Lloyd—who had cooked—had left the whole mess after telling everyone off. Yes, I had heard the story, but not from Ann and Lloyd. I thought we should have a meeting the next morning on chores and responsibilities, on the god-damned practicalities, the awful, inevitable practicalities which hold us down to the ground.

The storm passed and we drove back on a slick wet high-way. Across the wet ocean-field to the tent, where a single lamp was glowing over the ungainly beast of the entire op-eration. Only Gale was up to greet us. "Do you want supper?"

"Well . . . guess not."

End of the day. Truck lights out, engine off, into the bag and sleep.

In the morning everything seemed completely disorgan-ized. Pots and dishes were half done, equipment was wet and scattered, stoves were wet and gunked up with food, there were no matches, and everyone was dragging around, getting up to what I knew would be an angry meeting. There was something else too. Our idyllic spot—because of a long day, late start and therefore late arrival, and heavy rain-storm—had been wasted.

Jingles dropped by early and was deep in conversation with Tita about Tolkien; dishes and equipment were piled around the entrance to the tent, and no one could move in or out. Nothing was moving, nothing could move. Had Ann M., Howie, Lloyd, and a few others carried such a heavy load? I couldn't wait for us to meet. The walk had become dreamy, just a stroll, just "be free"—meals, gas, washing,

destination, roads, shopping, all those things would be done
. . . somehow.

"We have got to talk about jobs, cooks, dishes, equipment
. . . really about consciousness and apathy, awareness and
consideration. Howie and Ann M. have cooked, with the
help of two or three others. Gordon and Phil and a few
others have washed and cleaned up when someone else who
should have done it wasn't available. This afternoon we will
have to talk, at the campsite, about who is going to take over
. . . and if you don't know how to cook, you can sign on as
a helper. Today, think about what you have done, what you
haven't done for the group. It's the little things again.
Jingles coming back today. Not stacking dishes. Not getting
your stuff packed together and out to the truck. Jam in the
peanut-butter jar."

A few laughed. But it was typical of the little things that
brought us down. "Sure, it's ridiculous, but if these little
things could change, it would mean we were really consider-
ing each other. Jam in the peanut butter! A perfect little example. Sure, I'm pissed off. And I don't much care about
jam *or* peanut butter, but *I* hear about these things. We've
got to accept each other, but we've also got to change what
we *can* change in ourselves."

I told them about a certain student (they all knew him)
who, just before graduation, gave everybody hell at a student
body meeting for letting him do all the work. *But he had all
the strings in his hands!* And no one else could pick them up
because he was holding them all. Instead of "accepting" responsibility, he had come closer to stealing it; in that sense,
he had done a disservice to everyone who should have been
learning to pull his own load. Undoubtedly the student
thought as soon as he left school everything would fall flat,
since he was the last martyr in the world.

I was trying to cut it both ways; to give Ann M. and a
few others credit for everything that they had taken on but
also, in a strange way, to assign them some of the blame—
for lack of a better word. To show them that *they* had taken

on too much and then, slowly, had taken on a feeling of superiority which soon enough was joined with anger at the others who did nothing. The trouble with "blame" is that it doesn't at all apply until the person who has taken on too much begins to complain about it.

The student who had felt that everything would go downhill as soon as he left school would not be around to see that others would fill the vacant slots as soon as they were open. Here, on the other hand, we could relieve the ones who had taken on too much and parcel out the duties to others. The "martyrs" could see that the world still went on. They might realize that taking over was their pattern, as much as it was the pattern of others to avoid responsibility.

To accept others as they are, we must first accept ourselves. In order to accept ourselves, we must first *see* ourselves as we are—our longcomings and our shortcomings. And this can never happen in a classroom, even in intimate seminars. We can only see while doing. After doing, and observing, then talk can mean something. We were twenty-one different kinds of idiots, and we still must learn to live together.

My tirade was over. At the end of the day's walk we would decide who would cook from now on, and how it would go. It seemed the perfect time for a fast, so I proposed it. Whenever we were hungry we could think of the cooks; who should cook, why we hadn't volunteered to help cook.

"You mean, no lunch and no supper?"

"Yes, no lunch and no supper. And no snacks. Only water. We break the fast tomorrow morning . . . at break-fast. Can we agree?"

Some nodded, others spoke up in agreement. Gale disagreed: we need our food. Finally, though, we had a tenuous agreement to do it—a weak unanimity.

We set out, thanked the owners who, although there had been no trouble, no sign of us except when we bought milk and eggs, were somewhat cool. I'd bet money they had been arguing about us.

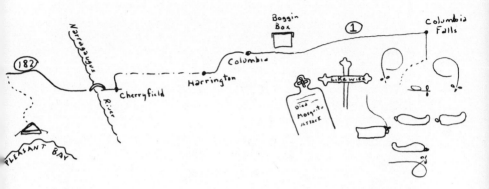

We were strung out, but we were starting together. For a long time I'd wanted to try to walk the entire distance without stopping; this would be the day.

Motorhead and I fell into a rhythm and walked into Harrington together, crossed the little bridge. Motor, whose lips were bloodless white, wanted to stop at a drugstore. I told him of my aim and we parted ways. He went in, he told me much later, to renew a prescription for penicillin. Even at this point he was pretty sick, but Dan was the only one who knew it. At the next corner I stopped at a store for a glass of water but felt embarrassed at my appearance and at the thought of asking for water without buying anything. So I bought a root beer and downed it in about five seconds. Why? We had agreed on water only, and I had broken the fast as soon as, if not sooner than, anyone. It would catch up with me later.

Way up ahead of me on the old, cracked, but very straight road were two figures. Walkers? We were the only walkers in the whole U.S.A., but how could they have covered so much ground?

It was Dan and Diana! They were as surprised as I was.

"How did you get here so fast?"

"How did you catch up with us?"

We stuck together, made only one bathroom stop at a filling station, and took off again. No lunch. No snacks, no candy bars, no potato chips, no fruit and no (more) soft drinks.

Fasting is not really difficult when one does almost nothing, but walking is very deceptive. Nothing about one's body is really sore or tired. Breathing still comes easily, but at some point there is nothing left. This is the point at which a person lies down and, in bliss, groans, "Oh, but these rocks are comfortable."

Long past the point where, for me, there was nothing left, we came to a little junk-antique-variety-store-café called The Bargain Box—"Boggin Box," the natives said. Dan and Diana stopped off and I clattered on the mile or so to camp, like the tin woodsman looking for oil.

Don was the only one there. He had been taken into Machias (Match-I-us) for a toothache, then dropped off. He was completely inside his sleeping bag, sweating buckets. Why? "Bugs," he said. Then they found me.

We were hungry, tired, thirsty, bitten. I tried to see it as an interesting time. Very interesting. Hot as hell. Slap! Smack! Stomach growling, lukewarm water to drink. More walkers came dragging in. We had absolute unanimity! The worst bugs of the entire trip. Even worse than New Boston; worse than the blackfly day out of Cooper's Mills.

Across from our thicket-yard, bugged site there was a bluff and a slight breeze. When almost the entire group had gathered there we started talking about the cooking teams, but the discussion was interrupted by some hesitant confessions.

"I had a Hershey bar."

"What? You sneaky sonofabitch."

"So did I."

"You too?"

"I didn't have a candy bar all day long."

"No, you just had a big bag of potato chips."

"I had a hamburger and a quart of milk. I couldn't help it."

It was time for my own breast-baring: "Well, I must confess, I had a root beer." And what a howl that caused! I might as well have shot my invalid grandmother. Others came forward with their little secrets. We were all laughing, pointing, accusing, slapping bugs, sweating. It was hell on earth. In fact, it was so miserable that we were practically in hysterics, laughing and rolling down the hillside over it. Some were really convinced that they were dying of hunger; the hell with it, they were going to walk back to the Boggin Box for hero sandwiches. I couldn't very well stop them, not after my little sin. They stayed in camp until we made up three teams of cooks and helpers. Howie, Gale, and L.J. were the chief cooks, and each had three helpers. Team 1 would take breakfast tomorrow morning, team 2 would make supper, team 3 would have breakfast the next day, and so on. Thus each team would cook only every other day and would continually alternate breakfasts and suppers. The driver of the day and whoever else was on the truck would fix lunches.

Howie, L.J., Herbie, Bill, and I took off for roads ahead. Big Ann, Tita, Diana, and a few others took off for the Boggin Box. Four miles of walking at the end of a long day didn't faze them.

Meanwhile we found an almost untraveled road through a blueberry patch on the side of a low mountain. It overlooked thousands of square miles off to our right—the most breathtaking stretch of road I had yet seen.

Herb and I were making some wild arrows on the dirt road when Bill drove off and left us. We could get to within ten feet or so of the truck, then it would zoom away. Once the back doors were flung open to a living work of art—L.J. and Howie faced us, or behinded us, bent over with their pants around their ankles. Later Howie got out to show us that they were really going to wait for us, and Bill and L.J. left him too.

We found another rugged individual just outside of Whitneyville who was glad to have us. The field was directly in back of his house, in a neighborhood of cracker-box houses, suspicion, barking dogs, and backyards full of wrecked cars. He was a young guy with a big family and looked like a cowboy hero—not a Marlboro country type who'd shoot holes

in you if you smoked some other brand, but a militant pacifist, as we discovered later.

We stopped in some little town for gas, and the fast was
broken by a few more. Bill, the bad cynic, especially wanted
me to see that he was not eating but stuffing, jamming, two
hamburgers down his throat.

Back at camp, Phil wanted me to admit that the fasting
experiment had been a failure. I didn't think so. "Not to
see yourself, in these experiments, is to fail at them. To eat—
even five minutes after saying you wouldn't—is to fail at it
only if you don't begin to see where *you* are. We fail only
if we remain that cocky. We said we would fast and we
didn't." I must say that Phil did.

Almost everyone was a little ashamed about not having
done it. Some claimed that they had "agreed" to the experiment only to the extent that they didn't object out loud. But
they must understand that by not objecting they had given
their assent. If they objected, they *had* to speak up.

"Let's try it again in a week or so."

"A week? We'll be in Canada in a week!"

We had walked over 400 miles already. We did discover
that ordinarily, all of us ate the equivalent of four meals a
day—so we *had* cut down. I'm convinced now that there
really is something to the idea of food as fuel, even immediate fuel. I guess I just learn hard.

Howie and his team turned out a delicious breakfast: eggs
on toast with thick chunks of bacon on the side, milk, fruit,
and coffee.

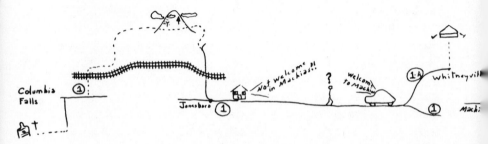

Memorial Day. Jake and I loped off together early enough, for once. We made that high blueberry path and breathed in the entire countryside—forests, hills, mountains. The whole area, the whole world, was off to our right; sloping, dipping, rising, down gently again, dipping, rising slightly, down, up a little in hills, valleys, ridges, mountains, and beyond them more rolling dappled hill country, still more mountains, and finally, sky. The last line of low mountains had to be nearly 50 miles away.

We did that stretch in silence.

The scene, the silence, brow-of-hill silence, undoes us, does us up again.

What do we really breathe? We breathe more than air. Oh yes! We breathe whole mountain ranges, we breathe fields, we breathe peace, we breathe sky and blue space, clouds and trees, we breathe birds, we breathe yellow and orange, we breathe the dreams of fruition of a million blueberries.

At the railroad tracks we saw three or four figures way down, coming toward us. They had to be walkers. Who else? We lay down to wait for them.

Logs by the side of the tracks. Piles of logs. Inhale. LOGS!! All piled on top of each other like kids' blocks.

I was looking at a pile of what we call rocks. Then I discarded the word "rocks" and just looked. Suddenly they were more than "rocks."

"Rusty barbed wire." I went over and looked at it without words, for words are categories.

"Language is a conspiracy." Is this what Fort meant?

The track walkers were almost up to us. Gale, Motorhead, Tita, and Phil. They joined us and sat for a while. The tracks probably cut off half a mile, and the four of them took at least half an hour longer to walk that way. Very direct, and a pain in the ass to walk. The same for power lines, except that power lines are often almost impassable.

"First time in three weeks I've cleaned between my toes," Jake announced, as if everyone would be charmed to hear about it.

We were, in an odd way.

Off we went down the road, which was a gentle incline in our favor. Houses were set back from it; there were side yards or wide fields between each one—ideal; lots of room. Just then a truck rushed by us, the first traffic of the day, with a sign on the back: CZECHOSLOVAKIA HAD A GOOD GUN CONTROL LAW!

It reminded me of other signs we had seen in the last day or so:

REGISTER COMMUNISTS NOT GUNS!

WHEN GUNS ARE OUTLAWED, OUTLAWS WILL HAVE GUNS!

While about ten of us were having lunch at a store in Jonesboro, where our back road joined Highway 1 again, a young man came up and said, "You must be the people they're talking about on the radio."

"What?"

"Over WMCS in Machias, the announcer has been talking every fifteen minutes or so about a bunch of dirty, disheveled-looking people heading for Machias. He ends with something about 'These people are not welcome in Machias . . . they are *not* welcome in Machias.'"

Although at first we smiled and shrugged it off, it was disturbing. Howie suggested that I give the guy a call, since we were headed directly for Machias and would go through it tomorrow—unless we were shot first. The student explained that the owner and manager of the radio station was an ex-major in the Marines and—surprise—quite militant.

Now that we were on the main highway we could see that his broadcasts—or something—were having an effect. Drivers were yelling at us, swearing, shaking their fists, giving us the finger.

Back in the Dark Ages again. Gun-lovers, people-haters. I decided to stop at the first spot I could and call the radio station; we had never seen a reaction like this one.

We were into the big Memorial Day weekend, and the national hysteria for road deaths was sweeping the country. The radios were keeping count of the dead; the announcers seemed confident that if we really tried, we could break the record.

I went in at the next roadside tavern. The manager was leery about letting me use the phone—maybe he'd heard the announcements. A call to Machias cost about 20 cents, he said, but still he hesitated. I gave him half a dollar and he allowed me to call.

First I got the secretary, then The Man himself. I told him who I was and said that we objected to his description of the group. What had we heard? To begin with, that we were "disheveled." Well, weren't we? Yes we were, and he too would be disheveled if he had walked 400 miles. After listening to a description of the project, that we didn't lug showers around with us, he did an about-face. I was salty; when he apologized I told him that I wanted the apology over the air, together with an explanation of what we were doing, and I wanted to know when we could expect to hear it.

"If you're listening in the next three or four minutes, you'll hear it then."

"Thank you very much . . . we'll be listening."

The tavern had no radio, and the people in the tavern whom we asked were scared of us. Phil, Big Ann, Tita, and I rushed out to flag a car so we could hear it. When the drivers saw four frantic wild people waving at them, they zoomed by even faster. It took almost four minutes to get someone to stop—the couple had passed us twice before they decided to risk it. The wife, who listened to Station WMCS often, twisted the dial and got it just as a song was ending.

"We would like to make an announcement by way of correcting an impression," said the voice. "We have just discovered that the group of people heading toward Machias are students who are on an experiment, an educational experiment, and are walking to Canada. They have been walking for more than four hundred miles. We understand that on a trip such as this it is impossible to remain 'bandbox fresh.' I myself remember my military experience in the field and realize this is impossible. We want to wish you the best of luck on your trip and . . . sorry!"

People told us that he made approximately the same announcement for the next three hours. The scary part about it was that our reception on the highway for the remainder of the walk that day (and the next) was awed stares, friendly waves, smiles, and shouts of welcome and "Good luck!"

It had all been changed by one telephone call.

At the campsite we told our young cowboy owner that there might be trouble, and his answer was as quick as it was decisive. "They come in here without permission, they'll regret it. I got a gun, too, and I wouldn't hesitate to use it."

For us, at that moment, his answer was more reassuring than alarming.

Bob B., Big Ann, and Diana had been throwing up for the better part of the day. From the Boggin Box sandwiches? No one was sure. Diana had recovered by late afternoon, but Big Ann and Bob B. were still on their backs—Bob in the tent, Big Ann in a bed in a little trailer. After Diana's recovery, Howie asked her why she threw up. "Because," said Diana, "I saw a buckskin pony and a Harley 350, and I couldn't decide which I liked best."

Big Ann, with the best of intentions, came to the tent to see if she could help her buddy in misery. "Can I help you?" But no sooner were the words out of her mouth than she threw up again, partly on Bob's sleeping bag.

"Yes, Ann, you can help by getting the hell out of here."

CANADA

Our problem was to get to St. George by ferry from Eastport or Deer Island, rather than by way of Calais. Some long-haired campers in a VW bus had told us: "Be sure and make Lubec and Campobello Island." At the time it looked impossible, but we'd stay on the coast as long as we could.

In Machias from a street phone booth I called Eastport for information about the ferry. No listing. Called the police —forty rings, no answer. No A.A.A., and no tourist bureau. We tried to call L'Etete, but no ferry service was listed. St. George? Nothing listed. Eastport police again. No answer. I was sick of the phone booth. Sunday. Emptiness, except for an A&P, which for some reason was open. Of course, out on the highways they were killing each other, trying to break that record.

We went into the store and bought candy. Through Gale, who had done the shopping, we found the friendly manager, who had heard the radio broadcasts and who offered his place, a house on Hadley Lake just out of East Machias, where we could stay for two or three days if we wished. He would come to our campsite at Whitneyville and take us out to see it.

Everything was up in the air, and we were saying yes to whatever came our way. Maybe we could even make the long night walk into Canada. We had two hours before we would go with the manager to see his place, which was 8 miles closer to Canada than our present site. There was time to drive to Lubec or Eastport for information. Let's go!

Ah, that was a heady drive! Harbors and sea scenes of Maine, but something more . . . CANADAAAA!!

We kept studying the map. Lubec had the flimsiest, thinnest land connection with Canada, or was it a bridge? We had stared at the map for so long that we were like blind men. Maybe we could walk across at Lubec onto Campobello Island—CANADA—rent a boat from there to Deer Island, and walk north across Deer Island to the free ferry (as some maps indicated) going to the little town of L'Etete, just south of St. George.

Lubec! Last of the US of A.

Over the international bridge to the little booth, where the customs man stuck his head in the truck, looked at the mess, and waved us on.

"Look at that red maple leaf! Isn't that beautiful?" We were shaking hands, clapping each other on the back even though, really, WE were still 40 miles away.

At Welchpool we came upon a small fishing fleet, stopped, and asked them if they could take about twenty of us over to Deer Island. One grizzled fisherman volunteered to take the lot for $20, "Canadian!" His cronies laughed. We laughed too. In fact, we were out of our skulls.

Back to camp, bearing gifts from the north—Canadian ale and goodies. The A&P manager was waiting for us, drove us to his lake house. Perfect! Back to camp. We'd have a short walk to his place tomorrow morning and then . . . maybe shoot for Canada in one long walk—at night. Even the sick people were getting well.

A discussion turned into a full-fledged meeting. Half the people wanted to do the short 8-mile walk, rest in the afternoon, take off for Canada that night, walk through the night, and be there by morning. The other half were up for the night walk but wanted to wait over all that day and leave on the following night. The argument was put off till the morning, and we slept.

It was broad daylight, our tent stood tall and beautiful; sunshine and clouds above us, Canada ahead, and for once no feeling of hurry-push-get-the-stuff-packed. Big Ann was much better, so was Bob B., Diana had recovered completely, and Motorhead was buoyed by some outside force. Lloyd cleaned our little Optimus stove and Motorhead was working on the Coleman stoves. Soon enough all stoves were working beautifully, and naturally the stove rivalry came up. Motor had "faith" in those Colemans; Lloyd, L.J., and I loved the little Optimus. Once and for all we would prove which was best—which would boil water quicker. The young owner walked back amid the preparations for the big contest and could hardly believe his eyes. There were water judges, container inspectors, lawyers, outraged citizens, bookies and oddsmakers quoting Las Vegas, speeches on why one container was better for conducting heat, what size containers should be used, and why a particular one would favor a certain stove. Finally each stove was filled with gas, pumped up to the fullest, lit, adjusted, checked out, turned up as high as possible. Motorhead was like an evangelist tent-healer: "Come on baby! I got faith in you, little Coleman . . . you're the greatest stove in the world, baby! I got FAITH!!!" He was screeching, jumping, pumping; two hundred times, fifty more for good measure.

The Optimus was hissing like a furious little coral snake, and the blue welder's torch flame was searing the supporting bars a molten orange. "*Listen* to that little sonofabitch!" said Lloyd.

"Noise don't boil water! *Noise don't boil water, baby!*"

The owner of the field was staring at us. No one else was surprised; this rivalry had gone on for weeks; now it was at a peak.

"Ready?"

"Okay!"

"Just a second . . ."

"Ahhhnn! Whatsa matter?"

"Okay, ready!"

"Let me pump it just . . ."

"Oh Hooooo!"

"Okay, ready!"

"Let's go."

"Five seconds . . . two . . . OKAY!"

Pots were put over burners. Everybody crowded around. "Stand back, give 'em air!"

In a minute bubbles were forming under the Optimus. "There it is! There it *is!*" Motorhead held his breath. Suddenly there was a swirling of water in the Coleman pot.

"Come on, baby, looka that! Looka that!"

"Lloyd, open it a little more . . ."

"It's all the way . . ."

Big bubbles in the Coleman pot.

Thousands of little bubbles in the Optimus.

"That's it! That's *it!*" Motorhead was out of his pale skin.

"No . . . just a second! Not yet!"

"Oh, shit, Lloyd . . ."

"Not yet!"

"There, looka that!"

"That's it! That's it! FAITH, BABY, FAITH!"

The Coleman was bubbling furiously.

Fifteen seconds later, the Optimus was too.

Everyone was jeering, cheering, laughing, screaming.

Lloyd and I trumped up some excuse and carefully prepared for another contest.

The Coleman won again! We were crushed. Motor was ecstatic.

What was Motor's blood like, right now? Something was running through him, jumping in him. His veins, his blood, were like a trout stream in the spring, the trout were bits of very joy in his blood; so many trout there was blood in his joy.

And all this time, too, he was really ill, and ready to quit the walk, because of a serious throat infection which only Dan and Diana knew about. Pale, wide-shouldered, skinny Motorhead with his almost colorless lips was really sick, but for a short spell he was the healthiest one of all.

After breakfast we had a meeting to discuss the night walk and Canada. Another deadlock. We couldn't conclude anything so we decided to break camp, go to the house on the lake, and continue the discussion.

An 8-mile walk? Piffle!

Our owner-host, again one of the have-nots, had been so good to us. The girls had taken showers and washed their hair, another group was almost a part of the family. The night before we had planned to have a game of kick-the-can with his whole family, but there wasn't time, darkness had closed in on us. They did come into the tent with us, sit around and talk. His wife brought pillows and helped tend the sick ones. There was no question of trust-distrust; we were them, they were us. Perhaps only with less affluence does this kind of sharing become widespread.

They were us, they were like us, loving, with a streak of fierceness—"Just let them try to come in this yard!" said he, this young owner of an old Buick with painted sharks' teeth across the front. How could we thank them? Words are not enough. Good-bye . . . and good-bye. Waving. All their children waving back; that little house, the TV, bathroom, good field, crazy wingless airplane on skis (like man to get off the ground in wild ways anyways), trailer-converted-dollhouse where Big Ann threw up, recovered, threw up, recovered; field of the famous Optimus-Coleman contest and nutty ecstatic Motorhead. We will remember them, they will remember us, and nobody needs to write.

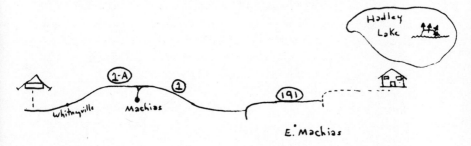

Northing around Machias, with or without a welcome; and sure enough the stateys, the ever-present stateys, pulled up before eight of us. They had heard the good news . . . we were all right. We told them we might make a night walk into Canada, and they told us they'd be on the lookout, and even waved to us when they drove off.

About a mile from camp Herbie and Bob B. pulled up in the truck. Could Gale and I go with them to Calais to get Plume inoculated? Neither of us felt up to it. Herbie pleaded. Okay. At the house supper was cooking, some people were going for a swim, but it wasn't quite the usual; there was a hum in the air . . . we might be picking up for the night walk in a few more hours.

Off to Calais. Suddenly Plume was getting more attention than he had in weeks. He usually walked with Bob B., sometimes went in the truck when we were on big highways, or when the traffic was bad. Plume seemed to understand a great deal. Once or twice we had had to go cruising back along our roads looking for him. When he'd see the truck he'd make a line for it, leaping, frisking; jump in, lick us all, everything but "Hi! Woooo man, I thought you guys had left me!" He'd lie on top of bags and clothes, lip-smacking, pink tongue out to the side, white teeth gleaming, eyes shining. Now we'd drive into Canada to the vet's and make Plume ours, officially.

The vet laughed at us for ooohing over "poor Plume" before the shot. Such a big to-do over a little shot.

On the way back we talked about Canada and the night walk. I didn't see how we could hold everyone back; the fever had broken out—Canada! Now! At the same time Big Ann was still shaky, and there was Motorhead. At the end of 8 miles he had crashed, completely.

Were we ready for it?

Back at the ranch the blackflies were almost stealing the equipment. Even when we went swimming in the lake they followed to sit on heads, get into noses and eyes.

After an early meal we had our heaviest meeting yet.

Impossible to put it all down. We went around the room

a number of times. Whether he really did or not, everyone was trying to speak for himself *and* for the group. It was terribly understandable, and there was no resolution.

We're *up* for this! It's going to be a beautiful night, a perfect night. It's clear, the moon is almost full. How do we know what the weather will be like tomorrow night? How do we know if we'll be as up for this tomorrow night? If we don't go now, we might lose the whole feeling for it. We've got the spirit now, you can *feel* it! We're ready! I know it's not a race to Canada . . . that's not it, it's just that we're *up* for it and we could make it on that alone.

And the other side.

Yes, I think we could make it tonight. *I* could. I'm not worried about that, but I don't think it would hurt us to rest tonight, straighten out clothes, clean the truck, map the whole thing tomorrow, find a place to stay, arrange for the boat, all that stuff. But mainly, I don't think we should go because Big Ann, Bob B., and Motorhead are still recovering. We've got to think of them.

"Let them speak for themselves."

Well, I mean, if the group is *up* for it, I'm game to try. I'll try.

I think I can make it. How far is it? If I can't make it I'll ride in the truck. I'm not going to hang the whole thing up.

There! It's the *time*! The *time* for it. Now! I say Canada tonight!

The Canada delegation marched up and down the aisles.

Gale spoke very well for the other side. She spoke also for a number of people who really needed the rest but wouldn't or couldn't bring themselves to stand out against the "spirit," the "now" people. Jake was exhausted (but, of course, would go along), Motorhead—after the morning—had died, sleeping as if he'd never come back. The Weasel was doubtful, although he said something that everyone there will always remember: "I'm really up for going but . . . there *are* a couple of clouds in the sky." Everyone rolled over laughing. Tita would try, if the group could agree. "I mean, whatever is decided."

"How far is it?"

"Thirty-two miles, almost exactly."

"To the border?"

"To Canada. To the international bridge."

"Then another couple of miles before we find a place."

We did agree, unanimously, that we'd wait at the bridge —whichever night—and all go across into Canada together. I was hoping that agreement on little things would help pull us together on the other. No luck. We argued for an hour . . . two hours. Around the room again. We had taken two or three votes.

Gale had become the chief spokesman for staying over. "It's not a race. Everybody knows that to say it, but I wonder how many understand it. We've really worked for this time. Even though Canada is not the destination, it's important. I think everybody deserves the chance to enjoy this walk, not to be dragged along just because he can 'make' it."

L.J. fought back. L.J. and Gale—the two Taureans—had really locked horns.

"*But who* CAN'T *make it?*"

"The ones who are sick! And I don't think I can either!"

"Then drive the truck!"

"I don't want to, I want to walk it."

"Then let's walk it! Tonight!"

Another vote. At least four people would not vote for to-night.

Could we get unanimity for flipping a coin?

"No!" said Gale. "I think this is too important to flip a coin over."

"*We* agreed to flip a coin when we wanted to go inland."

"Well, I won't."

Stuck! I must admit that I was secretly elated. I had even dreamed of this. Unanimity on the anvil, not in the classroom.

We tried everything. Five minutes of silence, suggested by Phil or Gordon (the Pisceans, the reconcilers), to think of what was best for the group; then once again around the room.

Nothing. Howie suggested that everyone go outside, into

the night, feel it, look at the sky, really ask ourselves if we could make it. We did. Walked around looking, staring, thinking, all the words inside—and soon enough, more words outside. Back in.

It did no good. L.J. was almost in a rage. If we talked long enough, it would be like a filibuster; the ones who wanted to stay would win, regardless. We discussed the idea of unanimity again. I mentioned that the possibility of going tonight could have been blocked long ago. I agreed that the advantage, *and* the responsibility, was on the side of inertia. But regardless of the bitterness, the feeling that we were pulling apart . . . we were pulling. Each person *did* have the responsibility to make himself felt *and* to be responsible to the group, so that we *were* like a family. And even if there was insanity in the family, we were stuck with it.

It was unfolding before us: one or two people really feeling strongly about something and holding up the group. The bitterness was a little surprising—but proof of the fact that the angry ones had not understood unanimity, only *known* of it—proof that the stronger ones did not understand some of the others for not being *up* when they were up; for their being tired or psyched out.

Slowly it dawned on us all. Ann M. got up, left for her bag. Lloyd passed the word that she would go along with whatever the group decided. Either way. That was nice. It was not disgust, I believe.

The meeting was breaking up. 11:30. We had hacked it for a solid four hours. The diehards stayed to argue. Howie wanted to take a walk, and he, Don, Dan, Tita, and I decided to walk into East Machias, about 3 miles away, and see if we could get a coke or ice cream. We set out. Howie had fought hard for Canada tonight; so had Don and Dan. I couldn't help feeling that we should stay over, but I had said so once and now kept it to myself. It was a walk without pressure.

In the recruiting letter I had mentioned that we would try not to say, "Isn't it beautiful!" But tonight we couldn't help it. The moon lit everything. Long sloping fields, shadows from trees and barns, then fields again; sparkling pale yellow fields, blue roads, blue-yellow roads, faces, legs. And songs all the way there.

We found a local hangout. Howie went to the men's room and didn't even stop up the toilet. The destination that night was as irrelevant as Nova Scotia to the walk. We strolled back, Don played his harmonica, we sang, talked, strolled. We almost had it both ways; we stayed over *and* walked that night. How would it be tomorrow night? Probably like this.

L.J., Gale, Phil, and Gordon had continued the meeting. Phil had really been drawn into it by now. They were tugging, pounding away at each other. It was 2:00 a.m. Some people were amazed: it had really been bad. Others thought it had been very good. Diana began to understand that she had never before truly said what she thought. One person *could* hold up the whole group. When would this happen with majority rule? Only when ten voted one way and ten the other; then the last guy could swing it.

L.J. came up to me outside of the house. We talked alone. "Look; I know this goes against the group . . . but I'm going tonight. I *have* to. I'll meet you all there." He was not quite asking and not quite telling me.

"Okay, go . . . we'll pick you up tomorrow when we go mapping."

"I've gotta go."

"I understand . . . take care."

"Okay."

"Have a good walk."

He waved and was off down the road. I knew that he felt torn—he was walking to Canada, he was back with us.

For a part of the next day everyone must have felt that we had been wrong not to go the night before. We got to sleep around 2:00 in the morning, woke up fairly early, swam, were eaten by blackflies again. Phil and I had a wrestling match which just about killed me; and the day was spent not in resting but in waiting.

But Motorhead finally confessed how sick he was; he could

hide it no longer. He wanted to be driven to a phone to call his parents for money to fly home. His throat was killing him, and it had been getting worse for ten days. The doctor had given him penicillin and warned him of rheumatic fever unless he stopped and rested for three days. Since then he had walked about 40 miles.

I talked him into trying one more doctor before calling home, "just to see." We got hold of a doctor in Machias (it was Sunday) and went to his house at about 2:00 p.m. In six hours we were scheduled to leave for Canada, but maybe Motorhead would be going the other way.

The doctor was hanging clothes out on the line when we arrived. Up the stairs we went, Motorhead, the doctor, and I, into his little office. All the time I was kicking myself for not noticing how sick Motor was. Other things were crowding in, too. How was L.J.? Where is he now? Can we actually make 34 miles without stopping? Make the boat connections? Find a place in Canada?

The doctor gave Motor a huge load of penicillin, laughed off the rheumatic fever, asked if Motor couldn't stay off his feet in some way for about three days. Sure, he could ride in the truck. Good, said the doctor. He had heard all about the trip and was anxious for us to make it all the way; he was from Nova Scotia.

"*From* Nova Scotia?" I don't know why, but it seemed miraculous.

"Yeahhh . . . Say, do you have any rock hounds in the group?"

"Well . . ."

He took us over to a large wall map of Nova Scotia and showed us where the good "rock" beaches are. Spring, he said, is the best time of year for rocks—agates.

The best thing he did for us was to calm fears, but he also gave heavier doses of penicillin and an old remedy for sore throat: to a glass of hot water add 1½ teaspoons of salt and ten drops of iodine, gargle this poisonous-sounding mess three times a day. We'd do it.

He saw no reason why Motor shouldn't finish the trip.

Keep going to doctors till one of them tells you what you want to hear. The horizon was clearing. Arrange for the boat, go back to camp, and "rest" till 8:00 p.m. The northern part of Campobello Island is the site of Wilson's Beach; it is closer to Deer Island, and maybe we can do better than $20.

On the highway to Lubec we got a slight taste of Memorial Day weekend traffic. Although this part of the country wasn't really in the game, the radios kept us posted on the highway deaths—the latest body count. According to the ads, all the kindly oil and automobile companies were very concerned and kept telling people to drive slowly, avoid accidents. No one had yet mentioned the only sure way to cut down on traffic fatalities; no gutsy radio station or big oil company came out and said, "Listen, folks, why not forget driving for this holiday . . . go out and take a walk." No, it was "slowly," but drive. "Carefully," but drive!

We got to Lubec, crossed the bridge, and there, slogging along all by himself, was L.J. He waved, jeered, cheered us and himself. His first words were, "I was wrong! I don't think the group could have made it." He had walked for over ten hours with only a few brief stops, and had averaged a little better than 3 miles an hour. An impatient but a courageous thing he'd done, to walk through the night on a strange road by himself . . . and a great experience. "It was a beautiful night, lots of wild thoughts, hallucinations, weird feelings . . . and fears." We still had it to look forward to.

After arriving at the little island's northernmost town, Wilson's Beach, we scouted around for a fishing boat to take us to Deer Island. Dyas Cook was our man. His son pointed to the horizon to show us where the boat was—a flyspeck against the sky—but it would be back tonight, and he thought his old man would do it. How much? $3.50, maybe $4. That would save us $16. We got his telephone number, and the trip over was set up for 4:00 the following afternoon.

We were assuming a lot of things: that we could walk 32 to 34 miles in ten or eleven hours, find a field to sleep in for

three or four hours, make the boat connection at 4:00, walk
the rest of Deer Island to the northern end for the last ferry
(meanwhile driving the truck to Eastport to pick up mail
and groceries and back in time to make the same ferry connections on Deer Island), and find a good place almost immediately in New Brunswick for a long sleep . . . IN CANADA.
All before nightfall. Nothing was certain—no ferry schedules,
no places to sleep—we didn't even have the boat yet.

Time, space, walking distances, chance, estimates—let
them be. We could bend, adjust, wriggle, scrape through for
a walk, boat ride, scenes, night, moon, and a great place at
the other end. So simple. Breathe deeply, then plunge in.

An old man of seventy years, in a house with windows so
old and so clean they were like jewels, let us have his high-
grass field. At the end of 33½ miles we could crash there for
four hours without the tent. In the early part of the walk
L.J. would be on the truck with Herbie; then at 2:00 Phil
would take over so both would have night walking time.

Back to the lake; we swam, ate, and packed up. We were
ready to begin but I was bushed—well then, rest while
walking.

It was the night before Canada.

7:30.

Howie was introducing people over his "show," giving up;
"Please say something to the folks—That's enough! Pardon
me; hey, you over there! What is this thing on your head?
Tell the folks. What? I'm sorry," shrugging his shoulders,
turning away.

"I am so *up* for this," Jake was saying, "I swear I'm'na *float*
to Canada."

"Whoopee, we're all gonna die."

"How does he *do* it?"

"Where's the toilet paper?"

"Nine minutes to eight!"

"Where we goin'?"

"CANADAAAA!"

Howie blew his whistle, brandished his stick, and we were
walking.

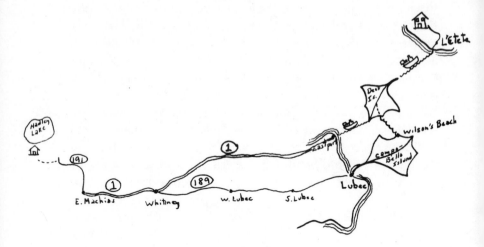

We walked out in the evening looking for night. Walking we knew, but not walking at night. Nothing could stop us, nothing could hurt us. But how in the world could we have launched into 34 miles so innocently? So confidently? Just "walk through the night," from the last of daylight through darkness and into the new day and Canada.

Through East Machias and past the store where, earlier, we had made a last run for candy, cigars, cigarettes. Two old men had passed Lloyd, who was waiting outside with the truck. "Goddamn hippies," said one. "Fuck you!" Lloyd said, in a loud voice. The two old men entered the store chuckling, and I heard one say, "Didn't like that, did he, Jed?" "Heh heh, no, he sure didn't." I asked Lloyd what happened and he told me. Good! All of us were sick of turning the other cheek.

Highway 1; gloaming. The moon off to our left seemed to take up about one eighth of the sky. My right little toenail was being driven back into my toe. Night came down, lights, hasslers in cars—license plates of cars threatening, zooming near us—Maine stateys patrolling and actually on our side. "Well be cruising back and forth . . ." Yeah? They were flying back and forth. Three or four cars out for "fun" earlier were gone by 10:00 or 11:00. So were the stateys. The road was ours by midnight, the moon was up high overhead, almost full. Stretch the arms out and hold the sky from one end to the other.

We also discovered that a mile was still a mile—that we couldn't just "walk through the night" but would have to drive ourselves through the night.

Panther screams? Unearthly howls, screams way off to our right. Eerie hallucinations, dancing lights, a house way out nowhere all lit up, an old man sitting by an upstairs window perfectly silhouetted . . . furious twenty-minute snatches of sleep . . . Christmas trees and hamburgers in the sky . . . flying saucers, oases, night mirages, hay wagons, sky trees, hot fudge sundaes dancing up out there in space . . . sopping wet fields of deep grass, and wild searches through them for rest, for the last sleep. The truck, the real oasis, with coffee, sandwiches, candy bars. The Weasel walking in his sleep: "My legs aren't tired but my eyes won't stay open; I just want to crash!" He did. Tita had already been picked up, and Big Ann. Gale would relieve Herbie at the wheel instead of Phil, who walked it all the way. When Gale and Big Ann were picked up, Herbie joined me and we told jokes for about two miles. Once I had him rolling around on the highway.

It's not just nice to have a road all to yourself; it's great!

From around 2:00 in the morning till 5:00, almost 6:00, it was ours. In that period there were not more than five cars. Lloyd and Ann M. would pass us, we'd pass them. Ann M. was sleepwalking, finally lay down in a ditch to sleep forever. Lloyd carried her part of the way. About once an hour the truck would come up, lights blinking: "How's it going?" "How many miles?" was the usual answer.

We caught up with Bob B. walking on blisters' blisters, staggering again—a shameful display. We hooked up with Phil, Gordon, Howie, and Jake and walked along together suffering, laughing, moaning. We were the only ones on the road; we were the only ones in the world! In so many ways the night is better for walking. In so many ways it is worse. Look up at the sky while walking. Nothing moves. The sky and the whole plan is laid out, as plain, as mysterious as anything about our lives; mysterious as our heads—our thoughts blown up a billion times and turned inside out. There's your head—with only pinpoints of light. Ever beginning, an endless beginning-ending, and all the time a black level treadmill was turning under our feet left-right-left, until the sun and Canada rise up and greet us. It was not exactly that the sun would bring Canada, but somehow . . . it would.

The truck came by just before dawn, with announcements of where everyone else was. Dan, Don, Diana were almost there. Rich had disappeared. Everyone else was strung out or dead in back of the truck. L.J. was at the field sleeping after helping to unload the truck.

By 5:00 we were reeling, but felt that we must be there. The man who broke our backs did it with the best of intentions. He worked at the international bridge and just thought he'd come by and tell everyone exactly how far it was to the bridge.

"Hi there! You're five and a half miles from the bridge. Exactly!"

"You've got to be wrong. It couldn't be more than a mile."

"Five miles? *Couldn't* be!"

"Exactly; five and five and a half tenths."

We made another half mile or so, staggered to the side of the road, and flopped, just at dawn—rocks felt like downy pillows, wet grass felt like clean starched sheets—too tired to bleed.

We walked up to the bridge around 7:30—Phil, Gordon, Howie, Herbie, Jake, and I. Bob B., Bill, Bob D., Rich, Diana, Don, and Dan (the last three made it to the United States side at 5:05) were sitting there. Four or five logs were in the truck. They were so *out* that their legs and arms could be moved without in any way disturbing them.

Overheard from the men's room, United States side: "There're some hippies in there . . . why don't you go get your gun?"

We were so sick of that kind of talk, so tired but so happy

to be where we were, that we gave them the double-whammy peace sign and "CANADAAA! ! ! "

After breakfast at a strange little cafe in Lubec, we collected again. Lloyd and Ann M. were sitting on the curb. "Was it a successful experiment?" Simultaneously Lloyd was nodding yes, smiling, Ann was shaking no, going, "Wooooooooo."

We did float across the bridge together, cheering, pounding each other, hugging into Canada—blisters, fatigue forgotten. Canada! Everywhere we looked. The red maple leaf fluttered in the breeze; and it is, it *is* something to hold and behold this red living leaf.

"The air is better!"

"The roads are softer!"

"People are friendlier!"

"Miles are shorter!"

"It's all downhill!"

"CANADAAA! ! "

Another mile, and we were humping along: 32 miles, then 3 more. Even Canada didn't help.

Sleep in that field was a sleep full of thanks. But four hours and we were up again. In two shifts we could haul everybody to Wilson's Beach. Gale, Motorhead, Bob B., and the truck, fully loaded, would go around by way of Eastport, shop, pick up mail, and catch the last ferry from Eastport, which left at 5:00 p.m. The last ferry from the north end of Deer Island ran till sometime around 7:00 p.m., and the island is 8 or 9 miles long—a 2½ hour walk. It would be close. Close?

We got to Dyas Cook's boat with five minutes to spare. We jumped aboard, the boat took off, the truck wheeled around for the race to Eastport, and we flew apart waving.

To sit down and still be moving was a rare experience. To sit down and to be moving over green water, green Canadian water—with coves, inlets, and little fir-tree islands everywhere—washed our minds out.

Dyas Cook charged us $4 for a 6- to 8-mile trip across water. But the real kick came from doing it this way. The map says you gotta go around here, go back up through there, take the ugh-way, and so on. There had been at least ten places where we managed to make connections when the map showed no roads, so we took old roads and trails just on the chance that we'd find ways to link them. Of course we knew that maps are only representations, but we began to understand it; our map-and-book minds were being stretched.

We got off the boat, walked up a dirt road to the highway, and headed north. Half an hour later I found a phone and called the Eastport ferry. Well, he says, the last ferry is just now loading up. Is there a blue truck on the ferry? No. No? No blue truck with painting on the sides? A blue truck that . . .? No!

"Are you sure that's the last ferry?"

"Yes, that's the last ferry."

What could we do? We walked.

The people on Deer Island, New Brunswick, are the wildest drivers I've ever seen. Motorbikes, trucks, cars, hot rods tore past us. There's not a cop on the island. They seemed quite happy.

Kids joined us, walked for miles with us, talked about their little island, and in every way welcomed us. Sure, they were always friendly when people came over and were willing to be friendly, they told us. But sometimes kids came over from Maine to start fights; then it was a different story.

We were plodding along, talking with the islanders, when suddenly our blue truck turned a corner and pulled up next to us.

Sure, no sweat; they had made it easy! In fact, they had been one of the first ones on the last ferry.

Okay; but now it was getting close to the time for the last ferry to L'Etete, so we geared up and humped along faster. When we arrived we saw a tiny ferry—room for eight cars at the most—and about twenty-four cars lined up, in addition to seventy or eighty people. Not a chance that we'd get on. Yet like a nightmare in reverse, when it came time for the ferry to leave, the cars pulled aside and allowed us to go on. These friendly and curious islanders had only come to see us off; they were waving and yelling "Good luck!"

The boat was ready to pull off just as we spotted Ann M. and Lloyd walking up, wrapped in blankets. They had been sleeping in some field close by. Three more seconds and they would have joined the islanders waving bye—for the night.

The fog and mist turned into a gloomy drizzle as the ferry headed out past mysterious-looking reefs, shoals, and islets. Up ahead was the Canadian mainland, and 45 walking miles beyond was St. John and the big ferry ride to Nova Scotia. It was a sobering, exciting, troubling fact.

The rain looked as if it would last all night. We had no place to stay yet, and it was getting dark. Groceries for supper were stashed away in the truck—an all-vegetable dinner, since we had been vegetable-starved for so long—now for a dry place to fix them in. Forty-three miles in the last twenty-three hours, and now rain. I would shoot for a barn within a mile of the ferry landing.

Almost exactly a mile away we found it, a beautiful barn. J. W. Andrews, said the mailbox. We had to have this place. Andrews himself answered the door, took us to the barn and up to the wide second story above a big fishing dory. He cleared away his dulse (a sea plant which the Canadians in this part of the country dry and eat), and told us we could have that floor.

Perfect!

It was pitch dark and raining. We found the entire group at a little combination hot-dog stand and coffee house just up from the ferry landing. The place was close, smoky, dimly lit, happy, and wild. Seventeen walkers in a room built to handle about six customers at a time. Rain, night, and as far as they knew they had no place to stay; but every one of them on the stools, sitting on the floor, leaning against walls had that silly slaphappy CANADA smile and dazed, happy eyes. We could walk through brick walls; what was a little rain? Besides, hot cocoa, hot coffee, hot dogs were coming up. Our shoulders rubbing together caused sparks, our sparks coming together gave us fire.

"We have a great barn, less than a mile from here!"

Great! But it didn't send them any higher. They were there . . . in a land of tired ecstasy. I offered to drive them to the barn. No, they were up for walking.

I would choose the barn we had that night as the most beautiful stopping place of the entire trip—for everything that happened there and before we got there. The barn was a perfect size; everyone had to pull in just a little, so it was people-warmed. The lamps cast a perfect light; downstairs Gale's team worked on our vegetable dinner, upstairs people were readying for night. Of all the meals this was certainly one of the best: broiled tomatoes, salad, cabbage, broccoli, squash, and a shrimp dish for the meat people. Maybe the best meal, and half the group missed it—sound alseep. I stayed awake as long as I could to savor all of it, just to turn it over. No, it wasn't Canada, but goddamnit, it was *Canada!*

Next morning it took us about three hours to find roads, but just out of St. George, we discovered a fine old back road and a ramshackle blueberry pickers' ranch house— deserted at this time of year—to stay the night. Inside one of the shacks I thought I had at last found my real hat, an old construction worker's helmet, but I couldn't quite go it. Lloyd put it on, and his red curls flowed out from under the old silver hardhat. Yes, it was Lloyd's. We also discovered —Ann M., Lloyd, Gordon, and I—that there would be wrestling at Blacks Harbor Arena this same night: WORLD FAMOUS MIDGET GIRLS—MIXED TAG TEAM MATCH. The orange placard had pictures of the girls in their wrestling outfits, ready for action. We taped the announcement to the front of the truck.

By now we knew that even on this out-of-the-way road, someone would report us unless we got permission. We decided to check with the Canadian Mounties at the station house in St. George, which was 4 or 5 miles from our shelter.

The Mounties told us that the owner was in St. John or Montreal, and that if we left the ranch as we found it we could stay there for the night. Score one for the Mounties.

"You say the place is open?" they asked.

"Uhh, yes." About ten minutes after we got there.

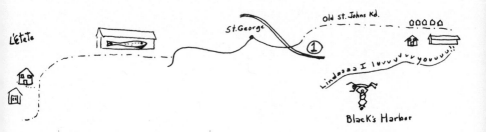

I made the walk from that wonderful barn—and the greatest two-seated outhouse I've ever seen, a pleasant, permanent outhouse—with Bob D. We took off for Blacks Bay, heard about the sardine cannery, and decided to go see it.

Some official led us through to watch the lady packers. Since the job demanded only their hands, the girls stared at us staring at the fish, their hands and flashing scissors chopping heads and tails off large sardines. They affected the bravado of a bunch of men thrown together, and Bob and I really got it: whistles, catcalls, remarks, while their fingers and hands never missed a beat—grab a fish and chop-twist-chop packitinacan. We passed the wife of the barn owner working away, and she told us we were welcome to their place—she even blushed nicely—while her hands worked without slowing, twist-cut-chop-pack: "Oh, it was no trouble." At the end of the tour we received two cans of sardines.

I don't know what anyone gets from such visits—I think of school kids and class trips. Fish are caught, the boat docks at the factory pier, long belts reach down into the holds. Fish are shoveled onto the belts which go into the factory, are chopped up and canned by people who work just like machines, then are sealed and cooked, labeled and boxed by people-machines or machine-people. But what does one do with that?

On one wall was the orange placard: WRESTLING! TONIGHT!

Can sardines all day. Watch the midget ladies wrestle at night.

We caught up with Bill, and the three of us walked the rest of the way to St. George together. St. George is a small shady town, not on any main path. Most of the day was spent there, recovering from our long walk, meeting up with each other, recrossing paths. If the townsfolk thought anything of this strange invasion, they didn't say so.

Tita was "grossed out" at the thought of seeing lady midget wrestlers. Diana, Ann M., Howie, and L.J. all took turns saying they'd stay at the blueberry ranch with Tita, because everyone else definitely wanted to go. But as afternoon turned into evening, even Tita decided she'd go see the midget ladies . . . instead of being disgusted, she'd take it in "a different way." Could the truck hold us all? We'd soon find out. Blacks Harbour was 7 miles away.

Many things were coming to a head now that we were in Canada and close to St. John. Ann M. had received a letter from her brother with news of a good job out on the West Coast, if she could get there fast enough. L.J. had to get a good job in New York for the summer so he could help pay for school next year. Dan had already been told when to report to his job; he would be leaving with Don, who was scheduled to be best man at a wedding in Connecticut.

Tita was finally feeling the pain of a thirteen-year-old among students none less than eighteen. What could be done? Hold her head till the mood passed, and so it did. The Weasel, twelve years old, had his buddies—L.J., Howie, Phil, and Lloyd—and somehow he adjusted or kept it to himself. If he had been a little older there might have been more of a problem.

But the black cloud on the horizon was that some people would actually be splitting off from the group—tomorrow. What did we owe to one another? What did each one owe to the group? The project? The idea? What would it do to them? To Us?

For the moment we put it all behind us, raced the truck across the high grass, gunned it, practically jumped the ditch from the blueberry camp to the road, and all, ALL, including Plume, piled in and set off to Blacks Harbour for GIRLS! ! ! . . . . WRESTLING! ! !

Ringside seats and a raucous crowd.

Herbie fell in love with Linda-the-Wrestler and stomped around, a marsh-walking, water-sloshing General MacArthur at the ringside: "I LOVE YOUUUUU, LINDAAAAA! ! !"

Once Linda stopped, turned, gave Herbie a peace sign, and went back to wrestling. We gave him a peace sign too, but he wouldn't listen.

Linda and her midget partner in the tag-team match were the bad guys, but we got the whole place behind us. So the strategy was reversed, and the bad guys were allowed to win.

At intermission a magician jumped into the ring, did a few tricks, and said he would show us how to eat fire. Would anyone volunteer from the audience? Who knows what Gordon had in mind when he leaped into the ring? Could Gordon "eat fire"? Juggle? Sardine canners and walkers were equally fascinated.

The man explained something to him. Gordon, hands shaking, head thrown back, mouth wide open, put the burning torch—black smoke billowing out from it—to his mouth. Closer. Closer! Everyone in the arena was going wild. Would he do it? Can he? Would he? Hands shaking. Head thrown back. Sardine packers screaming, torch just at his lips . . . He . . . He was . . . Hands shaking . . . torch just . . . head wayyy back.

Gordon would take the torch away, he and the magician would exchange a few words, the crowd would shout encouragement, and back at it again; hands shaking, head thrown back, torch flaming inches away from his mouth.

He really put on a show before he shook his head, defeated, and gave over the torch. Everyone in the arena— half the sardine packers from Blacks Bay and Beaver

Harbour, the canners from Lord's Cove and Bliss Island—cheered and cheered for Gordon, who acknowledged his fans and gracefully stepped out of the ring.

Meanwhile, kids who had seen the truck and were convinced we were a rock group called The Walk were busy getting our autographs. They came away awed at how easy it was. By the end of the matches there was a line of teenagers with scraps of paper for us to sign.

People were just beginning to file out when L.J. and Lloyd peeled off their shirts and jumped into the ring to give the fans an extra match. Linda told Herbie that she just couldn't go out with him; she had to wrestle tomorrow night, and it was a long way away. The local cops stopped L.J. and Lloyd, and we crammed into the truck and went off to blueberry fields forever. We even picked up a hitchhiker, who crawled in among the twenty strange bodies and never said a word.

Some of the walkers slept in the little blueberry pickers' shacks across the road, but most of us slept in the barn-shed and told ghost stories, old or made up on the spot, and passed the French brandy. Ann M. and L.J. told everyone why they were leaving, explaining their predicaments. Although there were reservations, everyone understood.

Breakfast was a sad affair. Ann M. talked with me and explained again why she had to go. There were tears in her eyes . . . and doubt. L.J. had to go, had to go—the job he had to get was ruining the trip. Okay. We drove them to the highway outside St. George (the main road) and left them there with sleeping bags and clothes. The walk would continue, but for a time we bumped along as if slightly derailed.

I thought of couples who talk so rationally about the "children": better to part than argue, better for the kids. How much is selfishness, how much is real concern for the family? We were a family; this was not divorce, but it was a splitting apart before our common "life" would come to an end at Yarmouth. We all talked rationally, agreed that it was for the best. But we really missed them, and it was much more than personal. Could L.J. and Ann M. have waited just a little longer? They felt they couldn't; it was "the time" to leave, so they did. And it hurt.

It was not a question of struggling on bravely. There was no question of making it, we would make it in style. Everyone felt great that Motorhead was almost well. One more day on the truck and he'd be walking again. That was our victory . . . but we had lost two others.

I think all of us felt grateful to the Mounties for not pulling "the law" on us. They trusted us to leave the place as we found it, and how often do the police stick their necks out in trust? But it was typical of our up-and-down luck. Thorny sticks and kisses, brickbats and orchids, knives, growling dogs, angry stateys, hearts-on-sleeves ecstatic old men, and kindly cops.

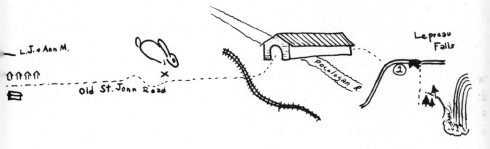

We traveled the old St. John road, as lonely a road as we had walked for a long time. Herbie's mapping notes show it:

> *Camp*
> *5.1 Rabbit, right side of road.*
> *8.0 Deer and rabbit crossing.*
> *9.1 RR tracks after covered bridge.*

More than 13 miles before joining the highway. I remember three cars passing us, not counting our truck, which caught us around one with sandwiches. Tita and I walked together most of the day, had good talks and silences, and then a celebration, an eye-sight: we rounded a bend and there, perfectly unexpected even though we had mapped it, was the covered bridge over the little river. The Pocologan River. No? Well, that's a nice name for a covered bridge to go over.

It is cool to walk inside it and inside our thoughts—I could hear Herbie's "Lindaa, I love youu," see Gordon about to swallow fire; we're here . . . we've made it to Canada and our lives will forever be different . . . and joined. We washed our feet in the Poco, and left no tracks on that unused gravel road.

"Dunrovin," "Holmes' Sweet Home," "Bless This Mess," in big letters across the fronts of the little vacationers' cabins on each side of the old road. We could almost hear them laughing—all the lonely people.

Up the road we found a greeting in rocks—artwork by Herb, Phil, Gordon, and Gale—and made the highway and Wagg's Store for fruit and cigars. Then on to the state park and our site next to a tremendous waterfall. This was one of the few nights that we didn't put up the tent; we slept in the pine forest next to the wide, boiling river down from the falls. Bob D. and Bill slept on the big rock as close to the falls as they could, and were drenched by morning. We played soccer that night with the kids from a big poor family living nearby. Then Howie, Herbie, and a few others sat in the truck and reviewed all of the places we'd stopped at, from the first night. We had running water and public outhouses, so Howie felt right at home even if the rest of us didn't.

In the morning we opened our eyes on a fresh pine forest, with the roaring of the falls in our ears—the day before the day of St. John. The plan was to stay over just outside St. John, then go into St. John for the ferry on the following morning.

Lloyd and I took the truck and found a broad, grassy field at a dairy farm about 8 miles from St. John. Just beyond the field the land fell away to a clear view of St. John harbor, big steamers at anchor, spits of land, water, ships, islands out of a dream. From the tall thick grassy field, the promise of ocean, a long ferry ride to Digby, beaches, bays, Nova Scotia, rocks for rock hounds, ocean waters for thirsty dreamers.

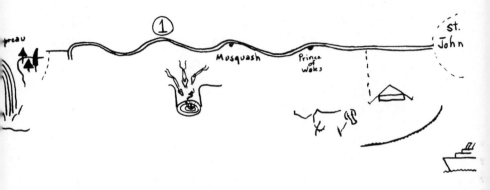

The walk to that field from our waterfall site, via a superhighway with its turnpike straightnesses and gradual curves (half an hour on one curve), with its cars flying by us at 70-80-90, made us feel that we were walking a tread-mill.

The Weasel and I walked it together and met up with Phil and Gordon. Just when it was hottest, we found some large pools of water under a bridge; dared, pushed, challenged each other until we were all swimming, yelling, freezing in the icy water, then cooking on tremendous hot rocks under a crystal-blue sky. Jake joined us and added his throaty, skinny screams to ours. The sun dried us and we were off again, with numbed feet for the next hour.

I wanted a picture of the whole group as we boarded the ferry for Scotia, so I stopped at a phone booth and called the local paper. They were more excited than I expected—than we needed. The papers told the radio station, which sent out a reporter to meet us at the site. We still had 8 foot-miles to go.

St. John, or its outskirts, might be rough. Some little nine- or ten-year-old kids went by us with clenched fists. Cars zoomed by, heads out of windows yelled the usual remarks.

The day had turned scorching dry. We went over to look at a large, limpid, clean lake, but sure enough:

NO SWIMMING

St. John Water Commission

Perhaps it was our attitude, but with St. John and the ferry ride and Scotia coming up, it was difficult to concentrate on the immediate, on each instant. Nova Scotia was in our grasp. St. John was all around us. We had denied that either of these was an aim, yet they got to us. Something else was going on, too. Secret conferences and quick trips into the city. Herbie and Howie invited me to keep my nose out of it, but told me that it was very important.

At that beautiful broad hayfield dairy farm, it was milking time and also interview time—tape recorder, mike, and eager reporter at the ready. The reporter told us he'd had a choice of doing a flower show or the walk. He had gladly chosen us, he said. Too bad it was the giddy time of afternoon.

"Now," he began hesitantly, "what is the purpose of this walk?"

There's the mike, all ready to listen. I don't know why, but the question downed us.

Howie told him he was doing it all wrong. "Gimme that." The reporter gave up the mike, and Howie with perfect composure started doing what he does for about two hours a day: "Excuse me, sir, but could you tell me what is the purpose of this interview?" He pushed the mike up to the startled reporter, gave him half a second, took it back, "Please, sir, you'll have to speak up . . . what is the purpose of this interview?"

"Wait a second . . . *I'm* giving the interview!"

People were rolling all over the field, laughing at Howie. In another minute the reporter realized he should have taken the flower show. Don and I went back with him to the radio station and taped an interview. The reporter told us it would go all over Canada.

Next door was a big "Y," and we talked our way into showers for 25 cents apiece, from 8:00 till 10:00 that evening. The reporter drove us back to camp.

We had milk about five minutes old, salad, a fruit dessert of watermelon, cherries, plums, grapefruit, pineapple chunks, grapes (peeled), oranges—enough for everyone to have three helpings.

The hot steamy showers were a celebration, and we stayed under the water till just a few minutes before 10:00. We hadn't had showers since the naval base at Winter Harbor, ten days before.

Outside the "Y" there was another interview and pictures; then we crawled into the truck. I don't even know who drove. After ice cream, we were back at our dairy farm overlooking the harbor, big boats, and dancing lights which beckoned and winked on the water. In fifteen minutes everyone was as still as baked stones.

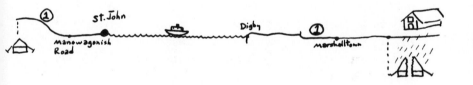

The ferry left St. John at 10:30, and we did the 8 miles to town (the last mile on railroad tracks) early enough to have two hours before its departure. But it was still a full morning: Plume was lost for an hour or more, we heard Don talk on the local radio station about "hostile people" and their fears of harmless walkers, and we walked by the famous Reversing Falls. We were amazed to find that a big plastics factory dumps its foamy chemical garbage into the bay, so that the swirling uphill rush of waters includes all the polluting foam direct-from-factory-to-you.

We had breakfast in town, and gawked at the first big city (90,000) we had seen for thirty days or so. Armed with Cuban cigars, we slowly drifted back to the docks around 10:00. I tried to arrange for icy champagne on the 2½-hour cruise to Digby, but there was no way; they had their regulations, and we'd have to pay $12 a bottle for it on the boat.

A photographer wanted one "spectacular" of a walker, feet first. Lloyd, the most obvious barefoot walker, wouldn't do it . . . no, absolutely not, get away. He was disgusted that I'd even ask him. I believe he even refused to pose for the group shot next to the boat.

Motorhead drove the truck on board with Plume, up came the gangplank, and we cast off from the mainland. Before we knew it we were out of sight of land. We retired to the bar, pulled tables together, and popped the corks. More whispering, and out came the results of two days' machinations. We were suddenly at the graduating ceremonies of the College of Walking. Our names were read off and diplomas were awarded by the members of the "administration": Herbie, Howie, Gordon and Gale. I received my Ph.D. and made a speech; there were toasts, speeches, champagne, speeches, more beer, old fashioneds, martinis, three more bottles of champagne, and more beer. We were goggle-eyed by the time we made Digby. Diplomas for Ann M. and L.J. were awarded in absentia. The St. John printer had spelled ambulatory "amulatory," so we were graduates of the "Amulatory College"—something between "amor" and "amble"; not a bad mistake. The diplomas had the seal of the school and signatures of the various deans, the president, and other dignitaries.

Nova Scotia looked like the promised land from the deck of that oceangoing steam ferry made in Scotland. But the real moment was when we stood on New Scotland, close to the docks, and watched our truck come off the ferry. Motorhead drove down the gangplank and everyone cheered. "Scotia!" "Scotia!" "Nova Scotia!"

Don and Dan told everyone goodbye, traded addresses and plans. Don still insisted that right after the wedding he'd be on his motorcycle to meet us before Yarmouth. Okay,

Don. For that little miracle we'd hold our breath. We knew
how he felt but didn't expect him back. The two of them
planned to hitch down to Yarmouth and take a plane from
there to Boston, but those plans changed a dozen times even
in the next few hours, mainly because we'd forgotten what
we looked like to the world. We had grown old together—
old, tattered, torn, scruffy—but to the normal earthling we
were just tumbleweed, or old rags, blown along the roads
and byways of the northeastern United States and Canada.

The road from Digby joins the main highway—South-
North 1—two or three miles out of town. Don and Dan
reached that intersection around 2:00 in the afternoon and
were still there when we passed them for the last time two
hours later.

For some reason Digby is a balmy, almost tropical city,
built along a main drag of open-air shops and cafés. It has
something of Bermuda and Nassau about it, something in
that wind, almost a spicy taste to the air. I wandered alone
for a while, stopped at a real estate office, saw pictures of
houses listed for five to twelve thousand, land, sites; no time
to inspect them, but I stayed long enough to find that there
is a small exodus of Americans fleeing to Nova Scotia to sit
out the revolution there.

Up came the truck. "Everybody's drunk; we better find a
place not too far out."

"Should I help find a place?"

"Yeah, maybe so."

Off we went. Gale was dead to the world in the back of
the truck, along with one or two other bodies. Leaving town
toward the highway, we passed straggling, wobbly walkers.
We passed shops that advertised agates and semiprecious
stones; we banged on one rock hound's door, but he wasn't
home. Past a Dari-Queen, where a bunch of walkers had
collected, out to the intersection past Don and Dan, who
waved a little sadly, and south on Highway 1.

We almost got a field near the intersection, but the wife
wanted the husband to okay it and he'd not be home till
5:00. On down the coast, mapping the last leg of this long

walk south to Yarmouth overlooking the Bay of Fundy. I
wanted us to settle in to ocean beach and quiet walking; and
I wanted us to get together, because something was building up—a not-good kind of pressure.

About 5 miles from Digby we found a place with a long
bayward-sloping field on one side of the road; the owner's
house and barn was on the other. Yep, the old man would
let us use his field, and if it rained we could use the barn,
a huge hay-filled structure with a skyscraping roof up above
the hay floor. We drove down a little road off the highway
and dumped everything, marked it with arrows, and set off
back to the group.

Don and Dan were sitting glumly on their bags. "These
guys, when they see *us*, they speed *up*," said Don. On to
the Dari-Queen and a ridiculous sight, or hilarious, or depressing. I had passed Phil walking along the main road
south and told him about the place; he was just as wrecked
as anyone else, but he agreed that it would do us all good to
"walk it off." He loped away with his easy draggy walk,
which I believe could carry him to the ends of the earth.
But there at the Dari-Queen were ten or twelve walkers
lying on the grass—out cold.

Instead of being hungover, I was filled with a raging
energy. Yes, both energy and rage. Why rage? I had the
feeling, an awful feeling, that the group was disintegrating.
We were leaves on a tree, and suddenly a little wind had
come along and scattered four of us. Now the rest were
fluttering to the ground.

The only thing was to walk. They had 5 miles to go before
camp. They were moaning, rolling around, or still sound
asleep. "You guys have got 5 miles to walk to get to camp.
You can sleep either here or there." I was about to leave
when one of them got up and said he was really dizzy, could
he ride?

"I think you should walk out of it, walk off and leave it."

Right or wrong, it makes me a little ashamed now, but
it's what happened, what I said; and I left. I wanted so
much for this project, and to see it crumbling was heart-

breaking. I went back to the site and helped put the tent up. Gale had done the shopping in Digby and the cooks would start fixing supper. The sky was threatening to break loose after a sun-and-clouds afternoon; the atmosphere was close, foggy, very damp—so was ours.

The sign at Dan and Don's intersection said 67 miles to Yarmouth. For some reason we had estimated the mileage as 45, a three-day walk. Maybe we could do three days at 15 per day and then a last day or night walk of 22 miles into Yarmouth. But even these, the last calculations, added to the feeling of disintegration and the idea that we were beginning to race again, with Yarmouth as the finish line. We *had* to have a meeting and get it straight.

For the following day we got a field out of Weymouth, on a side road behind the owner's house . . . no, he couldn't let us use his barn, too many things in it. Those roads were little used, and for the first 4 or 5 miles from the present site we could walk the beach. It could be a fine walk, ending with a stretch across a small bay on a railroad bridge without sides. A solid 16½ miles. That was the meal for the morrow.

At the tail end of daylight we ate our meal, in a rain that was as light as tiny snowflakes. Some had already gone to the barn. A meeting? Yes. Herbie pulled me aside just before going into the tent for what was, already, an up-for-angry meeting. "I think I'm going to have to cut out a little early . . ."

"What?" Et tu, Herbie? "We'll talk about it at the meeting."

The lamps were on and the rain was now coming down. From one of the four supporting chain links leading from the canvas to the center metal flange, there was a dangerous looking rip. It left the tent open from the cap two feet down; already rain was dripping in.

After a minute or so everyone got settled. In a way that I hadn't felt for some time, the overpowering groupness of our band hit me. But it would be rocked and shaken up before the meeting was over. I didn't answer the usual questions of where we'd get to by tomorrow night; how far from Yarmouth we were; how many more days, and so on.

"From the beginning of this walk, in almost everything we've done, there has been a magic about it. Some of you have felt it and talked about it many times. But tonight we have to decide, in all seriousness, whether it might not be better to stop here. We tried something; admit it was a failure, even if a good failure, and disband . . . it's nobody's business what we do from here on in. It's not the school's business, only *our* business. There's nothing forcing us on to Yarmouth . . . and there's nothing sacred about Yarmouth . . . I want to hear from each person what he thinks is best. Maybe the whole trip is really over. Someone else has just spoken to me about leaving early. We've lost four people; that would be five. Why not more? Why not let everybody go on home, any way he wants to? Nothing stops us from doing that! It's ours, and we can do what we want.

"I'm only sure of one thing. It is not going to peter out. The four people who left had all spoken to me earlier, much earlier, about the possibility of leaving . . . some *had* to, some felt they had to. But that is it. From this point, either we all go to Yarmouth together—really together—or else we split up right here."

A chilly rain was coming down; the mood was sticky, quiet, tense. But it was a thinking quiet, not a listening quiet, and the rain went almost unnoticed. Gordon had his hand up, so he began.

He spoke slowly, heavily, painfully, about creating a new spirit, really trying harder to get together; he felt that we should go on, share experiences, help each other.

Lloyd began by saying that no matter what happened, it couldn't be a failure. "If we stopped tonight it would still be a success . . . maybe the failure would be, maybe, if we *didn't* stop . . ."

It is hard to visualize Lloyd standing still or speaking. He is the original man-in-motion. But Lloyd, with words, had pitched it out farther. Suddenly I began to see the whole thing in a clearer light. I knew it might end as of this meeting.

Everyone listened to every word spoken. Every person spoke as if he opened his mind and heart to tell where he stood. "Unanimity" was bearing fruit. Each one had the power to stop it or help put it together again.

The rain came down harder. People moved in closer; there were at least three steady leaks. But the rain brought us closer together . . . for what did it matter? This is what was going on in the world: our decision. The rip widened a little. All of us looked up at it, wondering how long it would hold.

"I don't give a goddamn if the whole tent rips apart; I think we should sit here until we decide."

Tita and the Weasel spoke up. It was one of the few times they agreed perfectly, and one of the few times I felt they missed something that was going on. They both thought we should go on to Yarmouth. The Weasel put it straight out: "I really want to go on to Yarmouth . . ."

Only it wasn't "wanting" to. It was "us" going, all of us, or the walk breaking up here. It was *how* we went to Yarmouth. And the destination could not be allowed to interfere.

Six, then seven spoke up for continuing. Herb had come back in. He was ready to go; all the way, and together. Gordon was right. It was back to me.

"I didn't ever say we *should* break up. If we can really do it, and that includes two days after we get there . . . two days to talk about what we've done, and *then* break up, then okay."

Around the room again. Lloyd was game. No one else objected . . . *we* would go and we'd go together. "Let's make it a fantastic three days, then . . . the best three days. Let's get off the ground tomorrow! As if they were the last three days of our lives!"

"Let's make it a day of letting go," said Diana. "You want to make love to the person you're with, then *do* it! Anything! Go! Sit down! Run! BE!"

If we'd stayed there another ten minutes, we'd have been floating. Well, and what should a group do for each other?

Psyche each other up, higher, then separate, use what has been learned, come back, trade experiences, psyche each other yes, right, higher; separate, and use it.

"We've got to trade experiences more . . . What happened to you today? This is what I did. Did you try *this*? Try it!"

What we really faced at that meeting was the effect of four of the group leaving. The group was not sacred; people could split off. I'm sure that the ones who left did so in innocence—having no idea what they were doing to the ball of us. The forty-two-day marriage had been broken apart. But that meeting made it a marriage again, a tighter, smaller, rolling ball.

The meeting was over, but we took it away with us. The buzz was all through the tent. Yes, we could have started out that night.

People were dragging stuff up to the barn to sleep there in case the tent didn't last through the night. Howie, Gordon, Herbie, and I ended up at the little restaurant about a half mile south of our field. We got a bottle of wine, then another one, talked till about 1:00 a.m., and walked back. The rain had slowed and we flopped in our bags. There were some leaks, but we had our space blankets, and the rip at the top had not grown.

We were sleeping, then almost as suddenly, we were standing by the center pole. Sound asleep; then awake. We were still rubbing our eyes; some were still asleep; some were lying down but were asking what had happened. We stood facing the highway when we suddenly realized that those lights were not in the tent; they were the lights of a truck moving along the highway. Half the tent was down!

Finally someone produced matches and we lit the lamp, which was still hanging from the center pole. By that light a flashlight was produced. All this took a preposterously long time.

It had been an incredible day; an early walk to St. John, the ferry to Nova Scotia, the champagne crossing, Dan and Don leaving, the meeting, wine and talk afterwards; now what? Herbie was out cold. The conversation among all of us, plus his muffled answers, curses, grunts, while rain ran down our faces, made it all very curse-worthy, ridiculous.

"Hey, Herb! Get up! The tent's down! Gotta get up!"

"I know, I'm hip."

"But, Herbie, the whole tent is *down!*"

"Cool. Leave me alone."

He was going to sleep if he had to gather pieces of tent around him . . . if he had to float in his sleep.

It was funny until someone illuminated the big stone in one of the folds of the tent. Had it been thrown? How deep is sleep? Had I really heard cars? A car taking off? Someone else remembered it. These things register in some corner of the brain, but we just roll over, don't want to hear it. Shades of Limerick.

Then we found a cord tied to one of the end poles.

At times it is nearly impossible to believe the evidence that someone is intent on doing you in. Well, there it was.

Everyone but Herbie collected stuff and walked up the hill across the road to the barn. A neat, solid barn; and best of all, dry. Dry hay, dry strong wood floor, dry beams, and lots of room. It was 2:00 or 3:00 a.m., ahh, but those were happy minutes, settling into a safe dry place after being wet.

How much do we know? How much do we want to know? How do "things" break through to us? How much is felt, or intuited? Earlier, Rich and the Weasel had been arguing about ESP—"It doesn't exist!" said Richie. "Of course it does," said the Weasel. The argument was only a few hours old when I decided, suddenly, to go to the outhouse. I walked from the barn straight across to the outhouse, which was behind the main house and next to another barn. As I walked, something inside was almost speaking to me. Yes, you're going to the outhouse but there's something else . . . some other reason, because something is . . . something else is about to . . . something is happening right now.

I knew something, but I didn't know what it was. It was like trying to tune in and not being able to get a clear station. Then, just as clearly as anything I've ever known, I *knew* someone was down by the tent. I *knew* it. The rain was steadily coming down, deadening any noises from the road, which was more than a quarter mile away and separated by a low hill. Even the glare of headlights was not visible from the barn, yet I knew.

I started running down the road, came up to the brow of the hill, and there was a car with its lights on dim, parked opposite the little road leading to our battered tent. The car was more than 200 yards away, but I shone my little light on it and yelled. There were quick beeps on the horn, and in another five seconds the car was taking off. I was running toward it, but not in time to get the license number before it was gone, heading south. I crossed the highway and ran down to the mess of canvas, with Herbie somewhere in there. He was okay, but again had not known that anything was happening. He still wouldn't move.

Back to the farmhouse, woke up the old man, called the Mounties, ran to the barn to dress. Phil and Gordon were awake and dressed to go with me. We went out in ponchos, and within a minute or two after we reached the road, the Mounty was there.

He took off south going about 80, asking questions, totting up answers. He had some ideas but didn't get much help from us. The group he had in mind hung around a garage, and he headed for it.

The garage was closed; no lights, no people. We must have cruised around for an hour with no success. There was one car, parked next to a house, just sitting there, with three or more people in it. He checked it with a glance but drove off. Why? We all saw it. Perhaps it connects with the whole thing of ESP, or knowing more than we admit to ourselves. It was the only time the Mounties ever came close to dropping the ball.

Our Mounty friend—about twenty-three years old, and young enough to enjoy acing around at this time of night—let us off at the barn around 4:00 a.m., said to give him a call anytime. We climbed up to the hay floor and slept secure—even bastards who stone tents must get sleepy. At some point

Herbie, who had come up from the field, saw someone fooling around the truck; he ran after the man, who took off into the fields. Next morning one of the tires was almost flat.

Rain clouds clearing off, lugging wet stuff up from the field, talking about getting the tent patched, and a slow-gathering breakfast. The farmer and two of his sons came out to talk. They paraded their frisky seven-year-old Percheron into the yard for us—a huge, sensitive, playful animal.

At last the truck was loaded. A basket of pots, the one-burner Coleman stoves, and a few other things had evidently been stolen. What did it matter. It was the day of the new beginning; everyone was a little self-conscious, and ready to start.

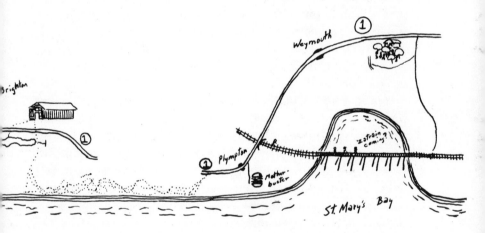

Bob B., Motorhead, and I were almost the last to leave, and we went together. We decided to have coffee at the restaurant just down from us and talk about the day. Bob B. had trouble homing in on something he really wanted to do. What stood in his way? A certain kind of laziness, a mental laziness, he admitted. Could he work with that today? Do it! Motorhead wanted to try the blindfolding again, work on descriptions to each other. I wanted so badly to get into ocean, to become rocks, sand, beach, to get inside sky-ocean-toes-beach-legs-seaweed-sun-clouds; to walk together but separately, silently, slowly. This whole long trip we had not had a session of beach without road. Now we could count on no traffic, because there could be none.

After a 4-mile stretch of beach, road and beach came together at a little park. We could leave the beach there or continue at that 4-mile checkpoint.

As we left the café and crossed the highway, a big bus steamed past us. GO ACADIAN, said a sign on back. We found out months later that Dan and Don had been waving frantically behind the closed tinted windows of that big exhaust wagon, going back to Digby and home via St. John again.

When we got to the beach we would go into a period of silence; instead it was a state—one state for the three of us which lasted for over two hours—two hours, a couple of weeks, seven years, or maybe we're there still—and covered no more than a mile and a half; for we wandered out of time, conscious-unconscious, probably never more than a hundred yards apart and not much closer.

Shells, rocks, boulders, logs; our eyes fastened, let go, picked up, were painted, dropped objects, seized others, dropped earth-beach-ocean, added clouds, heavens, suns, spaces between, dropped and tasted winds, gulped ocean and breezes, let them go through us, let them go holding on, stopped and stared at a log, sands, coiled shells or smooth sailing rocks, sailed them—a thousand, a million shades of brown, nine hundred purples.

Shells on a beach mark one location, as lines in each hand mark one person in all the world. If we knew enough, with even one handful of shells we could say this handful is from 5 to 7 miles south of Digby, Nova Scotia. Yes, but something better was happening.

Therapeutic? Like ping-pong for not-quite-lunatics? For semiconscious ants? Better. As if actual scales were falling away. Wind rushes between us. Separates, joins us. Sun. Blue. Dazzling beach. Water rolling, rolling.

And if they're not semiprecious stones? Just pretty rocks? Well, I can keep them . . . either here or there, just look them over good—the sun comes out, pages turn gold-yellow-silver—means I have them; they're on the beach south of Digby, within walking distance of where I left them. No? Then I have them somewhere else.

To possess without holding is a little like owning the world. But my pockets drag even while I debate carrying *all* I want, or none.

Suddenly I was afraid for the state I was in. The balance. The overwhelming with-it feeling. And the futility of words. The most generous time. The most selfish. The best day of the walk? Best morning? Best hour, minutes of my life? What is there to compare it with, and why?

Sounds of ocean. Three walkers tracing a way across the beach, staring, looking through sight, letting beach-rocks-ocean-shells in, letting them go. Letting eyes see, letting things pass in-out, no barriers, no words no names, letting ears hear, in-out, a gentle ear-breathing, an eye-breathing, in-out. Porous bodies with ocean breezes passing through.

We forget one another, quiet and pure, all powerful and empty. The emptiness is irradiated by the light of the heart of heaven. The water of the sea is smooth and mirrors the moon in its surface. The clouds disappear in blue space; the mountains shine clear. Consciousness reverts to contemplation; the moon-disk rests alone.

The sun hits us, strikes us, smiles on us.

When there is no consciousness of the difference between subject and object . . . then plants and animals behave like human beings . . . and everything is alive with ghosts and gods.

And categories fall away. Sick or well? No; sick-well, and the states of real health. Insane or sane? No; insane, sane, and the states beyond.

Around the world in 4 years; there's your background. Take on the world's languages, the world's bureaucrats, the world's mountains, paths, trails, lakes, oceans, highways and low-ways, the world's towneys, cops, saints, rock throwers; and walk. Walk! Just check it all out.

Match that, you colleges; Match that with your books!

Almost two hours of wandering. Motorhead walked up; we nodded; Bob B. comes over, and Motor breaks the silence: "Now, before I show you this rock, I want to tell you that rocks . . . well, you don't notice them so much . . . but you *know* that no two rocks are alike. I mean no two fingers are alike . . ." All three of us are laughing, grinning about our rock collections, handsfull, pocketsfull; but Motorhead was evangelistic about rocks: "I mean, rocks are *so* unique . . ." Then he shows us THE rock. "But LOOK!"

Bob B. showed us his, I showed mine; all of us were amazed that the others could only really SEE their rocks. Motorhead tried again: "But *that rock*," as the sun came out, "that rock deserved it! That rock *needed* it." Motorhead was well again.

And we had experienced very much the same things: the colors; having all the beautiful rocks but leaving them there; the uniqueness of each grain of sand. And such a strength in not knowing the names of things. That thing over there? Why, that's . . . one of *those* things. Was it precious? Semiprecious? Who knows? Do you *like* it? Keep it—in your pocket or there on the beach.

And now hunger. On the beach there were no towneys, no cars, and no lunch. We jumped over small streams flooding down to join the ocean. For two or three hours the tide was coming in, was still coming in when we reached the little park. Our walk had covered 4 miles. And how much more.

When we hit the road it was as if we were rejoining the world. What's happening to the others? What about the tent? Did they find a place to fix it? Have they been by with lunch?

Between Plympton and Weymouth there is a little intersection, with a store up a mile or so. We walked that road with purpose. At the store—totally French-speaking, a reminder of how far we'd walked—we picked up flat cakes of local bread, mayonnaise, mustard, bologna, canned tomatoes, lettuce, and cheese. Sloppy cake sandwiches which we ate at a table by the side of the store. Motherbusters!

Howie and Bob D. drove up with the truck. They eyed our Motherbusters and had to have some.

About a mile or two farther was a stream, Howie said; follow that stream to the bay-ocean. "You've got to see this place! . . . Gimme another bite of that." "That's a Motherbuster!" "Best Motherbuster I ever ate."

Past a church and through a heavily wooded section, with only the crazy belief that the bay was straight ahead. It had to be. We cut south and found the stream. Yes, it was a rusher, a rush-faster climber over rocks, hustling white rockbuster of a stream. But we had to bend under bushes to follow it. One more bush . . . one more . . . one last bush, and there was the whole bay.

The stream rolled, splashed out over a bank of rock into an almost round pool, making a fall of about three feet. The pool was four feet deep in the middle. At high tide it would be part of the bay, but at this time it was about three inches above sea level.

Water . . . in our eyes and ears all day, and still it was so different to sit by the stream and watch it splash, gurgle, run over the lip to the ocean and incoming tide. Motor and I dumped our clothes. Bob B. was content to sit and rub his poor feet while we dunked ourselves in the icy stream, knelt under the falls, and let the water come down our heads over our eyes, dimming the long view of bay water, of tide still on its way in. Then, out from under the falls lying in water up to the chin in this still but overflowing pool, from this tramp's natural palace, the eyes at water level sweep a low-lying island five miles off. Long Island, says the map.

The afternoon was a calm walk into Weymouth along the highway, with no hint of trouble, very few cars, fewer remarks. There were only some quiet stares; I guess that should have warned us.

Before the center of town, the railroad tracks took us to the minute station, then straight across a little bay on the railroad bridge without sides, to about a mile from our site.

If I was looking forward to anything that day, even in the back of my mind, it was this bridge without sides. We walked it a little before dusk, a perfect short walk. The waters of the bay were as smooth as glass and reflected evening sky colors in the middle, and banks of trees toward or near the banks. Under our feet were the smoky brown ties and beams. Out to the sides? Nothing.

Whoever walked the bridge spent at least half an hour on a fifteen-minute walk. We walked to the middle, sat down on the little island of wood, and talked.

Gale, Big Ann, and Diana had stopped for a wedding, and of course they had to toast the bride and groom . . . a few times. The bride's father ran a filling station, and he never quite left the job but never stopped celebrating. By the time they got to the bridge, it hit them, and Gordon (who admitted later he was "shaking on the inside") calmly led them across by hand. At one point Gale called back to the others: "Is there a train coming?" "What?" "*Is a train coming?*" By the time it was passed back to the end, it had become a statement and started coming back as news.

"A train's coming!"

The bridge is so narrow that they would have had to dive off or hang on to the very edge. A real-life Henny-Penny story. Very funny—afterwards.

The last quarter mile to the field was a comedown. The field we had been so happy about because of its privacy was the subject of close scrutiny by slow-cruising towneys, who made the special turn off the main highway just to see the freaks. All the signs were there—another night with the towneys. Before long we had the license numbers of ten cars whose occupants yelled from windows, cursed us out, or came by again and again staring—the quiet ones.

Cars with plastic Jesuses, beads hanging over the rearview mirror, wiggly dolls in the back or front; two-tone red and black hardtops and creamy white cars—American or Canadian—could usually be counted on for fun. Should we pass our scientific findings on to the National Commission on Causes and Prevention of Violence?

As it got dark, the remarks from the cars grew louder.

The hell with this; I'd call the Mounty now. The great day,

the walk on the beach, the bridge, the soft evening colors, sea, waterfall, all of that was tucked away and now was something else.

The owner's wife was reluctant to open the door so I could use the telephone, but finally the husband came down, peered at me through the glass, and let me in. Luckily I got the same Mounty who had helped us the night before. He'd be right down.

I had such mixed feelings: something of shame in having to call in the establishment, the notion that maybe I was overreacting, and irritation at the thought. Yet what is best can only be decided by hindsight, and we were not into to-morrow, we were here, now, at 9:15 p.m. All of the feelings from Limerick were back: about violence, ignorance, pacifism, consciousness, brutality—about what we say we are and what we really are. How far to retreat, who would get hurt, why, how, when. The only certainty is that all of us will, in one way or another, and time after time, make fools of ourselves.

In the same town a year before, five hikers, short-haired transients, had been chain-whipped by a group of the locals —beaten so badly they had to be carried out of town to a hospital. We didn't know that till late the next day.

Back at the field there was no diminution of traffic. I de-cided we should go into the woods behind the house. We would leave the lights and a few people near the truck until all but the last pieces of gear were over the barbed-wire fence and into the copse of trees behind the owner's house. Then, and only then, we'd move the lanterns and the truck. When cars came by we lay down until they went past; then we moved toward the woods again. When there were no cars passing, we took the truck across the field and down a steep incline, backing it so that it was facing the field. If we had covered the headlights with a dark cloth it might have gone unnoticed; more hindsight.

Tita and Diana got into the truck, four or five others were way across the field at various spots, but the knot of us were together near the truck arranging sleeping bags and air mattresses. All of us had some sort of makeshift weapon: a shovel, a thick walking stick, a knife. No excuses. If anyone came in after us, they would encounter at least one raving, stick-wielding, scared-to-death fighting lunatic.

We had planned on a meeting to talk about the day, this new-beginning day, and we did get started on it. Then a car came by, slowed down, and stopped. It received our full attention. The Mounty! He was about to drive away by the time I ran up to him. I yelled, he got out. I gave him the license numbers, repeated the threats, told him that we were back in the woods.

"Well . . ." he said, "if they come in there, don't be afraid to kill 'em."

What? If they come in there, kill 'em. Jesus . . . can't we do something other than that? Them killing us, or us killing them? We're just at the edge of a field in Nova Scotia, inky-black night, and a Northwest Mounty about half my age advises me to kill 'em. But he'll be around. To referee the fight?

Back to our little gathering. "What'd he say?" "He sayyy 'Kill 'em.'"

We began again, each one telling of his day, when suddenly, from the truck: kicking, struggling, fighting, screaming! *Inside the truck!*

My God! Tita and Diana!

Hating every step of it—the need for it—we were running to the truck with sticks and shovels, not to kill . . . but to . . . well, who can speak for his intentions or his sanity at those moments?

We flung open the doors; there were Diana and Tita and Motorhead . . . laughing. In fact, weak from laughter. And fright!

Motor had been watching the two girls, very slowly, very quietly, arranging things inside the truck so they could have room to sleep. "They would pick up a thimble . . . and creep to the other side of the truck and put the thimble down . . . verrrry quietly."

He watched as long as he could, then started yelling and

kicking things out of the way, thereby clearing a place for them inside of five seconds. "It would have taken them three hours, at the rate they were going!"

Back to our meeting; but every time a car came by, there was a lowering of voices, a drop-off of interest. The Mounty was waiting, lights off, around the corner next to the owner's house on the main highway.

Suddenly a car stopped. Way across the field, but at a spot where there was a driveway into the field. It had a rickety barbed-wire gate, easily opened. The gate was no more than a legal barrier. The car backed up, turned toward us, stopped. It was at such an angle that the headlights picked up the lights of the truck. They might not have seen us, but there was no doubt that they had seen the truck.

Five seconds. Ten seconds. Don't be afraid to kill 'em.

Yeah.

The car backed out onto the road, started toward us but still on the other side of the fence, cruising slowly. We watched them come closer; they were looking out at the field, the woods, at us. How were our glances crossing? Dark. Light. Hope. Fear. Anger.

The car almost stopped opposite the rickety gate closest to us. The locals were pulling off slowly when the Mounty gunned his car, swung the corner with his lights flashing, and stopped them. We nearly cheered. The exchange was almost close enough to be overheard. He talked to them a long time, and as the conversation went on they quieted.

At first we could hear them: ". . . Hippies! . . . Commies! . . ." Then he was checking their licenses, taking down names, and there was no talk at all. A few more words and they drove off. After an hour or so, at around midnight, the Mounty left. I had the sinking feeling that Canada was just another state of the union.

When it came my turn to "watch," it was close to 2:00 a.m. The night was neither cold nor warm, but I was shivering, naked, half in, half out of the sleeping bag, holding on to my 7-foot tree trunk of a "stick." Everybody was sound asleep.

I began by listening to every car that came by, then every cricket, every twig snap, every breath of every walker. I was listening to my pores closing, to my goose bumps rising, brushing aside the undergrowth of hair. I could hear ants farting.

What the hell was I doing? Naked, shivering, waiting. Holding a big stick and breathing softly. Astounding minutes, and somewhere at the back of me was a voice saying: Okay, okay, just like it is.

My hearing had become so acute that it was tuned beyond anything I really needed, or I would have heard the voices sooner. Finally I did hear them . . . a whole gaggle of voices. Twenty? Forty people, walking on the highway?

Well, of course! And what else would they be doing at that hour? Coming to get us, of course. The voices grew louder. The big clump of them were now in front of the owner's house.

Wake everyone up? Another thirty seconds and they'll turn right at the corner. They must be turning now. Another second or two.

Here was the feeling again. How do I find myself just here? But man, I *do* find myself here. Eyeless in Gaza. Naked in Scotia . . . with a big stick. Don't be afraid to kill 'em!

The voices weren't coming any closer. Not yet.

Fading? I cursed myself for hearing what I wanted to hear. Lying to myself. Of course they were heading for us. Where else? Who walks any more? At 2:00 a.m.? Or p.m.?

Fading. The voices were fading! For whatever crazy reason, those people, the whole gang of them, were continuing down the main highway. At 2:00 in the morning. Would they come back when they discovered their mistake?

Fifteen minutes later there wasn't a sound.

Dawn, early light, life, all of us in one piece. Oatmeal for breakfast. Coffee. We ate in a thankful silence; silence because we had planned it. Thankfulness? Oh Lordy. Sky, trees, eyes to see with.

The tent was just so much cloth, a big heavy neutral hunk

of cloth. With memories. We loaded it on the truck with no
definite plans for how, or even if, it should be mended. We
had at most three nights on the road. And then?

Just before the truck drove off, we broke the silence. The
group walking by at 2:00, someone decided, must have been
coming home from a dance. Gale would meet me at noon
and we'd walk together. Those on the truck would look for
a place to have the tent mended, maybe at the boat yards.

Sunday. Within 2 miles we were in a totally French-speaking part of Nova Scotia, and Long Island was falling away
from us. The waters out there were changing names: the Bay
of Fundy was coming to be Atlantic Ocean. The waters seem
to care not at all.

We walked into a little French store; signaled, pointed,
grunted for penny candies, drinks, stunted and dusty oranges
all the way from Florida—squashed most of the way, by the
looks of them. The oranges were expensive and we paid up.

Around noon of this calm, stiff day we walked over to
see a tremendous wooden church. The insides of these
churches are breathtaking. The sun, and blinding white
woodwork; worldly issues are obliterated at the threshold.
The door closes and the outside is forgotten. The difference
between the Bay of Fundy and the Atlantic is nothing. But

to leave the blinding sunny highway, the curious and huddled poor French at the grocery store, the flat stretching endless waters of Fundy-Atlantic, endless blue sky above, and walk under the arches and the far-off ceiling of one of those cathedrals is to walk into another state: mental state, physical state, geographical country.

Tita, Big Ann, Herbie, Phil, Jake, the Weasel, and I went in. The Weasel, true to the knight's code of a twelve-year-old, had to climb up into the high rafters and I, true to mine, had to shoot him down.

We seemed to have been there for hours, such time as unwinds all the usual timepieces, when the organ in this empty church—the arched roof of which goes up for at least 120 feet—sent out its whistling notes, piercing the air with a harmonized and easy version of "Sit by My Side."

There is a Spanish expression for the occasion when a person arrives unexpectedly just as a sumptuous meal is being served: "It's better to arrive in time than to receive an invitation."

Not only had we arrived in time, but if we had seen notices for an organ recital we would probably have walked on by. The ticket was *be* there, and we were.

The two organists played one folk song after another without a pause for announcements, and the six listeners listened as if they had nothing else in the world to do. I had never understood so clearly the feeling, whatever-comes-our-way: rain, sun, beach, church, organ music. Maybe, finally, we had begun to understand what our own talk was all about. Dig it! Be there! Walking at our snail's pace was finally paying off.

"Greensleeves." We drank up every note as if, at any instant, the organists might stop. No, they went through it and on to others. Then, just as suddenly, they did stop and were gone. I don't even know if they saw us. No applause, no acknowledgment.

An empty church is a certain kind of temptation, and we succumbed.

Herbie started it. He went up the aisle about thirty feet, stuck his weird wool cap on the side of his head, and came "limping" back toward us. It was such a strange, wild struggle-walk that even cripples would have laughed at him. He struggled up the aisle for ten feet or so, dragged himself into a pew, bent over and prayed to gawdalmighty, crossed himself about eight times, and suddenly straightened up. Cured! He could *walk*! He threw his "crutch" away and stepped up the aisle again, a new man.

No, not satisfied. He had to do it again. The second time he turned around and waved his thanks, as if God were some huge mechanic who (Who) had just pushed him out of a ditch.

After a few others had tried it, Herbie did it again.

Herbie is not a great student and not even a great actor, but he can do that sort of thing with such grace that God would smile on his effort.

Another 3 miles and Phil and I were picked up by Howie, who would now walk. He had found a barn in Comeauville for us. "Just look for Comeau, mailbox on the right side of the road, runs a grocery store." He gave us his sly grin, and we left him.

Comeau? Comeauville? On the outskirts of town we passed three mailboxes: Alex Comeau, Felix Comeau, Octave Comeau. But Howie said it was in the middle of town. Okay. And the mailboxes flashed by: Theo. Comeau, Dom. Comeau, Benoit Comeau, Harriette Comeau.

"Great! Did Howie give any other clues?"

"Said he ran a grocery store."

We stopped and asked a man (a Mr. Comeau), "Do you know a Comeau who runs a grocery store around here?"

"Which one? There are three."

"Which one is closest?"

It turned out to be *the* Comeau. Henry Comeau directed us to the barn, which was full of holes and bad planks, with plenty of hay to hide them—but there was not much of a drop. Never mind; it was a welcome sight.

There was no time to untangle gear; it had simply been dumped there, and that was it. A recurring dream, daydream, was that we might come back from mapping to find our air mattresses blown up and sleeping bags ready. Not today.

Out the other end of town: Braz. Comeau, Marie Comeau, Ed. Comeau, Nat. Comeau, Louis Comeau.

We went through the entire town without seeing any other last name. I don't know whether they are lying or whether it is a stunt, but *all* the people in Comeauville are named Comeau.

Phil would be driving tomorrow, and there were slightly less than two full walking days left. By the main highway it was 27 miles to Yarmouth. Maybe a short day tomorrow and then a night walk into Yarmouth? That would mean two places—one 10 or 12 miles away and the other in Yarmouth, where we would stay for two days.

About 8 miles out of Comeauville, just beyond a large and graceful river (Beaver River), over the bridge and up a slight hill, was a rolling hayfield. It curved down to the sea, giving a full view of the ocean from this high, gentle storm sea of waving green.

Often the mapping turned out to be spontaneous—a decision having to do with distance to be walked, the road, the place, its availability—all resolved by *"This is it!"*

As we walked to the house to ask for the field, we were in effect setting up the night walk to Yarmouth and thus the end of the walk.

The door was answered by a beautiful girl. How old was she? Just beautiful. Theirs was the first English family going south after Comeauville. How to explain the sweetness in the direct way she dealt with us; as if she knew us, and knew that we were okay? Her father wasn't there, but "I can answer yes for my family."

The decision seemed better and better as we drove away and headed for Yarmouth to pick up the mail. Meanwhile we worked on back roads and found some beauties. We left the main highway and clung to the sea. How would the moon be? About half full by tomorrow night. It would come up very late, around 1:00 or 2:00 in the morning. By way of the sea it was 19 miles to Yarmouth.

At Yarmouth we picked up the mail, including a nice letter from the Davis family in Orwell, Maine (and a picture of big Hurricane Herbie in the bow of the Davis rowboat, yelling to skinny Jake, who was almost out of the water, "Row, Jake, Row!").

The last mapping, the last walk we'd scout for; the last route for the last day was coming up. We were astonished and saddened. Was it really over? In a way I feel now that Ann M.'s departure was not so much from necessity but from a determination not to reach the end. Of course, we all had plans, but they were vague and rarely discussed. Don had talked about being best man in his friend's wedding mainly in order to tell us that he'd be returning to the walk on his motorcycle.

We found a camping place in Yarmouth where we could meet for two days. For reasons to follow, I'll call it Blackwell's. Mr. Blackwell would let the group camp, and we'd have hot showers, a laundry, and a campsite in a place that was well off the road. He was impressed with the group—on paper—and "very pleased" to have us until he saw all of us, at which time he cut off hot water, washing machines, everything. He told me, "Well, maybe I'm just a cranky old man, but I can't stand the sight of boys with long hair." He said there was no other reason for his action. I told him that his thumbnail sketch of himself couldn't be improved upon.

Phil and I were tired—a condition most of us had learned to live with—and hungry. We zipped back, checking the long scenic route with sprayed arrows and alternate trails. The vast sea stretched beyond the hump of Nova Scotia, and tomorrow before dawn, when we walked this stretch, there would be moonlight.

We pulled to a halt at a lonely café and ordered two large clam chowders. It was around 9:00 p.m. and we'd not be back before 10:30.

We sat at a table realizing how tired we were. It was not just two nights in a row of being hassled—the night of the rock and the night of the railroad bridge and the Mounty—it was a cumulative fatigue from 15- to 20-mile walks, day after day.

An old man sitting at a table across the little room was the only other customer and I looked at this stranger through all of our days on the road. At that moment, the Weasel was in the back of the truck, "bagged," or his body was, for I knew he was into the kind of sleep in which the mind goes all over the world, and at the same moment I was looking at the old man. For a long time (outside of other walkers) he was the only person that I had been able to sit still and look at without the barriers of conversation. It was a moment difficult to describe. Very tired, so a look without varnish, raw, without hope or sophistication . . . a time when the eyes simply look over and see someone. Some *one*. And see his humanness, not his goodness, his humanness, which is perhaps better.

In some way I saw him without judgment, as if I were only eyes; but because of the detached coldness of the look, being only "eyes," I was filled with mercy for him . . . and shortly after that, something like mercy for myself. "Heaven and earth will unite," says the Tao, "and sweet dew will fall." Sweet dew . . . sweet dew was what I felt. Why? How? What was the formula? Whole days in simple activity without pressure? Rocks on beaches, ocean-in-eyes-in-ocean? Days letting the waters of oneself settle and become clear? Is man a lake? Would we see clear to the bottom if the waters were calm for long enough?

The two days of meetings at the end of the walk were coming up. Given my distrust of words, what could happen in those two days that would be as vital as the time when things were actually happening? Something to clarify the entire undertaking. Experience, yes, but the words *after* it. Was that really the problem for those two days? What words can do? Words over it? Words after it?

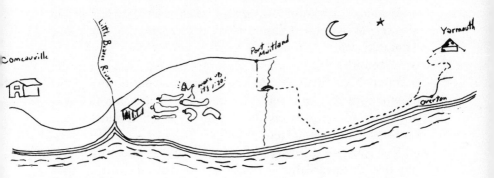

Next morning we outlined the plan—short walk, early sleep, night walk to Yarmouth—and everyone liked it. We left all the gear sitting in a big pile at the barn and took off to have the tent mended at a shipyard outside Weymouth. We lugged it up to the sailmakers' loft, and they looked it over. They didn't throw up their hands or try to talk us out of doing it; they just looked, calculated which machines could handle which rips.

"It might cost quite a lot," they warned us, "around $20."

"Go to it."

We made sandwiches and doled them out, and by the time we got to our beautiful field at Beaver River, some walkers were only a mile away from it.

When we went back to the sailmakers', the tent was patched with white sailcloth sections along the rips; seams and corners were mended with tough green cord, the cap was reinforced. $25. The work really looked good; we took it without an argument. Everyone had to see it, poke it, check the seams. But we decided not to use it, just sleep in the field for a fast getaway.

We had an easy-to-fix supper and were asleep around 10:00. The plan was for me to get up at around 1:30. I woke up at 1:20, slept another five hours in five minutes, jerked up at 1:25, and got out of the bag. Everyone woke up easily and we scrambled to get ready.

Herbie, to add to a lamplit, bewildering start, lost his glasses. We combed through the grass, and he swore and stomped around (crushing them?). All right, okay; they were found.

We got off a little after 2:00—no moon—and things settled down. I knew some would be tempted to take the highway to Yarmouth and cut off about 4 miles, but Phil and I talked it up for the "scenic" route.

Very early in the walk we had the roads to ourselves. When we turned toward the sea, and crossed an old bridge, there was not a living thing in sight. Down the long road to the sea and (perfect timing) up came the moon—a bent old man—around 3:00 to give us a dim glimpse of the vast, mysterious Atlantic. Our little road twisted and turned toward it. At close to 4:00, around a small lake, were the flashing lights of the truck, and Herbie with hot coffee and candy bars.

It was, and we knew it at the time, a quiet, beautiful walk, with the unreal quality of the first night walk, although it was not nearly so long. The most memorable view was from the road which took us straight down to the beach and to a lobster-canning factory. The road divided a huge field of hay which had been recently cut. The moon was at our backs and put the rambling house-factory with a hill of lobster traps against the dark sea.

This night there were freaky contacts with other people, or other dark blurs, when we did not know till the last instant who someone was. From an absolute stranger a blur would turn into a walker intimately known. A disconcerting exercise in how quickly we put on our armor, our prejudices, for and against.

Gale and I walked together and were by ourselves at dawn. Big Ann and Tita brought up the rear. We stopped and wandered near the ocean for a long time and they passed us. The glorious sun peeped up, rose higher, and we caught up with them and a few others. By this time we were staggering, resting, staggering on, joking, shot, silly, singing, then walking and resting again. We had been walking forever and Yarmouth was a name . . . a carrot at the end of a stick tied to our backs. We had been walking forever and we would die walking. Of course.

To stop was to lie down. To lie down was to go to sleep. The first one uncomfortable enough to wake up, woke the others and we staggered on.

It was broad daylight when we legged it into the outskirts of Yarmouth and a restaurant—unnoticed the day before— only a quarter mile from kindly Mr. Blackwell's campsite. It was open! I don't know why it should seem a miracle for a restaurant to be open at 8:00 a.m., but we felt it was. From this bias we went on to see everything that came from behind those magic doors as delicious, rewarding, fantastically good. Maybe it was!

Up the street, right turn, and home; our Army olive drab tent proudly bearing its white sailcloth patches, its campaign scars, which more than anything made it ours.

As if I were very drunk, I took all sorts of precautions to make this sleep just right: blew up the air mattress so that when I sat in the middle I could just hit bottom (there are various schools of thought on this); arranged the bag after fluffing it up; and only then crawled in among the other logs scattered under the tent's better-than-stone sides.

We got up and ate leftovers around 3:00 that afternoon and gathered in the tent not long afterward. I wanted two full days for the meetings, but I'd have to settle for a day and a half, since the plane left every other day and Howie and Big Ann were flying out on it.

We decided on one long meeting to review day-by-day happenings, campsites, and the external side of the walk. Next would come a meeting to discuss what the walk had meant, its strengths and weaknesses.

How easy it was to decide on who would shop and fix the food and when we'd meet again. I was not saying, "All right, troops, at 3:17 . . ." No, it worked itself out. This was the fruit of our time together. There were no bristling egos, no competition. More than intelligence and more than common sense, we had a kind of working grease. Sure, there were quiet remarks or snickers at something someone said or did that typed him for the thousandth time, but nothing cruel. There was love between us, among us, and it was easy to feel.

Even during the first meeting this realization set in as we recounted the days together, pegging them:

"Frost on the sleeping bags . . . The soccer field . . . Howie's eggs . . . Busted radiator hose . . . Cops in Jaffrey . . . Oughta *Hang* 'Em All! . . . *Off* the church lawn . . ."

From that point people who had walked together picked it up; others listened or got together, called across to ask or remind. At times the noise was fierce; then one person would catch everyone's attention and we'd all listen. But mainly everyone searched for "his" day, little things said or done. Journals were out, read through, scribbled in as people made notes now if they hadn't before.

"Oh yeah, those crazy cows . . . Chocolate pudding . . . Blackfly days . . . Toilet paper on the trees . . . The hate belt . . ."

"Are we still on the eighth day?"

Things would settle down only to build up again. I didn't want to stop it. We were working on memories, doing the walk all over again. In four hours we were exhausted—we'd walked about 240 miles. We broke it up, amazed that we'd only covered sixteen days. Some suggested that we would have to go faster, cover the days more quickly. Let it be.

We had supper and agreed to go for another two hours. The meeting was in our hands, not mine. At 9:00 we started again:

"Was that the day Gale was hit in the back with a hunk of wood? . . . Yeah, the day the house talked back to us . . . Raining all day . . . Maine! . . . And the Weasel pissed in both states at the same time . . . Matthew's gang . . . And Motor was arrested . . ."

There was no way to stop it; it went on long after midnight; we'd have to finish it early the next day, our last full day together. But even the next day it went on and on, the avalanche of things mentioned brought on more. We finished up late again, but I could hardly sleep. Next day: wake up at 5:00, have our last meeting from 5:00 till 9:30 and head for the ferry. Only a madman would try to capsule the whole thing. Why try?

What had the day-to-day meetings done for us? What had the whole thing been? Walkers were saying that the time had sneaked up on them, they had gotten into it so deeply that they dreamed it would go on forever. Was it learning? School? "This Can't Be Love, Because I Feel So Well"; and so this couldn't be school. All the things school teaches; all the things school ignores. "They don't educate, they indoctrinate,"—Dick Gregory. Enjoyment? Any connection between school-education-learning-enjoyment? The fear of joy. Fear of freedom. The personal threat which freedom imposes. Joy? Joy has left the classrooms. And why should it stay?

Everything students do in school has preconceived aims. Then we complain that they aren't curious. They aren't seekers. What we won't admit is that they are not seekers after our course goals.

We were up at 5:00 for the last meeting. Coffee, bread, jam; meet in the tent in half an hour. The Optimus was hissing fiercely under a big kettle of water. We brought the stove into the tent for coffee during the meeting.

It was very early, but there was a peculiar awareness about this last morning as a group—the LAST morning. What had we done? learned? I was almost sorry for the questions. It should have been just talk, tell about it, now that the physical trip is out of the way. I was not King Lear asking for loyalty but it was a feeling, in some way uncomfortably close to it. The trip . . . the trip itself. Words over it, words after it would not alter what was tucked away in those forty days. The trip was barely over (was it quite over?), we were sitting at the tail end of it. Now to ask them to pull it all together, in words, one day and a half after it? It was already 5:15, and everyone waited.

"This is difficult, because this was practice and not theory . . . because the substance was so general . . . maybe life itself. Well, let's go around the tent and then back to anyone who wants to add something." That was a concession to the critics of "around the tent" who claimed it was too mechanical—and yet how else? We did go around the tent, but perhaps the most impressive part of the meeting was the listening silence, a nest of silence, an embracing silence.

Bill spoke about our world in miniature, about a trial run for life, and a test of tolerance, inside and outside the group.

Diana spoke about a balance between books and life; about education and how "Once exposed to *this*, we can begin to see how unimaginative and insensitive the educational system really is." She also referred to her fight with fear—for instance, of truck drivers when she was walking alone—and to how she had overcome a good deal of it; how getting rid of fear was so closely connected with first admitting that fear was so much a part of her.

Bob B. spoke about seeing things without classifying, of "just looking" and of "the difficulty of being simple." He finished by reading, in a barely audible voice, a little note: "Maybe the end of the walk is a beginning."

Phil was involved in the relativity of time: ". . . realizing how important time is, if you take time out to spend it with yourself. And how ordinary responsibilities can reach out and destroy days, weeks, months, years. How a person's life can be lost that way . . . I think of days driving the truck instead of just walking. What a relief to be walking again. The value of being able to adjust to different situations: good weather, rain, cops, nice people, hassling towneys, all in the same twenty-four-hour period. Seeing so many narrow-minded people and seeing how often we have been narrow-minded about them . . . we have done so much in forty days. If Thayer [the old dairy farmer] could have seen this sooner, *his* life wouldn't have ended in such a way."

Big Ann mentioned her own search for peace, and said

that we should have had more meetings; also that if the walking day had been shorter, there might have been more time to keep up with journals.

Herbie had discovered that "I can see anything in myself, if I really want to. Faults as well as good traits. These (the faults) hurt. Maybe they're little things but I don't see them —I'm not seeing them—as little." A year later I got a letter from Herbie saying, "The walk was the best thing that ever happened to me."

Howie talked about feeling and a new-found ability to act on feeling, and about the idea of unanimity, which he hadn't understood before. Even though unanimity had been a source of great irritation at times, he finally agreed that it had been good.

Gordon agreed with Bob B. about the difficulties of becoming simple. He was another one who spoke about time: "In each day I have to use my own time of daylight . . . I have to *use* the present, and if I wait too long there's no time left." He was groping for ways of describing his own feelings and was far from the answers. "I think that in freedom in myself, . . . I've tried to be too much of a free person, and that kind of freedom, on this earth, is not possible . . ."

Gale spoke about our poor physical condition at the beginning of the walk—that it was a waste of time not to have our bodies at our service. "I would also like to have had more time alone. And silence. I believe that the walk should have been longer. Six weeks is not enough time to get into it. I found that considerations of time-space-distances occupied my thoughts, and a realization of the usefulness of the body itself. I wonder whether cars, riding, possessions, conformity, keep us from developing—physically and psychologically? And about our conveniences, so-called; how can we use them and yet keep them from interfering with our development?"

"When we get home we have our own standards of exclusiveness, our own snobbishness—our own way to shut people out of our lives. Will we ever relate it to our experiences of being shunned, feared, hated for nothing more than appearances?"

Some of what was said was unusually commonplace. Motorhead, for example, saying in astonishment: "How unique we all are!" Children "learn" that in first grade. And Lloyd delivering his one-word shots, each one so very much felt: Love. Hate. Silence. Fear. Freedom within, without. Time. Being ruled by time. But what was impressive was the quality that went with the delivery of the words, a quality of words joined with feeling, or feeling with words.

Although many of their "discoveries" seem almost elementary, these were not lessons learned from a book, but were things understood about themselves—and in this area, we are nearly all of us infants. "How unique we all are!" Obvious; yet difficult to put it any other way when it comes right out of experience—like Motor's discovery about stones on the beach.

It was as if almost every one of them was newborn and was talking about a new life. For me it was the realization that this was a course, and that in trying to tell about a course they were talking about their lives: time, happiness, perception, imagination, seeing themselves, changing themselves.

Courses . . . and happiness? Seeing themselves? *Their* time? *Their* lives? Not Shakespeare's? Not Joyce's? *Their* lives?

That's all I needed. I had my own notes of things to say, but now it seemed like so much scrap paper.

The curse of the Western world has always been the scholar with a burning drive to interpret, comment, and explain . . .

It was done. And now a mouthful of words? No, the experience was in those forty days, and what we could still do with them. To look on the days, go back into them, see the whole thing so clearly that it changes and, so, changes us.

I said what I felt: "Well, we did it. We kicked education in the ass. And that's a nice feeling. Our term was forty days;

our room was a crooked line from New Hampshire to Nova Scotia.

"And what did you learn? I think instead of learning, . . . that something was added to our lives."

For more than a year after the walk, notes and reminders continued to come in. Ann M. wrote a letter with the following description of walking.

Perhaps the rhythm of walking acts as a "mantra"—not each separate step but the total body movement involved. It is nearly always hypnotizing to walk alone, particularly in silence—one's thoughts begin to jam with the rhythm and poof! A slight awareness that one can control one's thoughts—a glimpse at the self—frequently a feeling of being submerged in the Sea of Chaos cheered by a subconscious Jules Verne awareness of the ecology (balance) of life which goes on unnoticed. I feel first a stirring impulse (of all places) in my left hip. It travels up the left side of my body—a breath—on to my head—accomplished: one more piston-stroke from the kinetic energy contained within—implosion —like a coal-burning furnace—raging yet still calling for coal and the inevitable stoker of the subconscious to feed it. While walking one can play mind games—extend a thought longer than what usual consideration you might give it—completely avoid those things you don't want to think about (swoosh, out of mind) replaced by what you want to think about . . . honesty, awareness.

A month after the walk was over and we were home again, Diana's car pulled up in the yard. She came flying in with a copy of *Journey to the East*. "Have you read this? *This is the walk!*"

A note from Bill months later, on whether this kind of project should be given credits or not:

To me this is a living experience. I hardly think about any living experience with respect to the credit I will receive. If I take this walk honestly, the credit will come. It doesn't do me any good physically or mentally; it's just there. . . . A diploma represents a very large amount of money spent. But, what you end up with inside is what the credit really stands for. The walk came to have an existence of its own, separate from anything I had ever done before.

Parts of a letter from Jake:

The big thing was time to myself. I've never really had time be-fore. I hardly realized I needed it. . . . The more I walked the freer I became. . . . I learned how relaxation, and what follows it, is related to being perceptive to things around you, and the more relaxed I was the more perceptive I became. . . . I am more of a person than before . . . with ideas, an imagination, flexible attitude . . . concentrating on what kind of a person I am and knowing my own ways with people made being myself the only way I could think of being.

Jake is no student, but he took eight hours out of one day and most of a night to write his long letter on the walk. The real Jake might be exasperating, but the realer Jake, the one that rises up out of frustrating, naïve, stuttering Jake, is a saint.

The problem with schools is not at all how they might teach more; it might even be that students are learning too much, to the detriment of something much more important. The missing ingredient is being. Living the learning, instead of reading the "learning"—which, no matter how beautifully it may be put down on paper, is not theirs. Not quantity, but intensity, vividness, quality: three dimensions instead of one.

Four months after our return Bob B., who knew I was writing about the walk, called up and asked, "Where are you? I mean, where are we right now?" I told him that I was working on the day of Dot's Diner, and he began telling me who he'd been walking with on that day, what they had been talking about, what he'd had for lunch at Dot's, and how he'd been walking with Ann M. that afternoon when she hurt her ankle.

I told Tita how much Bob still remembered about one day, and she proceeded to tell me, in even more detail, about the same day. "I remember every word of a postcard I wrote to my class, I remember my thoughts as I was walking in the rain, and I remember not only what I had for lunch but what Jake and Motorhead had, because they were sitting next to me at Dot's."

Walk days I still remember, very vividly. School days?

Whole months are simply folded away. Whole months of my life; one class after another.

The walk was over. At least, the walking was done with. We would take the tent down for the last time on the following morning, load the truck for the last time, get on the ferry and split up at Bar Harbor. From here on out it was rips and more rips in the fabric we had woven almost consciously.

The meeting broke up. We had to see Bill, the two Bobs, and Phil off on the ferry. It was a hilarious upturn. They stood on the ferry and we stood ashore waving. Plume, who was going home with Bob B., could be heard howling in the bowels of the ship. We would yell to them from the dock and they would answer:

"How does he *do* it?"

"I don't *know*."

"Amen, Brother!"

"Praise a Lord!"

"Boogie till the break of day!"

"Git back, Jo-Jo!"

"Bite the shit out of him, Banjo!" Sensational!

"Do you screw?"

"We got no distractions!"

The ferry pulled off, and they told us later that all they wanted to do was dive off and swim back to Yarmouth.

We ate in town then went back. In the afternoon Howie and Big Ann flew from Yarmouth to New York together. Before he left, Howie came over and asked about a big doubt that he had.

"Look, I know what the walk meant to me, even if I can't really put it into words. But what will I say when people ask me, 'What the hell did you do *that* for?'"

I answered from what I'd already experienced. "Either people see it or they don't. When some friend of yours hears about it and likes it—then tell him about it. As for the others, the ones who hear and then ask, 'Why?'—it's not worth the effort to explain."

It was at least a workable formula, and he called up one night about a month later to tell me so. In fact he was ecstatic over the discovery.

The following day the truck was loaded and on the ferry. At Bar Harbor we split again, and now there were only seven of us in the truck. We agreed to go back over as much of our route as possible and still try to be back in two days.

Have I been too hard on ordinary education?

Not hard enough.

It doesn't just keep us marking time. We march backwards, from promising beginnings, with all sorts of foolish notions about the world and ourselves in it. The latest scientific idiocies are forced down our throats: about time, memory, space, experience.

It was ghostly to go back past those places . . . to see our arrows so plainly marking our route, our once-route. Still fields, exact spots where the tent had been, where we had slept.

"That morning I walked with L.J. and Howie . . ."

"We rolled oranges across the road right here."

Through Limerick. "Matthew sucks," Motorhead suddenly yelled out the window at a bunch of swimmers. I gunned it through town.

I'm not only convinced that education should be very different, but that our ordinary learned-through-books conception of time-space-memory is wrong.

I looked and know that somehow we're still walking past those places, still sleeping in fields by streams, rivers, lakes, under pine trees near waterfalls.

"Life is real, only then when I am," says Gurdjieff.

We *were* then, and are still, in a real way, walking to Nova Scotia—and not caring if we ever get there.

A note on the type

This book was set in Caledonia, a Linotype face designed by W. A. Dwiggins. It belongs to the family of printing types called "modern face" by printers—a term used to mark the change in style of typeletters that occurred about 1800. Caledonia borders on the general design of Scotch Modern, but is more freely drawn than that letter.

This book was composed, printed, and bound by the Haddon Craftsmen, Inc., Scranton, Pennsylvania.